Service Composition for the Semantic Web

Brahim Medjahed • Athman Bouguettaya

Service Composition for the Semantic Web

Foreword by Schahram Dustdar

Brahim Medjahed
Department of Computer
and Information Science
University of Michigan - Dearborn
Evergreen Road 4901
48128 Dearborn Michigan
USA
brahim@umich.edu

Athman Bouguettaya
CSIRO ICT Center
CS & IT Building (108)
North Road
2601 Acton, ACT
Australia
athman.bouguettaya@csiro.au

ISBN 978-1-4419-8464-7 e-ISBN 978-1-4419-8465-4
DOI 10.1007/978-1-4419-8465-4
Springer New York Dordrecht Heidelberg London

Library of Congress Control Number: 2011921256

Printed on acid-free paper

Springer is part of Springer Science+Business Media (www.springer.com)

To my parents Malika and Mahmoud, my wife Ibtissam, my daughters Lina and Sarah, and my sisters and brothers.

Brahim Medjahed

To my father who taught me the love of knowledge.

Athman Bouguettaya

Foreword

The problem of service composition is viewed by many as the "holy grail" in Services Computing. There have been many attempts by researchers from various domains to perform research on this highly relevant and timely subject. One of the goals in Semantic Web research has been to provide concepts, methods, and tools to cater for automatic composition of services on the Web. This poses a hard problem since composition of services is naturally connected to issues of semantics and context (including functional as well as non-functional service properties) on the one side and technology on the other side. So far, there is no standard and agreed-upon way to perform service composition of the Semantic Web.

In this book the authors achieve a substantial step forward in the area of automatic service composition on the Semantic Web. Clearly, the goal of automation is engrained in computer science research, and is, as such, a worthwhile endeavor.

This excellent book aims at establishing the required foundations to address this problem. In particular, Medjahed and Bouguettaya present concepts and techniques that can be applied to a wide range of applications. In this book the contributions are presented in the context of e-government and bioinformatics cases but can easily be transported to other areas as well. The contributions include specification, understanding the semantics, matching, and generating composite service descriptions. These aspects all denote a rigorous and holistic approach the authors present in this book.

Medjahed and Bouguettaya succeed in guiding the reader through all relevant research issues in the field of service composition for the Semantic Web by basing the presented concepts, techniques and tools on case studies and, furthermore, by weaving conceptual considerations with implementation issues and algorithms. This style makes this book a worthwhile read and I hope that you enjoy reading this book as much as I had.

Schahram Dustdar

Preface

The world of computing has witnessed the emergence of a new paradigm called *services*. This phenomenon is part of an *evolution* journey that has taken us from *data* (bits and bytes) to *information* (wrapping meaning around data) to *knowledge* (reasoning about information) to the current era, i.e., **services** (the result of acting on knowledge). Services aim at taking computing to a *new level of abstraction* that is *closer* to the way *humans naturally think and interact* with their surrounding. The advent of this new paradigm has incidently happened concurrently with the rising need to support the new *service-driven economies*. The emerging *interdisciplinary service science* aims at using the latest research in service-related areas to inject efficiencies in dealing with the complex problems of *service creation and provisioning*. Service computing can be, in many ways, thought of as the *engineering* of solutions for the service economy.

A key plank of the service computing agenda is *service composition*: it aims at providing techniques, models, and architectures for the automation of multiple, autonomous, and dissimilar services to produce new and novel services. Service composition benefits include better techniques for service outsourcing and innovative and serendipitous services. Applications abound and span almost numerous areas, including e-government, life sciences, hospitality, disaster management, education, health, IT outsourcing, cloud computing, and many more. A key technology enabler for services is *Web services* which is tightly *congruent* with the service paradigm. There have been tremendous activities around Web service standardization which must be said, has probably gone beyond what was needed. Without any doubt, this over-standardization is now having a stifling effect on research.

This book is to the best of our knowledge, the first of its kind to address service composition, especially using the latest research in semantics to lay a much needed rigorous foundation which future research can build upon. We use scenarios from e-government (social services) and life sciences (analysis of protein sequence information) to illustrate the concepts and techniques discussed in this book. We analyze the main issues, solutions, and technologies for enabling interactions on the Web and Semantic Web periods.

Brahim Medjahed
Athman Bouguettaya

Acknowledgements

I would like to thank my parents Malika and Mahmoud for being an indefectible source of motivation, strength, and renewal. I am indebted to my wife Ibtissam for her constant dedication, tireless encouragement, and invaluable support. I also offer my thanks to my two lovely daughters Lina and Sarah for bringing joy and happiness to my life.

Brahim Medjahed

I would like to acknowledge the contribution of many collaborators who shaped our research in service composition. These were many research and coursework students at Virginia Tech who contributed to the realization to what was initially a largely amorphous idea. I would like to particularly acknowledge the contribution of Hao Long who did a splendid job in implementing a world-first digital government application using many early versions of the service composition techniques described in this book. I would be remiss if I were not grateful to my beautiful family consisting of my wife Malika, and sons Zakaria, Ayoub, and Mohamed-Islam for their support and understanding.

Athman Bouguettaya

Contents

Chapter 1
Introduction

Service-oriented computing is slated to shape modern societies in vital areas such as health, government, science, and business [199, 233, 140, 122, 30, 43, 150]. It utilizes services as the building blocks for developing and integrating applications distributed within and across organizations [102, 6]. The most common realization of service-oriented architectures is based on *Web services*. A Web service is a Web-accessible entity that provide pre-defined capabilities via message exchange [7, 196, 52]. It may wrap a wide range of resources such as programs, sensors, databases, storage devices, and visualization facilities [94, 55, 201]. Two factors are promoting Web services as the technology of choice inter-enterprise integration: the use of standard technologies and support of loose coupling [233, 53, 207].

Service computing has so far largely been driven by often competing standards evolving in silo-like ethos. While initial standards have been beneficial in the early adoption and deployment of Web services, innovations and wider acceptance of Web services need a rigorous foundation upon which systems can be build. There is a strong impetus for defining a solid and integrated foundation that would stimulate the kind of innovations witnessed in other fields, such as databases. Materializing this vision requires solutions to the different fundamental research problems to deploying Web services that would be managed by an integrated Web Service Management System (WSMS) [233]. Web services would be treated as first-class objects that can be manipulated as if they were pieces of data. A WSMS includes the architectural components necessary to tackle various service management issues such as service query processing and optimization, service composition, trust management, privacy/security, and change management.

One key challenge for Web services is interoperability. Interoperability refers to the extent to which Web services would cooperate to accomplish a common objective. It moves Web services beyond the elementary framework built on basic standards such as SOAP, REST, and WSDL. We identify two levels of interoperation: syntactic and semantic. Syntactic interoperation is currently achieved in Web services through the use of XML [233].

B. Medjahed and A. Bouguettaya, *Service Composition for the Semantic Web*,
DOI 10.1007/978-1-4419-8465-4_1,

XML provides the platform and language independence, vendor neutrality, and extensibility, which are all crucial to interoperability. However, semantic interoperation is still an open research challenge. The main impediment has been the lack of *semantics* to enable Web service to *"understand"* and *automatically* interact with each other. The *Semantic Web* is an emerging paradigm shift to fulfill this goal. It is defined as an extension of the existing Web, in which information is given a well-defined *meaning* [19]. The ultimate goal of the envisioned Semantic Web is to transform the Web into a medium through which data and applications can be *automatically understood* and *processed*.

1.1 Semantic Web Services

The development of concepts and technologies for supporting the envisioned Semantic Web has been the priority of various research communities (e.g., database, artificial intelligence). A major player in enabling the Semantic Web is *ontology* [71, 134, 19]. An *ontology* is defined as a *formal* and *explicit* specification of a *shared conceptualization* [19, 221]. Ontologies were first developed in the artificial intelligence community to facilitate knowledge sharing and reuse [71]. They aim to construct a shared and common understanding of relevant domains across people, organizations, and application systems. Nowadays, they are increasingly seen as key to enabling semantics-driven data access and processing.

Ontologies are expected to play a central role to empower Web services with expressive and computer interpretable semantics. The combination of these powerful concepts (i.e., Web service and ontology) has resulted in the emergence of a new generation of Web services called *Semantic Web services* [134, 147, 30, 136, 4]. Integrating ontology into Web services could not only enhance the quality and robustness of Web service management, but also pave the way for semantic interoperation. Applications "exposed" as Web services would be *understood*, *shared*, and *invoked* by *automated* tools.

Semantic Web services have spurred an intense activity in industry and academia to address challenging research issues such as the *automatic selection*, *monitoring*, and *composition* of Web services. In this book, we describe an end-to-end framework for *semantic Web service composition*.

1.2 Web Service Composition

Web service composition refers to the process of combining several Web services to provide a *value-added* service [35, 208]. It is emerging as *the* technology of choice for building cross-organizational applications on the

Web [67, 7, 140]. This is mainly motivated by three factors. First, the adoption of XML-based messaging over well-established and ubiquitous protocols (e.g., HTTP) enables communication among disparate systems. Indeed, major existing environments are able to communicate via HTTP and parse XML documents. Second, the use of a document-based messaging model in Web services caters for loosely coupled relationships among organizations' applications. This is in contrast with other technologies (e.g., *software components* [203]) which generally use object-based communication, thereby yielding systems where the coupling between applications is tight. Third, tomorrow's Web is expected to be highly populated by Web services [40]. Almost every "asset" would be turned into a Web service to drive new revenue streams and create new efficiencies.

We identify two types of Web services: *simple* and *composite*. *Simple* services are Internet-based applications that do not rely on other Web services to fulfill consumers' requests. A *composite* service is defined as a conglomeration of outsourced Web services (called *participant services*) working in tandem to offer a *value-added* service. `Tax Preparator` is an example of composite service used by citizens to file their taxes. It combines simple Web services such as financial services at citizens' companies to get W2 form (commonly used in the United States to list an employee's wages and tax withheld), banks' and investment companies' services to retrieve investment information, and electronic tax filing services provided by state and federal revenue agencies.

From a business perspective, Web service composition offers several advantages [177, 205]. First, composite services allow organizations to minimize the amount of work required to develop applications, ensuring a rapid time-to-market. Second, application development based on Web services reduces business risks since reusing existing services avoids the introduction of new errors. Third, composing Web services enables the reduction of skills and effort requirements for developing applications. Finally, the possibility of *outsourcing* the "best-in-their-class" services allows companies to increase their revenue.

1.3 Semantic Web Support for Automatic Service Composition

Web service composition has recently taken a central stage as an emerging research area. Several techniques have been proposed [16, 36, 118, 160, 191]. Standardization efforts are under way for supporting Web service composition (e.g., *BPEL4WS* [15], ebXML's *business process specification* [167]). However, these techniques and standards provide little or no support for the semantics of participant services, their messages, and interactions. Additionally, they generally require dealing with low level programming details which may lead to unexpected failures at run-time. A promising approach to dealing with the aforementioned issues is the *automation* of the composition process [134]. This tedious process would then be conducted with minimum human intervention. The less efforts are required from users, the easier and faster Web services are composed. In this book, we propose semantic Web approach for supporting the *automatic composition of Web services.* Composers would specify the *what* part of the desired composition (i.e., the tasks to be performed), but will not concern themselves with the *how* part (e.g., which services will be outsourced). They would provide "abstract" definitions of the actions they would like to perform. The process of composing Web services (selecting Web services, plugging their operations, and so forth) would be transparent to users. Detailed descriptions of composite services would be automatically generated from composers' specifications.

Several characteristics of Web service environments entangle the automatic composition process. First, the number of services available on the Web is growing at a very fast pace [40]. Service composers must delve into the potentially vast amount of available services, find services of interest, check whether they can interact with each other, and then compose them. Second, the Web service space is highly dynamic. New services are expected to avail themselves on the Web. This requires the ability to select the "best" and "relevant" available participants in a composite service at any given time [36]. Third, participant services are generally deployed in heterogeneous environments. Heterogeneity occurs at different levels including syntactic (e.g., communication) and semantic (e.g., content, business logic) levels. Composite services need to "understand" and deal with the peculiarities of each participant service. Finally, the execution of a composite service typically spans organizational boundaries and requires the capability of interacting with Web services that are autonomous. Participant services cannot be considered to be "subservient" to other services [195]. They should instead be perceived as interacting independently with each other.

1.4 Case Studies

While the concepts and techniques presented in this book are generic enough to be applicable to a wide range of applications, we use the areas of *e-government* and *bioinformatics* as case studies throughout this book. We give below a description of both case studies.

1.4.1 Case Study 1: E-Government

One of the major concerns of e-government is to improve government-citizen interactions using information and communication technologies [152, 25, 27,

174]. In the *WebDG* (Web Digital Government) project, we have teamed up with *Indiana*'s *Family and Social Services Administration* (FSSA) and *Virginia Department for the Aging* (VDA). The FSSA provides welfare programs to assist low income citizens, strengthen families and children, and help elderly and disabled people. VDA offers a large spectrum of programs and services to assist senior citizens. However, collecting social benefits is currently a frustrating and cumbersome task in both FSSA and VDA. Citizens must often visit different offices located within and outside their home town. Additionally, case officers must delve into a wealth of proprietary applications to access welfare programs that best meet citizens' needs.

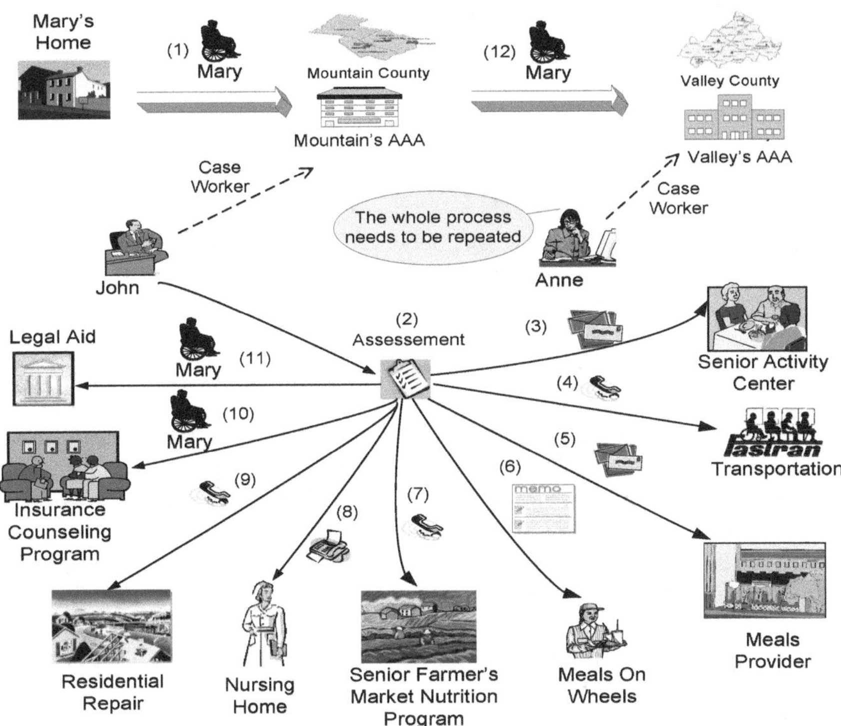

Fig. 1.1 Case Study - Government Social and Welfare Services

Let us consider the following scenario typical to VDA application domain (Figure 1.1). Assume that citizen *Mary*, a handicapped and indigent retiree, wants to receive services from an Area Agency on Aging (AAA). Typically, she would have to travel to *Mountain* County's AAA for an interview. In this case, John, a case worker at the agency, would assess the kind of services Mary would need. He would delve into a large number of social services and match the features of those services with Mary's particular needs. John determines that Mary may qualify for the following services: *FastTran* (transportation for the elderly and handicapped), *Meals on Wheels*, *Meals Providers*, *Senior Activity Center*, *Residential Repair*, *Nursing Home*, *Senior Market Nutrition Program*, *Insurance Counseling Program*, and *Legal Aid.* Mary's information is transmitted using different means of communication, including email, snail mail, fax, and phone. Mary may also have to visit some of the agencies such as the insurance counseling agency. Delay in processing is usually the rule and not the exception in these cases. To further illustrate the inadequacy of the current system, assume that Mary decides to move to *Valley* county because she developed high altitude sickness. The case worker at Valley's AAA would then initiate the same highly manual and error-prone process.

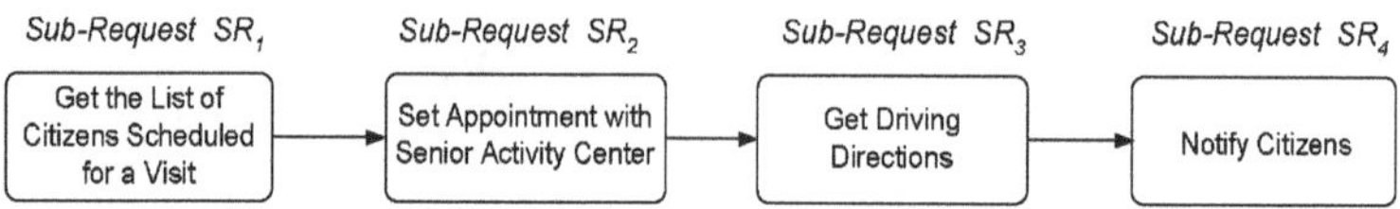

Fig. 1.2 Composing E-Government Web Services

This difficulty in collecting social benefits prevents senior citizens from becoming self-dependent with a consequent harmful impact on their welfare and health. To facilitate the use of VDA applications and hence expeditiously satisfy citizens' needs, we organize these applications into Web services. Those services may be used "individually" or combined together to provide value-added services. Assume that *John* is planning to organize a visit to a Senior Activity Center (SAC). *John*'s request includes several *sub-requests.* Each sub-request would typically be performed by executing one or more Web services (Figure 1.2). *John* first retrieves the list of citizens interested in visiting an SAC (SR_1). We assume that *John* gets the names and zip codes of those citizens instead of their full addresses. *John* then sets an appointment to visit a senior activity center (SR_2). Once a visit is scheduled, *John* gets the driving directions from each citizen's location to the SAC (SR_3). He finally notifies each citizen about the date and time of the visit and the driving directions to the SAC (SR_4).

1.4.2 Case Study 2: Bioinformatics

The second case study is related the analysis of protein sequence information in the bioinformatics domain. Consider a Gigabit Ethernet environment linking several bioinformatics institutions. Each of the contributing institutions has an entry point to this service grid to conduct scientific activities by invoking bioinformatics Web services. Access to the service grid is provided to authenticated biologists through a Web BioPortal. Such an infrastructure helps scientists avoid manual maintenance and execution of several Web service-enabled bioinformatics applications. Performing a complex process such as protein identification requires the combination of several bioinformatics Web services. BioPortal uses a service composition engine to handle the orchestration and management of such services. Figure 1.3 depicts an example of a composite service used for analyzing DNA sequences.

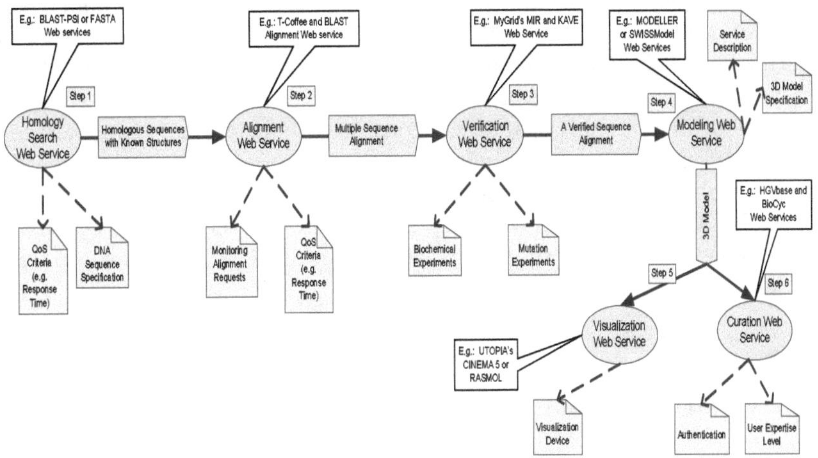

Fig. 1.3 Motivating scenario

The biologist first submits the DNA sequence specification to the BioPortal. The BioPortal interacts with the service registry (e.g., UDDI) to discover a relevant `homology search` Web service (Step 1). Homology search refers to scouring a sequence database to find sequences that are likely to be homologous (i.e., have a common ancestor) to a given sequence [92]. Contextual information of `homology search` includes quality of service (e.g., response time) and constraints about the sequence specification. BLAST-PSI and FASTA are examples of homology search services. The execution of `homology search` generates a set of the target-homologous protein sequences which genes' data are available. An `alignment` Web service follows to narrow down the search (Step 2). Alignment refers to the use of amino-acid data to determine the degree of base or amino acid similarity which reveals the degree of similarity between the target and the homologous genes [92]. T-Coffee and BLAST are examples of alignment services. The context of `alignment` Web service includes the specification of monitoring requests to check the status of alignment requests (e.g., estimated left time).

A large number of sequences may be aligned as similar to the target in the second step. To narrow down the search space, additional criteria in the target's specification are used. Such criteria refer to prior experimental results conducted on the target (Step 3). This task is performed by a `verification`

Web service such as ^{my}Grid's MIR and KAVE services. The `verification` Web service compares protein experimental reactions (e.g., biochemical and mutation experiments) and returns appropriate results to determine whether there are proteins that lead to similar experimental results as the target. The resulting proteins which succeed the `verification` service are then analyzed and used to infer a model for the target (Step 4). The `modeling` Web service provides a three-dimensional (3D) model of the target based on homologous sequences. MODELLER and SWISSModel are examples of such services. The resulting model is displayed using a `visualization` Web service (Step 5) such as CINEMA 5 and RASMOL. This service is constrained by the user's graphical device capabilities which constitute part of the `visualization` service context. Concurrently with the visualization process, the identified target is published in a curation database through a `curation` Web service such as HGVbase and BioCyc (Step 6). Curation is the process of tracking the provenance of bioinformatics results to accurately describe the purpose and design of bioinformatics data [92].

1.5 Research Issues

To illustrate the major research issues for developing a Semantic Web enabled service composition approach, let us consider the e-government case study (Figure 1.2). The *composition engine* would delve into the service space to determine participants that "best" serve each sub-request (Figure 1.4). The following simple services are found relevant to sub-requests SR_1, SR_2, SR_4, respectively: `Get-Citizens-List`, `Schedule-Visit`, and `Notify-Citizens`.

The "Get Driving Directions" sub-request (SR_3) returns the driving directions, given a citizen's name, zip code, and the address of the SAC. Since there is no simple service that offers such functionality, one solution would be to compose existing Web services in a way that would transparently fulfill the desired objective (i.e., sub-request SR_3). The composition engine finds the following two simple services as relevant: `People-Lookup` and `Direction-From-Address`. `People-Lookup` returns citizens' addresses, given their names and zip codes. `Direction-From-Address` returns the driving directions, given an initial and final address. The composition engine would then automatically compose `People-Lookup` and `Direction-From-Address` to execute the SR_3 (Figure 1.4).

To make the scenario even more challenging, let us consider relationships that may exist between Web services. For example, the invocation of the `Schedule-Visit` service *requires* the invocation of the `Lookup-SAC` service to get the list of senior activity centers. Such *pre-execution* relationships are generally dictated by the business logic of Web services (e.g., `Lookup-SAC` and `Schedule-Visit`). They may also reflect government regulations. For example, applying for certain welfare programs (e.g., unemployment benefits) may

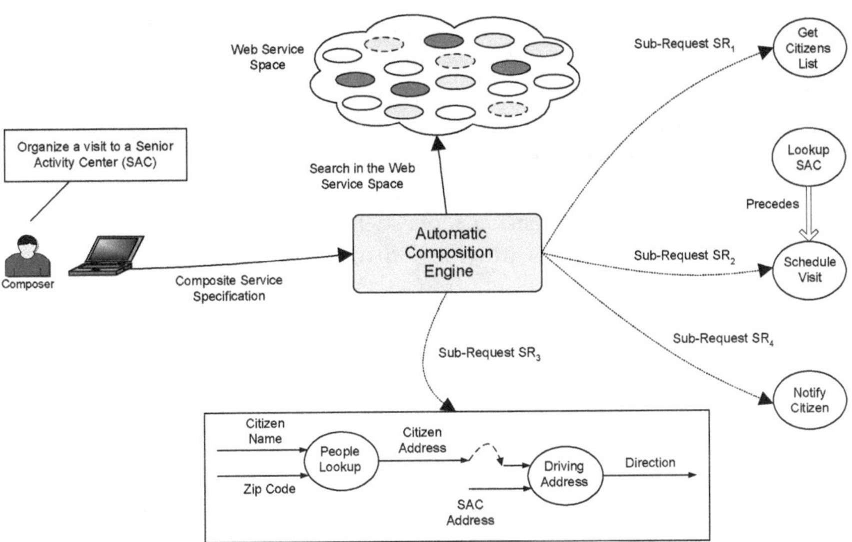

Fig. 1.4 Automatic Composition of Web Services

require access to the applicant record with a taxation office. Note that Web services may also be linked by *post-execution* relationships. The composition engine should be able to automatically include pre- and post-execution relationships in the generated composite service.

As illustrated in the aforementioned example, the automatic composition of Semantic Web services raises the following challenging issues:

- *Specification of Composers' Requests*: Composers should *specify* their *requests* for composition (e.g., "organize a visit to a senior activity center") in an unambiguous way. A composer's request may include several *sub-requests* (e.g., lookup for a senior activity center). The issues that need to be addressed are as follows: (i) whether composers specify all, some, or no participant services; (ii) how should the composition engine "interpret" each composer's request; and (iii) how would the different sub-requests be *orchestrated. Orchestration* refers to the execution order (sequential, parallel, etc.) of the different sub-requests and the condition under which a certain sub-request may or may not be executed.
- *Understanding the Semantics of Web Services*: Once the composition engine has received and "interpreted" a request for composition, it should delve into the Web service space to locate "potential" participants. Because of the large size of this space and sheer heterogeneity of Web services, there is a need to define a "meaningful" organization of that space to filter interactions and accelerate service searches. Web services should be described in a way that captures their semantics. In the e-government scenario, Web services may be located in the same county (local agencies), different counties within a state (state agencies), or different states (fed-

eral agencies). Additionally, those services may be offered by heterogeneous providers such as state and federal government agencies (e.g., Department of Health and Human Services), businesses (e.g., restaurants participating in a subsidized government program), volunteer centers (e.g., meal deliverers), and non-profit organizations (e.g., American Red Cross). The composition engine should be able to limit its search to Web services that are relevant to the composition request. It should also "understand" that `Direction-From-Address` provides "driving direction from one location to another".

- *Service Composability and Matching*: Let us now assume that the composition engine is able to understand the capabilities of Web services. The next step would be to select participant services. The selection process should be done while making sure that participants "can" actually interact with each other. We refer to such a task as *composability*. In the e-government scenario, the composition engine must verify that `People-Lookup` is *composable with* `Direction-From-Address` as depicted in Figure 1.4. The issue is to develop a model that clearly defines the Web service features that need to be compared for composability. For example, there is a need to make sure that the message parameter returned by `People-Lookup` is "similar" (e.g., in terms of their semantics) to the parameter required by `Direction-From-Address`. The composability process should compare Web service features at different "*granules*" (e.g., messages, operations, services) and levels (e.g., syntactic, semantic, and qualitative). Because of the heterogeneity of Web services, it would be unrealistic to assume that participants are "fully" composable. For example, `People-Lookup` and `Direction-From-Address` may agree on the semantics of their message parameters but use different communication protocol such as SOAP/HTTP, SOAP/MIME, and REST. The composition engine should not return a boolean type of answers regarding the composability of Web services. It should be flexible enough to cater for *partial* and *total* composability.
- *Generating Composite Service Descriptions*: The composition engine finally generates a *description* of the composite service. This description should include details such as the list of participants services, their orchestration (i.e., execution order), the way they are interconnected, and the mappings between their messages. The *orchestration* of participant services is an important issue that needs to be addressed during the generation process. We define two types of orchestration: *composer-defined* and *system-generated*. The composer-defined orchestration is specified by users in their composition requests. For example, Figure 1.2 states the execution order of sub-requests SR1, SR2, SR3, and SR4. The system-generated orchestration is automatically derived during the composition process. Several composite service descriptions may be generated for a given composition request. The composition engine should, in this case, be able to assess the "quality" of the generated composite services.

1.6 Preview of Chapters

In this book, we present an end-to-end framework for the automatic composition of Web services on the envisioned Semantic Web. We illustrate the major research thrusts to be addressed for a semantic Web enabled composition of Web services. We propose solutions for dealing with the underlying issues. The book is intended to be used for advanced or graduate courses on service-oriented computing and Semantic Web. The remainder of this book is organized as follows.

In Chapter 2, we present an in-depth study of interaction technologies on the pre Semantic Web and Semantic Web eras. We propose a framework for comparing Semantic Web interaction technologies. The framework identifies the interaction layers and proposes a set of dimensions to study interaction solutions. We compare major interaction technologies (e.g., workflow, software components, software agents, ontology, Web services), and illustrate the role of Web services in enabling interactions on the Semantic Web.

In Chapter 3, we propose an *ontological* framework for organizing and describing Web services on the Semantic Web. We introduce the concept of *community* to cater for an ontological organization and description of Web services. We develop an ontology, called *community ontology*, that serves as a "template" for describing communities and semantic Web services. We also propose a peer-to-peer approach for managing communities in highly dynamic environments. In particular, we present techniques for registering Web services with communities and coping with changes that occur in the Web service space.

In Chapter 4, we propose a *composability model* for Semantic Web services. We provide formal safeguards for meaningful composition through the use of *composability rules*. Composability rules are organized into five levels: *syntactic*, *static semantic*, *dynamic semantic*, *qualitative*, and *business process* levels. We introduce the notions of *composability degree*, and τ*-composability* to cater for partial and total composability.

In Chapter 5, We present a context-based matching framework for Web service composition. The framework relies on an ontology-based categorization of service contexts. Providers expose their service contexts as policies using context policy assistants (CPAs). CPAs implement a two-level mechanism for modeling Web service contexts. The matching process is performed via peer-to-peer interactions between a context-based matching engine (CME), CPAs, and community services.

In Chapter 6, we present an approach for supporting the automatic composition of Semantic Web services. The composition process is conducted in three separate phases: *specification*, *matchmaking*, and *generation*. We define constructs for the high-level specification of composition requests. We then propose a set of algorithms for checking composability and matching composers' requests with "relevant" compositions of Web services. We define a technique for automatically generating detailed descriptions of a composite service. We finally introduce a Quality of Composition (QoC) model for assessing the generated descriptions.

In Chapter 7, we describe the implementation of the proposed framework for service composition in the WebDG prototype. We also conduct an extensive performance study using two approaches: analytical model and simulation experiments.

In Chapter 8, we provide concluding remarks and discuss directions for future research.

Chapter 2
Enabling Interactions on the Web: A Taxonomic Perspective

The growth of the Web is revolutionizing the way organizations interact with their partners and customers. Businesses and government agencies are moving or have already moved their main operations to the Web to take advantage of the potential of more automation, efficient business processes, and global visibility [63, 64]. This has elicited the formation of alliances in which different partners join their applications and systems to share costs, skills and resources in offering value-added services. The ultimate goal is to have inter and intra-organization applications evolve independently, yet allow them to effectively and conveniently *interact* with each other. *Interaction* is defined as consisting of *interoperation* and *integration* with both internal and external enterprise applications.

Interactions among loosely coupled and tightly coupled systems has been, over the past twenty years, an active research topic in areas such as databases, knowledge-based systems, and digital libraries [24, 173]. However, the emerging Semantic Web has opened new research avenues because of issues such as semantics, heterogeneity, scalability, and automation. The Semantic Web requires the integration and interoperation of both applications and data. Disparate data representations between partner's systems must be dealt with. Interaction is also required at a higher level for connecting (i) front-end with back-end systems, (ii) proprietary/legacy data sources, applications, processes, and workflows to the Web, and (iii) partners' systems.

In this chapter, we survey the main issues and concepts to interactions on the Semantic Web [140, 233]. We propose a framework for comparing Semantic Web interaction technologies. The framework identifies the interaction layers, i.e., communication, content, and business process. It also proposes a set of dimensions to study interaction solutions. We present an in-depth study of interaction technologies on the pre Semantic Web and Semantic Web eras, and compare these technologies using the proposed framework. Previous work dealing with interoperation in loosely coupled systems mostly focused on databases and digital libraries [193, 175]. Recent surveys addressing in-

B. Medjahed and A. Bouguettaya, *Service Composition for the Semantic Web*,
DOI 10.1007/978-1-4419-8465-4_2,

teractions on the Semantic Web (e.g., [3, 31, 62, 65, 117, 194]) were mostly fragmented and lacked a holistic view of the problem.

The Chapter's organization reflects the historical evolution of interaction technologies in the pre-Semantic Web and Semantic Web eras. In Section 2.1, we present a typical architecture for a Semantic Web Interaction framework. In Section 2.2, we define the different interaction layers. We then identify a set of dimensions for comparing interaction solutions across these layers. In Section 2.3, we study several popular interaction solutions for the pre-Semantic Web, namely, EDI, components, and workflows. These solutions are evaluated against a pre-defined set of dimensions. In Section 2.4, we survey and evaluate the trends in supporting interactions in the Semantic Web. These include ontologies, Web services, semantic Web services, software agents, and XML-based standards. In Section 2.5, we describe current commercial platforms for supporting interactions on the Web. In Section 2.6, we overview Web service composition research prototypes. Finally, Section 2.7 provides a tabular comparison summary of the existing solutions for Semantic Web interactions.

2.1 Architecture of a Web-based Interaction Framework

Web-based applications generally involve several partners that interact via computerized systems (e.g., Web servers, networking services, databases) for conducting their daily business (e.g., exchanging documents, selling products, filing taxes) [29]. The building blocks for enabling such applications are provided through an *interaction framework* (Figure 2.1). These include modules for (1) defining and managing internal and external *business processes*, and (2) integrating those processes, and (3) supporting interactions with back-end application systems such as ERPs (*Enterprise Resource Planning*) [31]. A *business process* is defined as a multi-step activity that supports an organization's mission such as manufacturing a product and processing insurance claims [31].

We depict in Figure 2.1 the main components of an interaction framework. Translation facilities (e.g., application adapters) may be used to interconnect back-end systems (e.g., databases, ERPs) and internal business processes (e.g., workflows, applications). An external business process implements the business logic of an organization with regard to its external partners such as processing messages sent by trading partners' systems. Interactions between partners' external business processes may be carried out based on a specific *standard* (e.g., EDI [163, 49], *RossettaNet* [48]) or bilateral agreements. *Interaction standards* define the format and semantics of messages (e.g., request for quote), bindings to communication protocols (e.g., HTTP, FTP), business process conversations (e.g., joint business process), security mechanisms

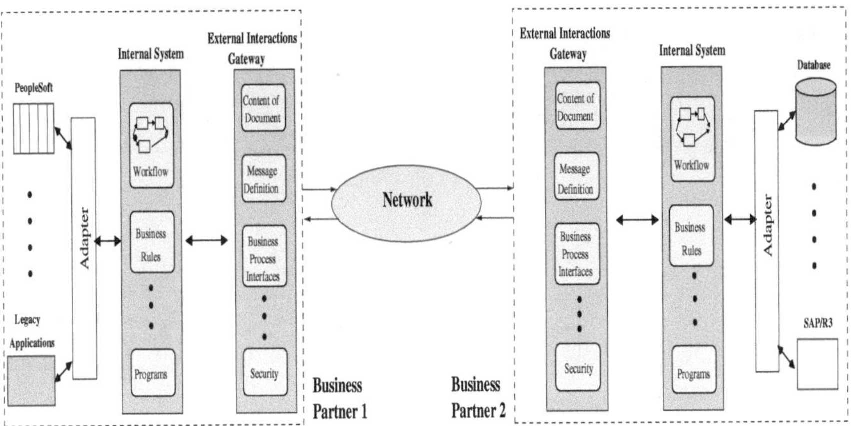

Fig. 2.1 Architecture of a Web-based Interaction Framework

(e.g., encryption, non-repudiation), etc. Interaction frameworks may have to support several standards and proprietary interaction protocols.

Figure 2.2 depicts an example of interaction between the `AreaAgencyAging` and `HealthDepartment`. Assume that *John*, `AreaAgencyAging`'s case worker, wants to organize a walk-in immunization for a group of disabled senior citizens. Such immunization is fee-based and provided by a separate agency, namely the `HealthDepartment`. *John* first issues a *request for purchase.* Upon approval of this request, a *purchase order* is issued and sent to `HealthDepartment` along with the list of citizens interested by the immunization campaign. The purchase order is transformed into an *immunization order* at `HealthDepartment`'s order processing system. After satisfactory *credit check*, an *order fulfillment* is issued by `HealthDepartment`. An *invoice* and *immunization schedule* is finally sent to `AreaAgencyAging`.

2.2 A Taxonomy for Semantic Web Interactions

In the first part of this section, we identify the different layers that make up an interaction framework on the Semantic Web. We then define the dimensions for assessing interactions across these layers. These dimensions are used as a benchmark for evaluating Semantic Web interaction solutions.

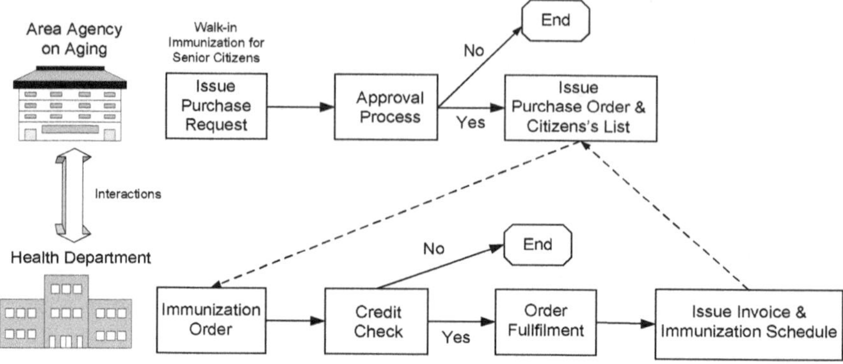

Fig. 2.2 Semantic Web Interactions: A Running Example

2.2.1 Interaction Layers

Interactions on the Semantic Web occur in three layers: *communication*, *content*, and *business process* layers (Table 2.1). For example, `AreaAgencyAging` and `HealthDepartment` need to agree on their joint business process: *John* expects to receive an invoice and immunization schedule from the `HealthDepartment` after sending a purchase order. `HealthDepartment` needs also to "understand" the content of the purchase order sent by `AreaAgencyAging`. Finally, there must be an agreed upon communication protocol to exchange messages between `AreaAgencyAging` and `HealthDepartment`.

Layer	*Definition*	*Examples of Enabling Tech.*
Communication	Protocols for exchanging messages among remotely located partners	HTTP, SOAP, REST, CORBA ORB, etc.
Content	Languages and models to describe and organize information in such a way that it can be understood and used	Ontologies, XML-based standards (e.g., eCO, cXML), etc.
Business Process	Enable autonomous and heterogeneous partners to engage in peer-to-peer interactions with each other	Web services (e.g., BPEL4WS), XML-based standards (e.g., RosettaNet), Inter-enterprise Workflows

Table 2.1 Interaction Layers

The communication layer provides protocols for exchanging messages among remotely located partners (e.g., HTTP, SOAP). It is possible that partners use different proprietary communication protocols. In this case, gateways should be used to translate messages between heterogeneous protocols. For example, `AreaAgencyAging` and `HealthDepartment` may use *Java RMI*

(*Remote Method Invocation*) [156] and IBM's *MQSeries* [104] respectively for internal communications. The objective of integration at this layer is to achieve a seamless integration of the communication protocols.

The content layer provides languages and models to describe and organize information in such a way that it can be understood and used. Content interactions require that the involved systems understand the semantics of content and types of business documents. For instance, if `HealthDepartment` receives a message that contains a document, it must determine whether the document represents a purchase order or request for quotation. Information translation, transformation, and integration capabilities are needed to provide for reconciliation among disparate representations, vocabularies, and semantics. The objective of interactions at this layer is to achieve a seamless integration of data formats, data models, and languages. For example, if `AreaAgencyAging` uses xCBL (*XML Common Business Library*) [47] to represent business documents and `HealthDepartment` expects documents in cXML (*Commerce XML*) [54], there is a need for a conversion between these two formats.

The business process layer is concerned with the conversational interactions (i.e, joint business process) among services. Before engaging in a transaction, `AreaAgencyAging` and `HealthDepartment` need to agree on the procedures of their joint business process. The semantics of interactions among `AreaAgencyAging` and `HealthDepartment` must be well defined, such that there is no ambiguity as to what a message may mean, what actions are allowed, what responses are expected, etc. The objective of interactions at this layer is to allow autonomous and heterogeneous partners to come online, advertise their terms and capabilities, and engage in peer-to-peer interactions with any other partners. Interoperability at this higher level is a challenging issue because it requires the understanding of the semantics of partner business processes.

2.2.2 Dimensions for Semantic Web Interactions

The Semantic Web covers a wide spectrum of interactions among different partners. The type of interactions depend on the usage scenarios, involved parties, and business requirements. Each framework makes specific tradeoffs with regard to the requirements of Semantic Web interactions. It is therefore important to determine the relevant requirements and understand the related tradeoffs when evaluating models of interactions. In this section, we identify the following set of dimensions to study interaction issues the Semantic Web (Table 2.2):

- *Coupling among partners:* this dimension refers to the degree of *tightness* and *duration* of coupling among business partners. Two partners are *tightly*

Dimension	*Definition*
Coupling among Partners	Degree of *tightness* and *duration* of coupling among business partners
Heterogeneity	Degree of dissimilarity among business partners
Autonomy	Degree of compliance of a partner to the global control rules
External Manageability	Degree of external visibility and manageability of partners' applications.
Adaptability	Degree to which an application is able to quickly adapt to changes
Security	Measures must be in place to boost partners' confidence that their transactions are safely handled
Scalability	Ability of a system to grow in one or more dimensions such the number of relationships that can be supported

Table 2.2 Interaction Dimensions

coupled if they are strongly dependent on each other. For example, one partner may control the other, or they may control one another. *Loosely coupled* partners exchange business information on demand. The *duration* of a relationship may be *transient* (also called *dynamic*) or *long term*. In *transient* relationships, businesses may need to form a fast and short term partnership (e.g., for one transaction), and then disband when it is no longer profitable to stay together. Partners need to dynamically discover partners to team up with to deliver the required service. In *long term* relationships, businesses assume an *a priori* defined partnership.

- *Heterogeneity:* heterogeneity refers to the degree of dissimilarity among business partners. The need to access data across multiple types of systems has arisen due to the increased level of connectivity and increased complexity of the data types. Applications use different data structures (e.g., XML, relational databases), standard or propriety semantics (e.g., standardized ontologies). There may also be structural heterogeneity at the business process layer (e.g., use of APIs, document exchange protocols, inter-enterprise workflows). In addition, organizations may, from a semantic point of view, use different strategies for conducting business that depend on business laws and practices [34].
- *Autonomy:* autonomy refers to the degree of compliance of a partner to the global control rules. Partner systems may be autonomous in their design, communication, and execution. This means that individual partners select the process and content description models, programming models, interaction models with the outside world, etc. In a fully autonomous collaboration, each partner is viewed as a black box that is able to exchange information (i.e., send and receive messages). Partners interact via well-defined interfaces allowing them to have more local control over implementation and operation of services, and flexibility to change their processes without affecting each other. Usually, a completely autonomous collaboration may be difficult to achieve because it may require sophisticated translation facilities.

- *External Manageability:* this dimension refers to the degree of external visibility and manageability of partners' applications. In order to be effectively monitored by external partners, an application must be defined in a way that facilitates the supervision and control of its execution, measurement of its performance, and prediction of its status and availability. For example, `AreaAgencyAging` may need to get the status (e.g., pending, approved) of the purchase order sent to `HealthDepartment`. This requires that `HealthDepartment` exposes sufficient information pertaining to measurements and control points to be used by `AreaAgencyAging`. While desirable in principle, high visibility may require complex descriptions of partners' applications. However, the overhead to provide such descriptions may be well justified if it provides other advantages such as *Quality of Service* (QoS).
- *Adaptability:* adaptability refers to the degree to which an application is able to quickly adapt to changes. Semantic Web applications operate in a highly dynamic environment where new services could come on-line, existing services might be removed, and the content and capabilities of services may be updated. Businesses must be able to respond rapidly to changes whereby both operational (e.g., server load) and market (e.g., changes of availability status, changes of user's requirements) environment are not predictable. For example, if `HealthDepartment` decides to stop its walk-in immunization activities, `AreaAgencyAging` would then need to adapt to such change. Changes may be initiated to adapt applications to actual business climate (e.g., economic, policy, or organizational changes). They may also be initiated to take advantage of new business opportunities. Since applications interact with both local back-end systems and partner applications, it is important to consider the impact of changes in both local and external applications to ensure local and global consistency. In general, the impact of changes depends on the degree of tightness among applications.
- *Security:* security is a major concern for inter-enterprise applications. Before Semantic Web applications reach their real potential, sophisticated security measures must be in place to boost partners' confidence that their transactions are safely handled [227]. For instance, `HealthDepartment` may need to check the authenticity of the purchase order before processing it. Semantic Web applications must support mutual authentication, fine grain authentication, communication integrity, confidentiality, non-repudiation, and authorization. Interactions may be based on limited mutual trust, little or no prior knowledge of partners, and transient collaborative agreements. Shared information may include limited capabilities of services.
- *Scalability:* scalability refers to the ability of a system to grow in one or more dimensions such as the volume of accessible data, the number of transactions that can be supported in a given unit of time, and the number of relationships that can be supported. More importantly, changes in

business climate are forcing organizations to merge to be effective in the global market. Thus, the cost and effort to support new relationships is an important criterion to consider when evaluating interaction solutions in the Semantic Web. Clearly, a low cost establishment of new relationships is desirable. However, in case of long-term relationships, the cost of establishing a new relationship is not of great significance.

2.3 Interactions in the Pre Semantic Web Era

Technologies for interactions on the pre-Web era have been around for almost three decades providing businesses, such as the banking industry, with a secure framework for sharing and exchanging data electronically. The most widely used and earliest framework is the *Electronic Data Interchange* (EDI) standard that runs on dedicated computer networks. Later, advances in software technology gave rise to a new breed of affordable software for distributed messaging and computing that can securely run on public computer networks: *component-based frameworks*. With corporate takeovers and consolidations coupled with the need of agile, just-in-time inter-enterprise cooperation on the Web, pressure mounted to provide solutions for enabling *inter-enterprise workflows*. Tomorrow's silver bullet applications such as *Virtual Enterprises* [17, 81, 82], will heavily draw on these solutions. In this section, we describe major interaction frameworks developed in the pre Semantic Web era: EDI, components, and workflows.

2.3.1 Electronic Data Interchange (EDI)

EDI [163, 49] is commonly defined as the inter-organizational application-to-application transfer of business documents (e.g., purchase orders, invoices, shipping notices) between computers in a compact form. Its primary aim is to minimize the cost, effort, and time incurred by the paper-based transfer of business documents [2]. EDI documents are structured according to a standard (e.g., ANSI X12 [49] and UN/EDIFACT [163]) and machine-processable format.

Figure 2.3 depicts two trading partners `AreaAgencyAging` and `HealthDepartment` exchanging business documents via a *Value-Added Network* (VAN). The document (e.g., purchase order) must be created in the business application of the sender (i.e., `AreaAgencyAging`). The *mapper* software is used to describe the relationship between the information elements in the application and the EDI standard. The EDI *translator* software converts the document into an EDI message according to the standard used.

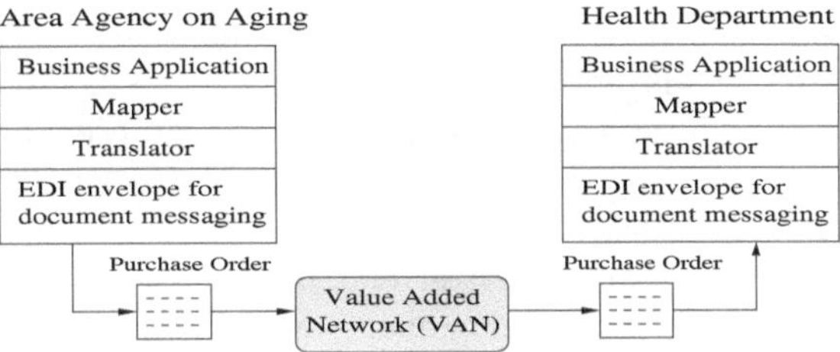

Fig. 2.3 EDI-based Interactions

The translator wraps the EDI message in an electronic envelope that has an identifier for the receiver (i.e., `HealthDepartment`). The actual transmission of the electronic envelope is performed by the *communication* software. This software maintains the trading partners' phone numbers to dial-up and exchange operations. The communication software can be a separate application or part of the translator. The VAN reads the identifier on the envelope and places it in the mailbox of `HealthDepartment`. At the `HealthDepartment` side, the reverse process takes place.

2.3.1.1 Interactions in EDI-based Solutions

EDI focuses mostly on interoperability at the communication and content layers. VANs are used to handle message delivery and routing among business partners. EDI standards provide a single homogeneous solution for content interoperability. They define a set of types for describing business documents. However, there is a limited (albeit large) number of predetermined documents supported by EDI standards. While these documents represent a large number of business transactions (e.g., shipping invoices, health care claim status reports), companies are limited to that set of EDI documents for which standards already exist [2]. It would be difficult for trading partners to conduct transactions whose parameters are not included in an EDI document. In that regard, EDI is hardly flexible in its ability to expand the set of supported document types. The introduction of a new type or changing an existing type of business transaction is complex and time consuming [2]. This kind of changes requires modification to the configuration of the translation software and must be validated in the related standard or EDI guideline committee which usually takes a long time [2]. For example the *EDI Guideline Consistency Subcommittee* (EGCS) is responsible for the content and maintenance of all TCIF (*Telecommunications Industry Forum*) EDI-maintained code lists [9]. Any modification to these code lists has to be reviewed by the EGCS. The EGCS is also responsible for notifying the *TCIF*

Secretariat of any changes in the electronic documentation. Interoperability at the business process layers is supported through pre-defined business processes. For example, if `AreaAgencyAging`'s purchase order is accepted then the `AreaAgencyAging` expects a purchase order acknowledgment, an invoice, and the immunization schedule.

The EDI approach is particularly strong along the criteria of security and heterogeneity. EDI is based on document exchange over private or value-added networks. Business partners do not concern themselves with those security issues encountered in public networks. Moreover, business partners do not need to directly reference each other systems. Therefore, critical security issues are bypassed. All partners are required to comply with the EDI standard. As a result, heterogeneity is not a problem. However, understanding all information in an EDI document is not a simple task. For example, there are data elements (UNH and UNT) in EDI document whose sole purpose is to indicate the start and end of a message. The impact of local changes is limited as partners do not directly reference each others' systems.

Although several EDI implementations have shown impressive results as set in the example of SEWP [162], the cost of establishing a new relationship usually requires a significant overhead. Because EDI is based on proprietary and expensive networks, organizations, predominantly small and medium, could not afford EDI. They were, *de facto*, excluded from being partners with larger organizations that mandate the use of EDI [2, 114]. Typically, VAN services entail three types of costs: account start-up costs, usage of variable costs, and VAN-to-VAN interconnect costs for the number of characters in each document [114]. The final cost of an EDI solution depends on several factors such as the expected volume of documents, economics of the EDI translation software, and implementation time. Maintenance fees and VAN charges can vary considerably and as such affect the cost of EDI systems. Some VAN providers do their billing on a per document basis. Others charge based on the number of characters in each documents [114]. It has been reported that 90% of the Fortune 500 companies in the United States uses EDI; only 6% of the other 10 million companies can make that claim [2]. Efforts to reduce the cost of using VAN networks include Internet-based EDI solutions such as EDIINT [109] and OBI [168].

Each EDI deployment involves negotiation and agreement on a set of implementation conventions describing the extensions to the standard documents and actual formats that would be exchanged. This negotiation and agreement process represents a significant cost in EDI deployment. To address this issue, EDIFACT and ANSI X.12 have undertaken an effort to standardize sets of documents for various industries. For example, ANSI X.12 has recently released a set of standard EDI document definitions for the health care industry. Using these industry standard document definitions, the customizations required per relationship can be reduced, although per-relationship work is generally still required. Additionally, once implementation conventions are decided upon, custom integration work must be performed at both partner organizations for the existing enterprise systems to process the EDI documents. This typically involves purchasing a commercial EDI system, integrating it with the enterprise systems, and writing custom code to translate the EDI system document definitions to the corresponding enterprise system records.

2.3.1.2 Internet-based EDI Initiatives

EDI has been extended in many directions. For instance, business documents in EDI standards have been mapped to XML documents (e.g., XML/EDI [50]). More specifically, the combination of EDI and Internet technologies seems to overcome several shortcomings of the traditional EDI (e.g., VAN charges). Indeed, several organizations are already using EDI for transacting over the Internet. For example, EDI purchase orders and invoices are now routinely exchanged via the Internet by NASA, Sun Microsystems, and Cisco systems. Major Internet-based EDI initiatives include EDIINT (*EDI over the Internet*) [109] and OBI (*Open Buying on the Internet*) [168].

EDIINT [109] – EDIINT is essentially the same as traditional EDI, but uses the Internet as a communication medium instead of VANs. The aim is mainly to reduce EDI communication charges due to the use of VANs. EDIINT was initiated by the *Uniform Code Council* (UCC) to standardize the method to exchange EDI documents over the Internet. EDIINT is similar to EDI in terms of interoperability at the content and business process layers. At the communication layer, the first EDIINT standard (emerged in 2000) was EDIINT AS1 (*Applicability Statement 1*). EDIINT AS1 set the rules to exchange EDI documents using SMTP protocol. The second standard (completed in 2001) was EDIINT AS2 standard. It supported communication of EDI documents using the HTTP protocol.

Initially, there was reluctance to use the Internet for exchanging critical business information due to concerns about security. To deal with this problem, EDIINT AS2 specifies standard mechanisms for securing documents using PGP (*Pretty Good Privacy*) encryption and digital signatures [110]. The standards referenced by EDIINT AS2 include RFC1847 and MIME Security with PGP [110]. EDIINT offers lower entry cost than EDI since it is Internet-based. However, the quality of service (e.g., automatic error detection and correction) associated with VANs is lost. EDIINT offers similar characteristics as EDI with respect to the other dimensions (i.e, coupling, heterogeneity, autonomy, external manageability, and adaptability).

OBI [168] – OBI is a standard that leverages EDI to define an Internet-based procurement framework. It is clearly stated that OBI aims to complement EDI standards, not replace them. OBI is intended for high-volume, low-dollar amount transactions, which account for 80% of the purchasing activities in most organizations. At the communication level, OBI uses HTTP protocol for exchanging messages. OBI relies on the ANSI X12 EDI standard to describe the content of order documents. Order documents are encapsulated in OBI objects. OBI objects also encapsulate other non-EDI messages such as buyers' and sellers' digital signatures. OBI does not introduce a specific model for describing locally maintained information (e.g., product and price information). This information may be described in the partner's database. At the business process level, OBI defines a simple and pre-defined operational protocol for Internet-based purchasing. This protocol consists of a number of commonly agreed upon activities (e.g., select a supplier, create order) for purchasing non-strategic material (e.g., office supplies, laboratory supplies). In fact, this protocol only specifies the way partner OBI systems interact. It is the responsibility of each partner to integrate its internal applications (catalogs, inventory and order management systems, etc) with OBI servers.

OBI makes a strong attempt to provide a robust security infrastructure. It uses the SSL (*Secure Sockets Layer*) [164] over HTTP for securing communications. It also uses digital signatures and digital certificates for ensuring messages authenticity and integrity. OBI rates higher than EDI with regard to the scalability and adaptability dimensions. First, the extensibility of order documents is not an important requirement. OBI targets simple and predefined purchasing transactions. Second, it offers lower entry cost as it is an Internet-based framework. OBI offers similar properties as EDI and EDIINT with regard to the other dimensions (i.e., coupling, heterogeneity, autonomy, and external manageability).

2.3.2 Software Components

Software components (simply, *components*) are program modules that can be independently developed and delivered [22, 203]. They may be newly developed or wrap existing functionalities provided by databases, legacy systems or packages. Although most of the fundamental ideas that define object technology are applicable to components, components are not necessarily created using object-oriented tools and languages [153, 96]. For example, components may be realized using a functional language, an assembly language, or any other programming language [203].

The development of component-based applications generally requires the interconnection of geographically distributed components. The availability of a *middleware* that provides more effective ways of programming is important to the development of distributed component-based applications. A *component middleware* is an infrastructure that supports the creation, deployment, and interactions among components [210]. Figure 2.4 depicts `AreaAgencyAging`'s and `HealthDepartment`'s applications assembled from components. Each component represents an independent unit of a business

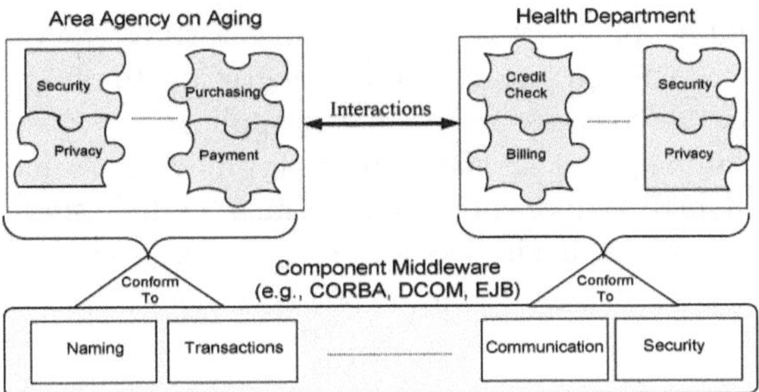

Fig. 2.4 Component-based Interactions

functionality such as *payment*, *purchasing*, *privacy*, and *security*. The different components work together to serve the needs of `AreaAgencyAging`'s and `HealthDepartment`'s business processes. They are built on top of a set of basic services. Functions provided by these services include distributed communication, security, transactions, and naming schema.

Three major component middleware frameworks have been developed during the past decade:

- CORBA (*Common Object Request Broker Architecture*) [170]: CORBA is the standard promoted by the OMG (*Object Management Group*), an international industry consortium. It is part of a general architecture called the *Object Management Architecture* (OMA). The backbone of CORBA is the *Object Request Broker* (ORB) which allows communication between client and server components.
- DCOM (*Distributed Component Object Model*) [154]: DCOM is Microsoft's technology for distributed components. It is an extension of COM, the Microsoft's component software architecture. COM and its DCOM extension are merged into a single runtime which provides both local and remote access.
- EJB (*Enterprise Java Beans*) [184]: EJB is one of several technologies which make up Sun's J2EE (*Java 2 Platform, Enterprise Edition*) specification. It provides a component model for the Java programming language. In EJB, pieces of business logic or functions can be written in Java and encapsulated to become components known as *beans*. The *container* is the core of EJB component model. It provides a runtime environment that hosts and controls the beans.

The component-based approach is more appropriate for a small number of partners within an enterprise [45]. However, with companies being merged and acquired at the current rate, there is a need to address interactions within an enterprise. Components mainly cover interactions at the communication layer. They exhibit limited capabilities dealing with interactions at the content layer. They focus on the syntactic integration to wrap heterogeneous applications. At the business process layer, applications (e.g., scheduling an immunization campaign for `AreaAgencyAging`) may be assembled from independently developed components (e.g., payment, purchasing, privacy, security) [198, 79]. However, businesses generally would need to develop *ad hoc* solutions for defining intra and inter-enterprise business processes.

2.3.2.1 CORBA-based Interactions

At the communication layer, the use of ORBs in CORBA hides the underlying complexity of network communications from application developers. When a client issues a method invocation on a server component, the ORB intercepts the invocation and routes it across the network to the appropriate server. It is also possible that components distributed on different ORBs communicate over the Internet through the *Internet Inter-ORB Protocol* (IIOP).

CORBA provides a *trader service* through which businesses can find each other by assigning a set of properties to each component. However, these properties are simply defined as (name,value) pairs. They do not provide support for semantic description of components. Recent efforts have been made to add semantic features to CORBA through the ECDTF (*Electronic Commerce Domain Task Force*) reference model which includes a *semantic data* facility [170]. However, the model is still at its very early stage. Additionally, very little work has been done so far to define a specification for the semantic data facility.

CORBA enable tightly coupled and long term business relationships between components. Once interfaces are expressed in IDL (*Interface Definition Language*), they are compiled by an IDL compiler into *stubs* and *skeletons.* The *stub*, used on the client side, invokes remote operations via the ORB to the corresponding skeleton on the server side. The *skeleton* gets the call parameters, invokes the actual operation implementation, collects results, and returns values back to the client through the ORB. Efforts are being made to add messaging capabilities to CORBA [45]. The new messaging specification defines a number of asynchronous and time-independent invocation modes for CORBA. It allows both static and dynamic invocations to use all modes. The use of message driven interactions among components allows the support of loosely coupled relationships. CORBA components are mostly based on static operation invocation. Although the *Dynamic Invocation Interface* (DII) in CORBA allows components to learn about other components' operations at run time, the utility of DII is yet to be exploited due to its complexity.

Components shield application developers from implementation details. Interfaces are the only considerations businesses must make when interacting with each other. Business partners have the latitude to implement their interfaces in ways that best fit their internal needs and requirements. Each CORBA component has an IDL that includes the name of the operations to be called by clients together with the name and types of all parameters and return values. However, all participants in a certain market need to agree on a predefined interface. This means that businesses are bound to interfaces published by their trading partners. In terms of heterogeneity, CORBA was designed to be independent of implementation languages, operating systems, and other factors that normally affect interactions. Components can be implemented using diverse programming language such Java, C++, and Smalltalk.

External manageability is partially addressed in CORBA through the *event service*. The CORBA *event service* allows components to inform each other of the occurrence of specific events. It divides components into suppliers and consumers. Suppliers generate notifications of events while consumers register to be notified about the occurrence of events so that they can perform specific actions in response of those events.

CORBA provides little or no support for adaptability. As mentioned before, businesses are tightly bound to interfaces published by their trading partners. Hence, any change to a partner's interface may need the corresponding interface to be re-compiled. To date, CORBA does not provide mechanism to respond rapidly to changes in component interfaces.

Security is addressed in CORBA through the CORBA *security service*. This service provides a number of mechanisms such as authentication, authorization, and encryption of messages to build secure Web-based applications. Major CORBA vendors provide implementations of the security service.

The complexity of CORBA development increases the cost of entry in CORBA-based solutions. For example, developers in CORBA must generate binary code packages and deploy them on client sides when building new applications or when modifying the interfaces of existing applications. Although the dynamic invocation interface in CORBA alleviates this problem, programming calls with such interface is fairly complicated.

2.3.2.2 DCOM-based Interactions

Similarly to CORBA, DCOM-based solutions mainly deal with interactions at the communication layer. They present little or no support for interactions at the content and business process layers. For a DCOM client to access an operation of another component at the communication layer, it must use virtual lookup tables to obtain a pointer to that operation. The DCOM runtime environment ensures that the pointer is local to the invoking process by using proxies [121].

DCOM components enable tightly coupled and long term business relationships. Proxies need to be created at the client side to communicate with stubs on the serving end [121]. The operation invocation process is static in DCOM which prevents establishing dynamic relationships among components. In terms of heterogeneity, current DCOM implementations are mostly based on Windows platforms although some experimentation have been done to port DCOM to other platforms (e.g., UNIX). Also, the languages that are mostly used to write DCOM components are Microsoft J++ (Microsoft's implementation of Java), C, C++, and Visual Basic. Additionally, DCOM's IDL is neither CORBA nor DCE (*Distributed Computing Environment*) compliant [121]. Security in DCOM relies on the Windows NT security model. Although this allows developers to build secure applications on Windows platforms, it is not clear how security will be provided when DCOM is used on other platforms. DCOM has similar characteristics as CORBA with respect to autonomy, external manageability, adaptability, and scalability.

2.3.2.3 EJB-based Interactions

At the communication layer, EJB uses the *Java RMI* [156] to enable interactions among beans. The use of RMI makes the location of the server transparent to the client. Similarly to CORBA and DCOM, EJB is fairly limited in terms of interactions at the content and business process layers.

Similarly to CORBA and DCOM, EJB caters for tightly coupled and long term business relationships. Developers must define an RMI remote interface for each bean. The RMI compiler generates a stub for each remote interface. The stub is installed on the client system and provides a local proxy for the client. The stub implements all the remote interfaces and transparently delegates all method calls across the network to the remote bean. A new specification of EJB (EJB Version 2) has recently been made available. It uses JMS (*Java Messaging Service*) to add support for message driven beans, extending the EJB component model to support both tightly and loosely coupled applications [45]. Static operation invocation is found in most EJB implementations. However, some implementations such as *JBoss* integrate more dynamic features.

In EJB, each bean has a *remote* interface which defines the methods that carry out the business logic of the bean. The EJB remote interface provides functions that are similar to those provided by CORBA and DCOM IDL. Hence, EJB is similar to CORBA and DCOM in terms of autonomy. EJB does not support heterogeneous platforms although it is fully based on Java. Indeed, most of the current EJB implementations do not offer direct interoperability with non-Java platforms. In addition, communicating between components deployed on heterogeneous application servers, such as invoking a *BEA WebLogic* component from an *IBM WebSphere* server, requires operations in degraded mode.

Several implementations of an event service have also been provided for EJB to support external manageability. An example of EJB's event service is the *Drala Event Broker* [66]. EJB provides some support for adaptability by associating a *deployment descriptor* to each bean. The descriptor describes the way in which a bean interacts with its environment. Application developers declaratively define contracts in their descriptors. This contract describes the type of services (such as the form of transaction management to be used) required by the bean. It can be changed independently of the business logic.

The EJB container provides security features to EJB components. Each deployment descriptor contains declarations about the access control for the corresponding enterprise bean. When a client calls an operation of that bean, the container is responsible for checking that the requester has the right to invoke that operation by accessing an access control list. Finally, EJB offers similar properties as CORBA and DCOM with respect to scalability.

2.3.3 Workflow

Workflow management is concerned with the declarative definition, enactment, administration and monitoring of *business processes.* A *business process* (or workflow process) consists of a collection of activities related by data and control flow relationships (Figure 2.5). An activity is typically performed by executing a program, enacting a human/machine action, or invoking another process (called sub-process). Programs, persons, machines, and data used to perform workflow processes are called *workflow resources.* For example, `AreaAgencyAging`'s business process includes several activities such as issuing a purchase request, approving it, and issuing a purchase order. The information sent from `AreaAgencyAging`'s *Issue_Purchase_Request* activity to the *Approval_Process* activity includes the number of citizens eligible for immunization service. The scripting of activities and resource policies through *business process analysis, modeling, and definition tools* defines a *business process definition* (workflow schema) [57]. The *workflow enactment service* enables different parts of the business process to be enacted by providing interfaces to users, applications, and databases distributed across the workflow domain (Figure 2.5).

Workflow is a key technology for automating business processes that involve access to several applications. However, traditional workflow systems are ineffective when we consider the needs of Web-based applications, with their complex partnerships, possibly among a large number of highly evolving processes. Current efforts (e.g., the Business Process Initiative - BPMI.org) promise to deliver a next generation workflow systems (*Inter-Enterprise Workflow Systems* - IEWSs) that have the ability to thread together cross-organizational business processes, supporting the integration of diverse users, applications, and systems [227]. IEWSs focus mainly on interactions at the business process layer. Their purpose is to automate business processes that interconnect and manage communication among disparate systems.

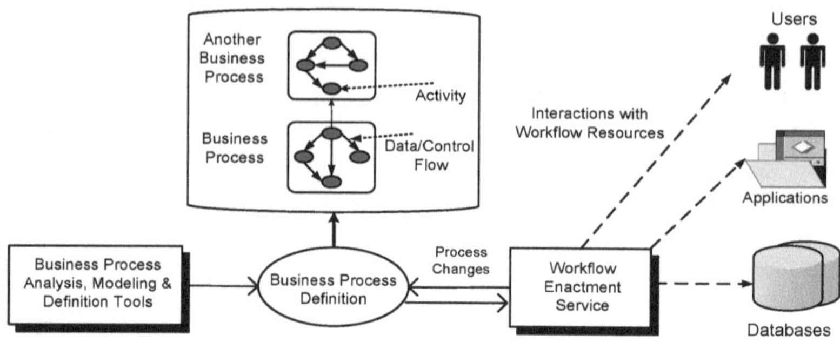

Fig. 2.5 Workflow System Characteristics

2.3.3.1 Distributed Workflow Systems

The emphasis in *Distributed Workflow Systems* (DWSs) is on partitioning the overall workflow specification into several sub-workflows, each encompassing all the activities that are to be executed by a given entity within an organization [160]. DWSs impose that each organization participating in a distributed workflow deploy a full-fledged execution engine, capable of interpreting the workflow definition. The same workflow model must be adopted by each participant in the global workflow. This approach assumes that global and sub-business processes use the same process definition and data exchange model. This is a quite restrictive assumption in the context of Web-based applications where: (i) partners may use disparate data and process representation models (e.g., `AreaAgencyAging` uses EDI and `HealthDepartment` uses RosettaNet), and (ii) private business processes may require access to proprietary/legacy data sources and applications (e.g., Oracle database for `AreaAgencyAging` and SAP application for `HealthDepartment`). In addition, DWSs assume a tight coupling model among the distributed sub-workflows. Thus, modifications to back-end applications, sub-workflows, and global workflow need to be coordinated. The cost of establishing a new relationship may be significant as business processes must be modeled and deployed in concert across all participants. DWSs are appropriate for the development of a business process of a single organization that needs to integrate multiple distributed sub-workflows.

2.3.3.2 Collaborative Process Management

Inter-enterprise business processes management features the separation between *public* and *private processes* [31, 57]. A *public process* defines an external message exchange of an organization with its partners according to a message exchange protocol such as EDI and RosettaNet. A *private process* describes internal executable activities that support the activities of public processes. Public and private processes interact through *process wrappers*. Process wrappers consist of pre-defined activities that can be used in a private business process to send/receive messages to/from public business processes. For example, if a public process uses *xCBL* [47] to represent business documents, and the private business process expects documents in *cXML* [54], the conversion between these two formats is handled by a wrapper. Private processes may also interact with back-end applications through *application adapters*. In this approach there is no requirement that local process management engines (e.g., engines which are responsible for managing private business processes) be identical. It is possible for example, that one engine is based on IBM's *MQSeries* [104] and another based on HP's *Process Manager* [100].

The separation between back-end applications, public, and private processes has the advantage that local changes (i.e, those that concern only private processes) have no impact on public processes and back-end applications. However, changes related to interactions (e.g., changing the formats of incoming and outgoing messages) between a public process (or a back-end application) and a private business process may require the modification of some wrappers. The separation between components of a Web-based application (public processes, private processes, business rules, and back-end systems) contributes to the scalability of this approach. The support of a new interaction protocol (e.g., EDI) requires only the creation of a new public process and process wrappers. The support of new a back-end application requires the creation of new application adapters. The creation of a new relationship with a new partner may require a few adjustments. If the new partner does not comply to an already supported interaction protocol, a new public process must be created to support the protocol used by the new partner. The support of a new back-end application requires only the creation of a new application adapter. The above discussion shows that the addition of interaction protocols, back-end applications, or partners does not require the modification of private business processes.

The separation between public and private business process provides for a greater degree of autonomy and bridging of heterogeneity. With regard to security, IEWs may leverage techniques used in other frameworks (i.e, document-based or component-based frameworks). External manageability can be provided by adding specific activities in public processes.

2.4 Trends in Supporting Semantic Web Interactions

The traditional approaches for Web-based interactions were not devised for Semantic Web. They provide little or no support for capturing the semantics of messages exchanged among partners or partners' business processes.

Therefore, recent research has focused on developing concepts and techniques for enabling interactions on the Semantic Web. In this section, we overview major Semantic Web technologies, namely, ontologies, Web services, agents, and XML-based interaction standards.

2.4.1 Ontology

The Web is evolving from a set of single isolated application systems into a World wide network of disparate systems interacting with each other via information exchange. This requires means to represent the semantics of the exchanged information so that it could be automatically understood. This is where the concept of*ontology* would play a crucial role, providing a machine processable semantics of the information communicated between heterogeneous systems.

Ontologies were initially developed in Artificial Intelligence to facilitate knowledge sharing and reuse. They have since then been recognized as a popular research topic in various research communities such as knowledge engineering, e-commerce, natural language processing, cooperative information systems, and information integration. In this section, we define the concept of ontology and give the motivations behind it. We then overview major languages and standards for describing ontologies on the Web. Finally, we evaluate ontology-based systems using interaction layers and dimensions.

2.4.1.1 Modeling Semantics Through Ontology

An *ontology* is a *formal* and *explicit* specification of a *shared conceptualization* [60, 171]. "Conceptualization" refers to an abstraction of a domain that identifies the relevant concepts in that domain. "Shared" means that an ontology captures *consensual* knowledge. The development of ontologies is often a cooperative process involving different entities possibly at different locations (e.g., businesses, government agencies). All entities that agree on using a given ontology commit themselves to the concepts and definitions within that ontology. "Explicit" means that the concepts used in an ontology and the constraints on their use are explicitly defined. "Formal" intends that the ontology should be machine understandable and described using a well-defined model or language called *ontology language*.

An ontology typically consists of a hierarchical description of important concepts in a domain, along with descriptions of the properties of each concepts. Formally, an ontology Ω contains a set of *concepts* (also called *classes*) $\{c_1,...,c_n\}$ which constitutes the core of the ontology. The notion of concept in ontologies is similar to the notion of class in object-oriented programming.

Each concept c_i has a set of *properties* $P_i = \{p_{i1},...p_{im}\}$ associated to it. This set describes the different features of the class. Each property p_{ik} has a *range* R_{ik} (also called *type*) indicating a restriction on the values p_{ik} can take. An ontology relates classes to each other through *ontology relationships.* Examples of relationships include "subclassof", "superclassof". Properties are also related through similar relationships such as "subpropertyof" and "suprepropertyof".

We identify three different types of ontologies depending on their generality level: *vertical*, *horizontal*, and *metadata* ontologies. Other types of ontologies such as *representational*, *method* and *task* ontologies also exist but are out of the scope of this book [71]. *Vertical* ontologies capture the knowledge valid for a particular domain such as medical, mechanic, chemistry, and electronic. *Horizontal* ontologies describe general knowledge that is valid across several domains. They define basic notions and concepts (e.g., time, space) applicable in many technical domains. *Metadata* ontologies provide concepts that allow the description of other concepts. For example, *Dublin Core* is an ontology for describing the content of on-line information source.

2.4.1.2 Ontology Models and Languages

Several ontology-based approaches have been developed for Web applications during the past few years. A common claim for all these approaches is the need for models and languages to specify ontologies. In this section, we overview a representative set of these languages and models: RDF/RDF Schema, Description Logic, DAML+OIL, and OWL. An exhaustive list of ontology languages for the Semantic Web is presented in [84].

RDF and RDF Schema [71]: RDF (*Resource Description Framework*) provides a domain-neutral framework to model metadata about *resources* on the Web. It is recommended by *World Wide Web Consortium* (W3C) working groups. A *resource* is any "thing" on the Web that has a *Uniform Resource Identifiers* (URI) such as Web pages and files. Besides resources, RDF's basic model includes *properties* and *statements.* A *property* is a characteristic, attribute, or relation that describes a resource. A *statement* consists of a specific resource with a named property plus that property's value for that resource. This value can be another resource or a literal value (free text). An RDF description is a list of triples: *(resource, property, value)*. RDF does not provide mechanisms for defining relationships between properties and resources. This is the role of *RDF Schema.* RDF Schema is a type system for RDF. It provides a mechanism to define domain-specific properties and classes of resources to which we can apply those properties. Basic primitives of RDF include *class* and *subclass* which together allow the definition of class hierarchy, *property* and *subproperty* to build property hierarchies, and *do-*

main and *range* to restrict the possible combinations of properties and classes.

Description Logic (DL) [10]: DLs are a family of logic based formalisms for describing knowledge. A DL considers unary relations (called concepts) and binary relations (called roles). A DL terminology includes a set of *primitive* concepts and roles and definitions of *complex* concepts and roles. The definitions of complex concepts and roles are given via *descriptions* that are built using a set of *constructors*. Consider an example in which the primitive concepts are *person*, *smart* and *footballPlayer*, and *child* is a primitive role. Various constructors can be used to define new concepts by imposing some restrictions on the number of fillers of a role, or on the classes to which fillers of a certain role have to belong. For instance, ($\leq$ 3 child) is a complex concept built by applying a number restriction constructor on the role child: it defines the set of objects that have at most 3 fillers for the role child. ($\forall$.child.smart) is a description which is built from the *universal quantification* constructor $\forall$, and defines the class of objects for which all fillers of the role child belong to the class smart. $\exists$child.footballPlayer uses the *existential quantification* constructor and defines the set of objects for which there exists at least one filler of the role child which belongs to the class footballPlayer. The following describes the complex concept c1, which is defined to include set of persons such that all of their children are smart, have at most 3 children, and have a child who is a football player: c1 $:= person \sqcap (\forall child.smart) \sqcap (\leq 3child) \sqcap (\exists child.footballPlayer)$. A particular description logic language may include several constructors other that the Boolean ones such as the Number restrictions or roles also known as cardinality constraints (e.g., $\geq$ 3 hasChild), Qualified number restriction (e.g., $\geq$ 3 hasChild.Female), Nominal (e.g., c := Italy), Inverse roles (e.g., $hasChild^{-}$(hasParent)), Transitive role, and Role composition (e.g., $Uncl := hasParent \circ hasBrother$). Particular DL languages are characterized by the set of constructors allowed for building complex concepts and roles from simpler ones and by the set of axioms for asserting facts about concepts, roles and individuals.

DAML+OIL [99]: DAML+OIL is the result of a merger between DAML-ONT, a language developed as part of the US DARPA Agent Markup Language (DAML) and OIL (the Ontology Inference Layer), developed by a group of (mostly) European researchers. It builds on earlier Web ontology standards such as RDF and RDF Schema and extends those languages with richer modeling primitives (e.g., cardinality). DAML+OIL adopts an object oriented approach, describing ontologies in terms of classes, properties, and axioms (e.g., subsumption relationships between classes or properties) [97]. When a resource R is an instance of a class C, we say that R has type C. From a formal point of view, DAML+OIL can be seen to be equivalent to description logic (DL), with a DAML+OIL ontology corresponding to a DL terminology (Tbox). As in a DL, DAML+OIL classes can be names (URIs) or expressions, and a variety of constructors are provided for building class expressions. Example of DAML+OIL constructors include *intersectionOf*, *unionOf*, *complementOf*, *oneOf*, *minCardinalityQ*, *maxCardinalityQ*. The meaning of the first three constructors (intersectionOf, unionOf and complementOf) is relatively self-explanatory: they are the standard boolean operators that allow classes to be formed from the intersection, union and negation of other classes. The oneOf constructor allows classes to be defined existentially, i.e., by enumerating their members. The minCardinalityQ, maxCardinalityQ, cardinalityQ constructors are known in DLs as qualified number restrictions. The minCardinalityQ (maxCardinalityQ, cardinalityQ) constructor gives the class whose instances are related via a given property to at least (at most, exactly) n different resources of type C. The number n and class C are specified in the constructor.

OWL [98]: OWL (Ontology Web Language) is a revision of the DAML+OIL web ontology language incorporating lessons learned from the design and application of DAML+OIL. The SH family of description logic is the basis of OWL. OWL has three (increasingly expressive) species: OWL lite, OWL DL, and OWL full. OWL lite: equivalent to SHIF(D_n). Inference in SHIF(D) is of worst-case deterministic exponential time (ExpTime) complexity. OWL lite includes all the vocabularies of RDFS schema. From DL boolean operators, OWL lite allows only the usage of the intersection operator via its axiom *intersectionOf*. The cardinality that can be placed on properties is restricted to "0" or "1". With OWL lite one can declare a property to be *transitive*, *symmetric* or *inverse* to another one. OWL DL: equivalent to SHQIN(D), where the inference is of worst-case non deterministic exponential time. OWL DL allows the different boolean operators and it allows to specify different values for the cardinality on properties. OWL full is union of OWL syntax and RDFS. OWL full is undecidable.

2.4.1.3 Interactions in Ontology-based Systems

Ontologies are mostly developed to support interactions at the content layer. At the communication layer, they may rely on existing communication protocol (e.g., HTTP). Ontologies may be used, at the business process layer, to provide a set of pre-defined business documents to be exchanged among partners. Each document would contain the actions that should take place during message exchange.

Participants in an ontology-based system are bound to the concepts and properties defined within the ontology. This may impact their autonomy and heterogeneity. Ontologies are often not stable definitions. Indeed, a shared conceptualization of a domain has to be reached in a process of social communication. Changes in the domain generally trigger the modification of the ontology. The evolution of ontologies causes operability problems, which hamper their effective reuse. Solutions are still required to allow changes to ontologies without making current use invalid. The cost of entry in an ontology-based system may be significant since participants must describe their applications according to a given ontology. Finally, the issues of external manageability and security are not addressed in ontology-based systems.

2.4.2 Web Services

The precise definition of Web services is still evolving as witnessed by the various definitions in the literature. One such definition is that a Web service is a "business function made available via the Internet by a service provider, and accessible by clients that could be human users or software applications" [40]. It is also defined as "loosely coupled applications using open, cross-platform standards and which interoperate across organizational and trust boundaries" [208]. The W3C (*World Wide Web Consortium*) defines a Web service as a "software application identified by a URI (*Uniform Resource Identifier*), whose interfaces and binding are capable of being defined, described and discovered by XML artifacts and supports direct interactions with other software applications using XML based messages via Internet-based protocols". The aforementioned definitions can be seen as complementary. Each definition emphasizes some part of the Web service characteristics (discovery, invocation, etc). In this section, we define Web services as business functionalities that are:

- *Programmatically accessible*: Web services are mainly designed to be invoked by other Web services and applications. They are distributed over the Web and accessible via widely deployed protocols such as HTTP and SMTP. Web services must describe their capabilities to other services including their operations, input and output messages, and the way they can be invoked.
- *Loosely coupled*: Communication among Web services is *document-based.* Web services generally communicate with each other by exchanging XML documents. The use of a document-based communication model caters for loosely coupled relationships among Web services.

2.4.2.1 The Web Service Reference Model

Interactions among Web services involve three types of participants: *service providers*, *service registry*, and *service consumers* (Figure 2.6). *Service providers* are the parties that offer services. They define descriptions of their services and publish them in the *service registry*, a searchable repository of service descriptions. Each description contains details about the corresponding service such as its data types, operations, and network location. *Service consumers* use a *find* operation to locate services of interest. The registry returns the description of each relevant service. The consumer uses this description (e.g., network location) to invoke the corresponding Web service. For example, `HealthDepartment` may advertise a Web service that includes a `scheduleImmunization` operation. `AreaAgencyAging`'s provider would then access the registry, discover `HealthDepartment`'s service, and invoke its operations.

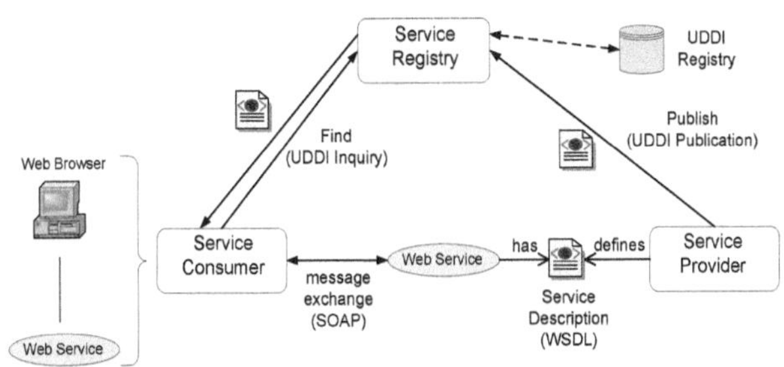

Fig. 2.6 The Web Service Reference Model

Three major standardization initiatives have been submitted to the W3C consortium to support interactions among Web services (Figure 2.6):

- WSDL (*Web Services Description Language*) [217]: WSDL is an XML-based language for describing operational features of Web services. WSDL descriptions are composed of *interface* and *implementation* definitions. The *interface* is an abstract and reusable service definition that can be referenced by multiple *implementations*. The *implementation* describes how the interface is implemented by a given service provider.
- *UDDI* (*Universal Description, Discovery and Integration*) [216]: UDDI defines a programmatic interface for publishing (*publication API*) and discovering (*inquiry API*) Web services [216]. The core component of UDDI is the *business registry*, an XML repository where businesses advertise services so that other businesses can find them. Conceptually, the information provided in a UDDI business registration consists of *white pages* (contact information), *yellow pages* (industrial categorization), and *green pages* (technical information about services).
- SOAP (*Simple Object Access Protocol*) [215]: SOAP is a lightweight messaging framework for exchanging XML formatted data among Web services. SOAP can be used with a variety of transport protocols such as HTTP, SMTP, and FTP. A SOAP message has a very simple structure: an XML element (called *envelope*) with two child elements. The first ele-

ment, the *header* includes features such as security and transactions. The second element, the *body* includes the actual exchanged data.

2.4.2.2 Web Service Stack

The Web service architecture is organized into a layered stack. The four key layers, including communication, messages, description, and processes, are shown along the perpendicular direction in Figure 2.7. The layered stack is an extension of the W3C service stack [218]. Service operations including publication, lookup, and binding could get support from the service stack. The upper layers rely on the lower layers to realize their functionalities:

- *Communications:* The underpinning of the Web services stack is the network, where the underlying communications take place. A set of network protocols help realize the network accessibility of Web services. The wide adoption of HTTP makes it the first choice of standard network protocol for Internet available Web services. Other Internet protocols could also be supported, such as SMTP.
- *Messaging:* The massaging layer provides a document-based messaging model for the interaction with Web services. The messaging model works with a wide variety of transport protocols. For example, the messaging model can be combined with HTTP to traverse firewalls. In another case, combination with SMTP enables the interaction with Web services that support asynchronous message exchanges.
- *Representation:* The representation layer is for describing Web services. It wraps Web services and specifies their functionalities, operations, data types, and binding information using a service interface. The WS discovery will rely on the WS representation to locate appropriate Web services.
- *Discovery:* The discovery layer is for locating and publishing Web services. It enables the usage of Web services in a much wider scale. Service providers can store the service descriptions in a service registry via the publication functionalities provided by WS discovery. Meanwhile, service requestors can query the service registry and look for their interested services based on the stored service descriptions.
- *Processes:* The processes layer supports more complex interactions between Web services, which enables Web service interoperation. It relies on the basic interaction functionalities provided by the technologies at lower layers in the Web service stack. For example, it needs Web service discovery and representation for querying and locating Web services based on their descriptions. The selected Web services are used to construct the process, which consists of a sequence of coordinated Web services.

The variety of Web service technologies constitutes a rich solution space of Web services. Each technology has specific design requirements depending on the usage scenarios. Therefore, it is important to determine the relevant

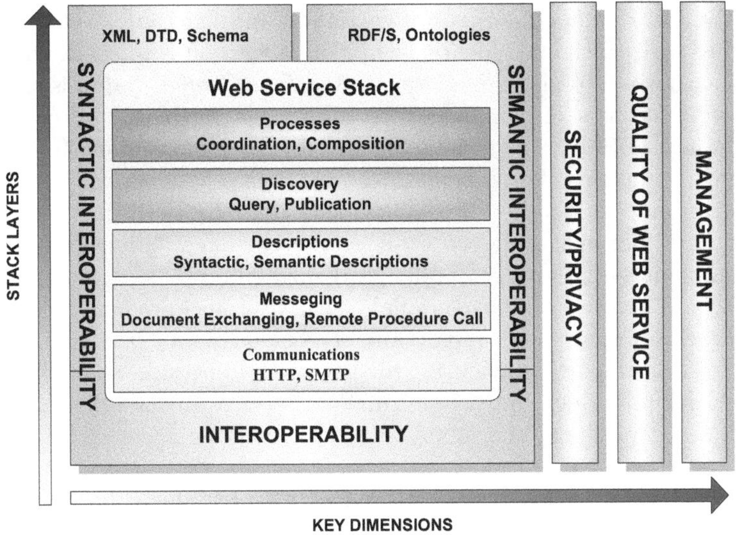

Fig. 2.7 Web Service Stack and Key Dimensions

requirements for deploying Web service. We identify a set of dimensions to evaluate Web service technologies. These dimensions are in line with the key requirements for deploying Web services. The dimensions are defined in line with the vertical layers across the Web service stack (see Figure 2.7), which include *interoperability*, *security & privacy*, *Quality of Web Services (QoWS)*, and *management*.

Interoperability: Web services are designed to bring together applications from geographically distributed and heterogeneous environments and provide interoperability between them. Therefore, interoperability is a core requirement that Web services aim at achieving. Interoperation occurs at two levels: *syntactic* and *semantic levels*. *Syntactic interoperability* is concerned with the compatibility of the input/output of the operations, the binding types, the data format, and so on. XML would help achieve this interoperability by encoding this syntactic information into XML messages. *Semantic interoperability* is the most challenging issue for achieving the truly seamless interoperation. It would rely on some machine interpretable languages to address the semantic issues. The envisioned Semantic Web could be a good resource for providing Web service description languages with rich semantics.

Security & Privacy: Security is an important issue for deploying Web services. Web services enable interoperation at the risk of letting outside intruders attack the internal applications and databases since they open up the network to give access to outside users to these resources [80]. Web service security needs to be concerned with the following aspects:

authentication, *authorization*, *confidentiality*, and *integrity*. *Authentication* is used to verify a claimed identity while *authorization* is to check whether a user is authorized to perform a requested action. *Confidentiality* is to ensure that information is disclosed only to authorized recipients by encrypting the message. Lastly, *integrity* is to protect the information from being tampered by putting digital signatures on the messages. Privacy is another major concern of Web service deployment [182, 132]. During the service interactions, personal data or business secrets (e.g., billing information, shipping address, or product preference) might be unintentionally or even inevitably released [1]. Conventional privacy protection mainly relies on the law enforcement and restriction of social values. Lack of sufficient technological support, privacy is still left in a vulnerable state. Emerging technologies for preserving privacy in Web services include digital privacy credentials, data filters, and mobile privacy preserving agents [183].

QoWS: The proliferation of Web services will introduce the competition between large numbers of Web services that offer similar functionalities. The concept of QoWS is considered as a key feature in distinguishing between competing Web services [231, 234, 185, 232, 172]. *QoWS* encompasses different quality parameters that characterize the behavior of a Web service in delivering its functionalities. Examples of parameters include availability, latency, and fees.

Management: Web service management refers to the management of Web services through a set of management capabilities to *control* and *monitor* service qualities and service usage. Web service management mechanisms are highly coupled with QoWS of a Web service. *Control management* aims to improve the service quality through a set of control mechanisms. Typical control mechanisms include Web service transaction and coordination, Web service change management, and Web service optimization. Transactions help improve the reliability and fault-tolerance of Web services. Change management deals with highly dynamic environment of Web services. It takes a series actions to identify the changes, notifying the coupled entities, and adopting appropriate operations to response the change. Web service optimization helps users identify Web services and/or their combinations to best fulfill their requirements. *Monitoring management* aims to rate the behavior of Web services in delivering its functionalities in terms of each QoWS parameter. Monitoring Web service behavior would be crucial in either calculating QoWS parameter values or assessing a Web service claim in terms of promised QoWS.

2.4.2.3 RESTful Services

REST (Representational State Transfer) or RESTful Web services may be considered a lightweight version of SOAP Web services in that they do not require XML messages or WSDLs [73]. RESTful Web services use HTTP to transfer information between other RESTful Web services. Critics of SOAP Web services state that they are too complex. Another concern is the brittleness of the WSDL itself-minor changes to the WSDL residing on the server or an upgrade to the Web service stack can cause each client using the Web service to have to make changes to its code. Further, there are concerns over the performance of SOAP Web services. Once the requestor has received the SOAP message response, an XML parser must be used to parse the response, and retrieve the results. Searching the UDDI repository to look up a service is also costly. REST has been chosen by many developers for it requires less overhead. REST is used by Google, Amazon, and Flickr, among other mainstream Web sites. RESTful services tend to use custom developed tokens that are passed in the URL QueryStrings. REST uses HTTP variables such as GET, POST, UPDATE, DELETE, and OPTIONS. The REST architecture is based on four principles [73]:

- Resource identification through URI - Resources are identified by URIs, which provides a global addressing space for resource and service discovery.
- Uniform interface - GET retrieves the current state of a resource in some representation. POST transfers a new state of a resource.
- Self-descriptive messages - Resources are decoupled from their representation so that their content can be accessed in variety of formats (e.g., HTML, XML, plain text, PDF, JPEG).
- Stateful interactions through hyperlinks - Several techniques exist to change (e.g., URI rewriting, cookies, and hidden form fields). State can be embedded in response messages to point to valid future states of the interaction.

2.4.2.4 Semantic Web Services

Semantic Web services integrate ontologies into Web services to pave the way for automated selection, composition, and monitoring of Web services [134, 147, 136]. The ontology-based Web service representation enriches the Web service description with machine interpretable semantics. It uses ontology language constructs to describe the functionalities of services. Web service discovery can locate appropriate Web services based on the functionality information of Web services. The ontology-based model can also specify the behavior of service operations, including the preconditions and effects of performing an operation of a Web service. Web service processes can rely on the behavior information to decide the order of different Web services that participate in the process. Major semantic Web frameworks include *OWL-S* [56], *WSMF* [72], and *WSMO* [89].

OWL-S [56] – OWL-S is an OWL-based ontology for describing Web services. It is an extension of DAML-S, a DAML+OIL upper ontology for Web service. The `Service` class sits on top of the hierarchical structure. It consists of three components: a `ServiceProfile`, a `ServiceModel`, and a `ServiceGrounding`.

The service profile represents the capacities of the service. It helps a searching agent discover services that fulfill certain requests. Specifically, an OWL-S profile contains three types of information: information about the service provider, functional description, and a host of the service characteristics. The provider information contains the contact information of the service providing entity. The functional description specifies the transformation introduced by the service. It provides the required inputs and the generated outputs. It also specifies the preconditions needed to execute the service and the expected execution effects.

The service model describes the execution process of the service. OWL-S defines the `ProcessModel`, as a subclass of `ServiceModel` to give a detailed perspective on how a service operates. A process can generate two kinds of effects: data transformation and state transition. For data transformation, the process receives some inputs and produces some outputs, whereas for state transition, the process starts based on some preconditions and produces some effects. The process model consists of three types of processes: *atomic*, *simple*, and *composite*. An atomic process is directly invocable by receiving an input message and returning an output message. The atomic process needs to be grounded to a WSDL operation to enable the execution. Similarly, the input and output of the process also needs to be grounded to the corresponding WSDL messages. A simple process mainly serves as a tool for abstractions. It may provide a view of some specialized uses of atomic processes. It may also simplify the presentation of some composite services for planning and reasoning. Simple processes are not grounded to any WSDL operations, so they are not invocable. A composite service combines several other processes (either composite or non-composite) with a set of control constructs. OWL-S defines a minimal set of control constructs, which consist of Sequence, Split, Split + Join, Choice, Unordered, Condition, If-Then-Else, Iterate, Repeat-While, and Repeat-Until. A composite service is not associated with a grounding. Therefore, it is not invocable either.

A grounding enables access to the service. It specifies the description elements needed to interact with the service. The grounding specifies the concrete level of the service description. In contrast, the service profile and service model specify the abstract part of the service description. The core function of a grounding is to realize the abstract inputs and outputs of an atomic process as concrete messages. The messages serve as a vehicle to carry the inputs and output in some transmittable format. OWL-S depends on WSDL to ground its atomic processes due to the similarity between the grounding and WSDL's binding.

WSMF and *WSMO* [72, 89] – Web Service Modeling Ontology (WSMO) is an ontology for describing several aspects of semantic Web services. It takes Web Service Modeling Framework (WSMF) [72] as a starting point. The WSMF consists of four main parts, including *goals*, *ontologies*, *mediators*, and *Web services*. The *goal* defines the problems that a Web service is expected to address. The *ontology* defines the formal semantics for the terms used in other elements of the WSMF. The *mediator* is used to address interoperability problems, such as data mismatches and process sequence mismatches. The *Web service* part defines several elements to describe a Web service, including the precondition, post-condition, data flow, control flow.

WSMO refines the WSMF and defines these elements in a formal fashion. The WSMO definition of a Web service consists of four parts, including *nonFunctionalProperties*, *usedMediators*, *capability*, and *interface*. The `nonFunctionalProperties` describe the properties that are not directly related to a Web service's functionality, such as service providers, cost, performance, reliability, security, etc. These properties are mainly used to help software agents discover and select Web services. They can also be used for negotiation. The `usedMediators` define the mediators used by a Web service. For example, a Web service can use the concepts and relationships elsewhere by importing ontologies through ontology mediators (`ooMediators`). It can also use `wgMediator` to address interoperability problems between a Web service and goals. The `capability` defines the functionalities of a Web service. It helps software agents locate a desirable Web service. A capability can be modeled by using preconditions, postconditions, and effects. The `interface` describes how a Web service functionalities can be fulfilled. It can be used to help software agents invoke and combine Web services. The WSMO definition describes the interface of a Web service from a twofold view, including *choreography* (from user's prospective) and *orchestration* (form other service provider's perspective). The choreography describes the information about how to interact with a service to make use of its functionalities, such as Message Exchange Pattern (MEP). The orchestration describes the information about how a Web service is outsourced to provide a value-added service. It has a tight relationship with the Problem Solving Pattern (PSP), which specifies a sequence of activities to achieve a given requirement. *Web Service Modeling Language* (WSML) [88] provides a formal syntax and semantic for WSMO. It is based on well-known logical formalisms, including first-order logic, description logic, and logic programming.

2.4.2.5 Web Service Composition

Web service composition is a process that combines outsourced Web services to offer *value-added* services [67, 7, 140]. Web service composition is different from traditional application integration, where applications are tightly coupled and physically combined. Web services adopt a document-based messaging model, which supports the integration of loosely coupled applications that are across multiple organizations. Major standardization efforts for service composition include BPEL and ebXML's *business process specification.*

BPEL [15]: BPEL models the behavior of a business process based on the interactions with the involved business partners. It establishes grammar guidelines to describe the business process based on XML, including its control logic and message format. It uses WSDL to model the services in the process flow. It also depends on WSDL to describe the external services that are needed by the process. A major design goal of BPEL4WS is to separate the public aspects of business process behavior from the internal ones. The separation helps businesses conceal their internal decisions from their business partners. Moreover, internal changes of the process implementation no longer affects the public business protocol. Therefore, BPEL4WS has both abstract and executable business processes to support the separation. An *abstract process* also refers to the business protocol. It specifies the public aspects in the business interactions. Specially, an abstract process only deals with the exchanges of public messages between business partners. It is isolated from the execution of a process flow. Therefore, an abstract process will not release any internal details of the process to its partners. An *execution process* contains the logic and state of a process. It specifies the sequence of the Web Service interactions conducted in the business process of each business partner. A business process consists of several steps called activities. BPEL4WS supports two types of activities, including *basic activities* and *structured activities.* Basic activities manage the interactions of the process with its external resources. Its major task is to receive, reply, and invoke Web services. Structured activities control the overall process flow. They specify the sequence of Web services in the flow. BPEL4WS also defines a set of control constructs to enable the sequencing mechanism, which is similar to XLANG. BPEL4WS provides a set of mechanisms to support transactions and handle exceptions. It uses a *scope* element to aggregate several activities in a transaction. When an error occurs, a compensation procedure will be invoked, which is also similar to XLANG.

ebXML's business process specification [167]: ebXML's business process specification is another process-based composition approach. The business process specification schema is available in UML and XML versions. The UML version only defines a UML class diagram. It is not intended for the direct creation of a business process specification but provides a representation of all the elements and relationships required for its creation. The XML version allows the creation of XML documents representing ebXML-compliant business process specifications. ebXML provides a set of common business process specifications that are shared by multiple industries. These specifications, stored in the business library, can be used by companies to build customized business processes. Interactions between business processes are represented through choreography. To model collaboration in which companies can engage, ebXML defines Collaboration Protocol Agreements (CPAs). A CPA is an agreement by two trading partners which specifies in advance the conditions under which the trading partners will collaborate (e.g., terms of shipment and payment).

2.4.2.6 Automatic Web Service Composition

One of the major challenges for a wide adoption of the service-oriented approach is the automated composition of Web service, i.e. the development of concepts, techniques, technologies, and tools that support an easy-to-use, low-cost, dynamic, and time-efficient composition of Web services [177]. However, the development of automated composition techniques is still an open problem. In this section, we overview major research techniques for supporting automatic service composition.

Interactive Service Composition – The interactive composition scheme blurs the distinction between composers and common users. Composers are required to have a clear goal and know the tasks that need to be performed to accomplish the composition. Common users can be guided through a set of steps to finish a composer's task. The composition scheme will work interactively with the common users to help them achieve the orchestration model. The orchestration process can start from users' goals and work backward by chaining all related services. It can also start from some initial states and achieve the users' goals by adding services in the forward direction. At each step, the scheme will choose a new service based on the task specified by the users. The interactive scheme can also capture the constraints and preferences during the interaction process. The constraints and preferences can serve as additional criteria to select services for the composition. An interactive composition approach is proposed in [197]. It adopts the OWL ontologies to model the component services. The service model specifies the input, output, precondition, and effects (IOPE) of services. The proposed approach also implements a tool for automatic translation from WSDL to OWL-S, which enables the support of WSDL-based component services. The data types are defined by XML-schema and message exchange between component services relies on the data flow approach. The composed service are specified using OWL-S. The interactive composition can be performed by chaining component services in either the forward or the backward directions. At each step, the composition scheme adds a new service based on the users' selection. Existing component service in the orchestration model can serve as a criterion to filter candidate services. Only the services that match the IOPE properties of existing services can be selected by the system and presented to the users.

AI Planning Techniques for Service Composition – Another trend for dealing with the automatic service composition is the use of Artificial Intelligence (AI) planning techniques. The composition engine treats service composition as a planning problem. *SHOP2* adopts the concept of HTN (Hierarchical Task Network) as a planning methodology [226]. It decomposes tasks into smaller and smaller subtasks, until primitive tasks are found that can be performed directly. SHOP2 uses a knowledge base which contains *operators* and *methods*. Each operator is a description of what needs to be done to accomplish a primitive task. Each method describes the process of decomposing a compound task into partially ordered subtasks. *Estimated-regression* is another planning technique for service composition [133]. The situation-space search is guided by a heuristic estimator obtained by backward chaining in a relaxed problem space. The resulting space is so much smaller than situation space that a planner can build complete representation of it, called a regression graph. The regression graph reveals, for each conjunct of a goal, the minimal sequence of actions that could achieve it.

Techniques Dealing with Service Behavior – A number of techniques dealing with service behavior have been proposed (e.g., [103, 33, 230]). These techniques deal with services whose life-cycle consists of several related calls. Models and formalisms for describing service behaviors have been discussed, including *finite state machine*, *Mealy machine*, and *pi-calculus* [103]. This book focuses on "isolated" operations, that is services whose life-cycle consists of independent operation invocations. The techniques described in [103] can be adopted to define dynamic semantic rules dealing with the composability of service behaviors. A pi-calculus model for extending CORBA IDL with protocol descriptions is proposed in [33]. The model is based on the concept of role which allows the specification of the observable behavior of CORBA objects. Techniques for testing the compatibility of behaviors are also presented. *Protocol Specifications* is another approach for describing object service protocols using finite state machines [230]. This approach describes both the services offered and required by objects. It also defines techniques that allow participants to be checked for protocol compatibility. However, the aforementioned techniques deal with objects and components *not* Web services.

Matching Techniques for Web Services – Several techniques have been proposed to deal with Web service matching. LARKS defines five techniques for service matchmaking: context matching, profile comparison, similarity matching, signature matching, and constraint matching [202]. Matching services to requests is performed by using any combination of the above techniques. The ATLAS matchmaker defines two methods for comparing service capabilities described in DAML-S [179, 176]. The first method compares functional attributes to check whether advertisements support the required type of service or deliver sufficient quality of service. The second compares the functional capabilities of Web services in terms of inputs and outputs. [42] presents a service matching technique for pervasive computing environments. Service descriptions are provided in DAML-S. They also include platform specific information such as processor type, speed, and memory availability. The composition manager uses a semantic service discovery mechanism to select participant services. This mechanism is based on DReggie, a Jini-based semantic discovery framework [41]. [124] adopts techniques from knowledge representation to match DAML-S service capabilities. In particular, it defines a description logic (DL) reasoner; advertisements and requests are represented in DL notations. Another DAML-S based matchmaker implementation is KarmaSIM [161] where DAML-S descriptions are described in terms of a first-order logic language (predicates) and then converted to Petri-nets where the composition can be simulated, evaluated and performed. Other service matching techniques are also presented in [12, 135, 95]. However, they techniques mostly focus on comparing syntactic attributes of Web services.

2.4.2.7 Interactions in Web Services

Web services allow interactions at the communication layer by using SOAP or REST as messaging protocols. RESTful services do not require XML messages or WSDLs, but as in the case of SOAP uses HTTP to transfer information between other RESTful Web services. The adoption of a messaging over well-established protocols such as HTTP enables communication among heterogeneous systems. At the content layer, Web services use WSDL language. WSDL recommends the use of XML Schema as a canonical type system (to associate data types to message parameters). However, the current version of WSDL does not model semantic features of Web services. For example, no constructs are defined to describe document types (e.g., whether an operation is a request for quotation or a purchase order). Semantic Web service frameworks such as OWL-S, WSMF, and WSMO deal with semantic interoperability.

Web services are still at a maturing stage. Hence, they still lack the support for interactions at the business process layer. To date, enabling interactions among Web services has largely been an *ad hoc* process involving repetitive low level programming. Standardization efforts such as BPEL4WS (*Business Process Execution Language for Web Services*) [15] and ebXML's business process specification are underway for enabling the definition of business processes through Web service composition.

The use of a document-based messaging model in Web services caters for loosely coupled relationships. Additionally, Web services are not statically bound to each other. New partners with relevant features can be discovered and invoked. However to date, dynamic discovery of Web services takes place mostly at development time. Heterogeneous applications (e.g., Java, CORBA objects) may be wrapped and exposed as Web services. For example, the *Axis's Java2WSDL* utility in *IBM's Web Services Toolkit* enables the generation of WSDL descriptions from Java class files. *IONA*'s *Orbix E2A Web Services Integration Platform* may be used to create Web services from existing EJBs or CORBA objects. In terms of autonomy, Web services are accessible through published interfaces. Partners interact with Web services without having to be aware of what is happening behind the scene. They are not required to know how the operations provided by the service are internally implemented. Some operations can even be transparently outsourced from third parties.

WSDL does not currently include operations for monitoring Web services such as checking the availability of an operation or the status of a submitted request. Additionally, neither UDDI nor WSDL currently define quality of service parameters such as cost and time. In terms of adaptability, changes may occur in operation signatures (e.g., name), messages (e.g., number of parameters, data types), service access (e.g., port address), and service and operation availability. The process of dealing with changes is currently *ad hoc* and manually performed. More efforts need to be done to cater for automatic detection and handling of changes.

Security in Web services needs to be addressed at different levels including communication, description, and firewall. At the communication level, enabling security in XML and HTTP is an important factor towards securing Web services. Current standardization efforts include securing XML-based messages through the creation of an XML digital signature standard and S-HTTP, a protocol for transmitting data securely over the Web. Other work is also being done to extend SOAP to include a security specification at the receiving endpoints (e.g., specify which users are authorized to receive and process messages). At the service description level, WSDL does not include security-oriented information such as role-based access control and other authorization information. Finally, since SOAP messages carried over HTTP traverse firewalls, network administrators would need to configure their firewalls so that malicious requests (e.g., code embedded in SOAP messages) are not tunneled through SOAP messages. For example, *application firewalls*, sitting behind networks firewalls, have been developed (e.g., *iSecureWeb*). Application firewalls check all HTTP traffic to validate and authorize messages based on security policies.

Security with REST is limited compared to SOAP Web services. Access Control Lists (ACLs) may be used when the POST method is used. Filtering of the QueryString on the server-side can be used, which is a similar approach used for HTTP Web applications. An audit trail should be kept when RESTful services are used to trace security violations. When the POST command is used, ACLs may be used which protect against unauthorized use of a service. Also, since there are no standards for RESTful services security, each API may use a different security model.

The emergence of tools to describe, advertise, and invoke Web services facilitates the development of Web service-based solutions. However, the use of a tagged language such as XML increases the volume of information to be exchanged among Web services. This might overload the network in presence of a large number of services, hence penalizing the scalability of the Web service approach. Additionally, SOAP defines only simple data types. Using complex data types may require the XML parser to get the corresponding XML Schema definitions from remote locations. This might add an overhead for processing SOAP messages. The registry presents another scalability issue. A centralized registry might result in a single point of failure and bottleneck for accessing and publishing Web services. A distributed registry would cater for a more reliable and scalable solution. However, this incurs an additional overhead of managing distributed repositories. An intermediary solution is adopted in UDDI where the registry is physically replicated over multiple nodes. This solution solves the problem of centralized registry. However, it still requires the nodes to exchange data with each other to maintain registry consistency.

2.4.3 Software Agents

The concept of *software agent* (or simply *agent*) emerged as an important paradigm for organizing many classes of distributed applications such as e-commerce, digital libraries, information retrieval, and data mining. It is defined as a piece of software capable of acting exactingly to accomplish tasks on behalf of its consumers. Consumers may be end-users, other agents, or applications using the agent. A more comprehensive definition would be to view an agent as an umbrella term which covers a range of properties. Agents typically possess several (or all) of the properties summarized in Table 2.3. Ideally, an agent should exhibit all the properties equally well, but this is an aspiration rather than the reality [165]. Other properties such as *emotion* and *character* (knowledge, belief, intention, etc.) have also been defined [224]. They are mainly used in artificial intelligence applications and so, are out of the scope of this book.

2.4.3.1 Agent Communication Language

A multi-agent system is a collaborating set of agents in which the membership may change over time. Individual agents in the community view each other as peers and are responsible for providing specific services according

Property	*Synonyms*	*Definition*
Continuous	Not Available	An agent is a continuously running process
Autonomous	Not Available	Agents operate without the direct intervention of humans or others and exercise control over their own actions
Co-operative	Communicative Socially able	Agents interact with each other via some kind of agent-communication language
Reactive	Sensing and acting	Agents perceive their environment and respond in a timely fashion to changes that occur in it
Adaptive	Learning	Agents change their behavior based on their previous experience
Pro-active	Goal-oriented Purposeful	Agents do not simply act in response to their environment, they are able to take initiatives to achieve a certain goal
Mobile	Not Available	Agents are able to transport themselves from one site (in a network) to another

Table 2.3 Agent Properties

to their role. The processing of a request in such an environment is distributed among the different agents. The success of a multi-agent system relies on how the agents interact and interoperate. This involves the ability of agents to communicate with each other via an *Agent communication language* (ACL). An ACL consists of three major parts: a *vocabulary*, an inner language called *KIF* (*Knowledge Interchange Format*) and an outer language called *KQML* (*Knowledge Query and Manipulation Language*). An ACL message is a KQML expression in which the arguments are terms in KIF formed from words in the ACL vocabulary.

Agents should share a common understanding of what is being communicated. Ontologies facilitate agent communication by providing a common vocabulary. The vocabulary is an open-ended dictionary or list of words appropriate to common application areas. Each word has an English description for use by humans and formal annotations (written in KIF) for use by programs. The dictionary allows for the addition of new words within both existing and new application areas. KIF is a prefix version of first order predicate calculus, with various extensions to enhance its expressiveness. It provides for the encoding of simple data, constraints, negations, and quantified expressions. A KQML message is a piece of dialogue between a sender and a receiver. Each message is a list of participants enclosed in matching parentheses. The first word in the list indicates the type of dialogue (ask, tell, recommend, bid, etc.). The subsequent entries are the arguments, that is KIF expressions appropriate to that dialogue.

Below is an example of KQML message where a sender (Mary) is asking the receiver (Bookstore) to send information regarding all books related to "Agents" which costs below $30:

```
(ask
  :sender Mary
  :receiver Bookstore
```

:content "select * from book where topic="Agents" and price<30"
:language "Oracle SQL"
:ontology "online bookstore")

2.4.3.2 Interactions in Multi-Agent Systems

Multi-agent systems cater for interactions at the communication layer by having a standard communication language, namely ACL. This assumes that the underlying communication and transport protocols are already established. At the content layer, ontologies are used to facilitate communication between agents and add semantics to their messages. Multi-agent systems lack support for specifying complex business processes. A process is generally spread through the implementation code of every agent involved in the process. This *ad hoc* definition of business processes does not scale because of the size of partners that may be involved in business processes. One solution would be to have a separate *control* agent that handles the business process. However, the control agent's design is time consuming. Additionally, the business logic is embedded in the control agent, making it hard to reuse for different business processes [180].

Multi-agent systems assume that relationships between different partners have to be pre-established. Additionally, data to be interchanged among agents generally needs to be manually or semi-automatically mapped to a common ontology. This makes agents suitable for long-term and tightly coupled relationships. Agents may be added to existing applications to add new functions or customize the execution of existing functions with little impact on the autonomy of those applications. However, they must adhere to the concepts and properties of a common ontology which may limit their autonomy.

Agents may wrap proprietary and heterogeneous applications. The adoption of an ontology enables the abstraction from heterogeneous information representations. Event subscriptions and monitoring agents may be used to address the issue of external manageability. However, adaptability is not adequately addressed in multi-agent systems. Agents are typically preprogrammed with certain functionalities and can hardly be configured to switch roles or change interaction patterns. Agents interact to carry out sophisticated tasks on behalf of users. In the course of this interaction, they may exchange sensitive information about these users. More research is needed to ensure that multi-agent systems support the security features required in Semantic Web interactions. The cost of entry in an agent-based system is significant. Agents must be able to exchange information via Agent Communication Language. They also need to formulate queries or requests based on the common ontology. They finally must have a way of matching queries/requests with their known ontologies (i.e. reason over its repository of ontologies).

2.4.4 XML-based Interaction Standards

A large number of contemporary interaction standards are based on XML. The vision behind this approach is to allow the use of services on the Web without dedicated transformation and mediation facilities or custom integration of partners' systems. Business partners would form a *trading community* based on their capabilities to produce and consume those XML documents. The business process of the trading community is specified by the shared document definitions. The partners are interconnected in terms of largely agreed upon documents. The business logic implementation at a partner side is invisible to other trading partners. In general, a complete XML-based integration requires standardized domain-specific ontologies (such as an agreed upon DTD or XML Schema), mappings between different ontology descriptions, and means for processing XML documents and invoking appropriate services (e.g., workflows and legacy systems) to handle requests.

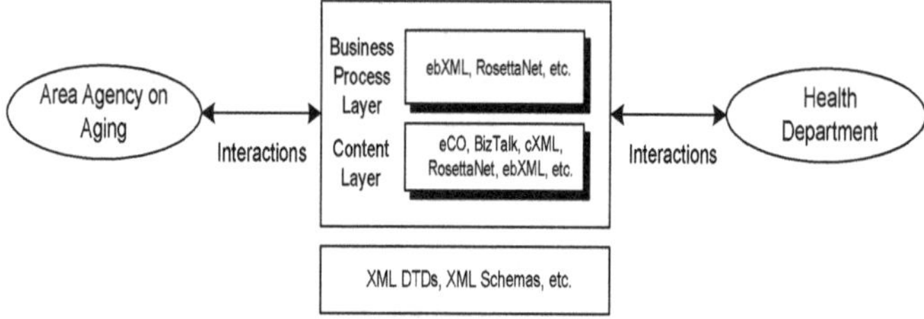

Fig. 2.8 XML-based Interaction Standards

Most of the existing XML-based interaction standards were developed for business-to-business (B2B) interactions. However, they may be extended to deal with other types of applications such as e-government and digital library. In what follows, we describe a representative set of those standards (Figure 2.8). The proposed standards generally deal with enabling interactions at the content (e.g., *eCO*, *cXML*) and business process (e.g., *RosettaNet*) layers. However they sometimes overlap or even compete with each other [31]. The issue of interoperability has thus shifted from the level of applications to the level of standards. A trading partner has to deal with several standards at the same time. In case one trading partner exchanges messages across industries, the variety of standards is likely to increase even more [31].

2.4.4.1 eCO

eCO [47] aims at providing means to businesses to discover and access services regardless of the standards and protocols each potential partner adopts. At the content level, eCO introduces xCBL (*XML Common Business Library*) to define business documents. xCBL consists of a set of XML *core documents* that are used to represent common interactions in business transactions. It does not target vertical industry domains. It attempts to provide a generic framework for describing the content of core business documents. The main motivation for establishing core documents is that some concepts are common to all business domains and thus can be expressed in a common format. Examples of such core documents are: *purchase orders*, *invoices*, *date*, *time*, and *currencies*. Business partners may use and extend these documents (e.g., adding new elements) to develop their own business documents. For example, `HealthDepartment` can use xCBL to create an XML document of its service catalog by customizing the generic *xCBL catalog DTD* with specific information about the search method (e.g., immunization services by type). Businesses are not limited to a specific set of pre-defined documents. However, this may hamper interoperability since companies would need to be aware of newly created documents.

At the business process level, eCO focuses more on providing a common building blocks for interactions among businesses. Businesses can advertise their online services as *Business Interface Definitions (BIDs)*. BIDs are XML descriptions that specify business services in terms of documents they accept and produce. It does not mandate a global business process definition. eCO uses xCBL as a basis to define both the interfaces of processes and content of data elements. Since every partner is forced to use the same tag to define the same type of information, the structural heterogeneity is not a problem. As is any standard, there is however a non-trivial issue: the meaning and types of services and their interfaces can vary among businesses although a group of partners in a specific marketplace may select to adopt common conventions. In generic frameworks such as eCO, it is difficult to address semantic heterogeneity because of the wide range of E-commerce applications. One solution is to use several schemas (or *ontologies*) including horizontal (i.e., across domains such as computer manufacturing and healthcare) and vertical (i.e., within a specific domain) domains. This solution requires the support of data normalization, mapping and conversion between schemas or ontologies.

Although, eCO requires that services be described using XML schemas, it does address, albeit in a limited way, the issue of autonomy. eCO separates the description of services and their implementations. Note that a marketplace may adopt some common conventions for describing services. This may as a result, negatively impact on the partners' autonomy. For example, a change in the name of a tag, requires all partners to make that specific change at the same time. In eCO, the use of security mechanisms is optional.

However, business partners do not need to directly gain access to each other systems. The establishment of a new relationship with an existing partner does not require any additional work. The creation of a new service requires the provision of its description (types, interfaces, etc). It also requires the integration of the interfaces of the service with internal applications. The integration cost in an XML-based approach tends to be less significant than other approaches because of widely available XML processing tools. The eCO framework rates high in adaptability. The impact of local changes is limited as partner systems are loosely coupled. In addition, eCO offers extensibility to accommodate changes.

2.4.4.2 cXML

cXML (*Commerce XML*) [54] consists of an XML-based schema language and a protocol for online purchasing transactions. It targets business transactions that involve non-production Maintenance, Repair, and Operating (MRO) goods and services. In a nutshell, cXML can be considered as a simplified XML and Internet-based version of EDI. cXML assumes the existence of intermediaries (*E-commerce hubs*) that act as trusted third parties between procurement systems and supplier systems. The functions provided by an E-commerce hub (e.g., Ariba Network, Extricity Software) are similar to those provided by the BizTalk repository. However, cXML does not prescribe a specific intermediary architecture.

cXML supports two communication models: *request-response* and *one-way*. The request-response provides for synchronous communication through HTTP. The one-way provides for asynchronous communication through HTTP or other protocols. Currently, the one-way model supports HTTP and URL Form Encoding.

At the content level, cXML defines a set of XML DTDs to describe procurement documents in the same spirit as xCBL (e.g., order request, order response). It provides the following elements for describing product catalogs: *Supplier*, *Index*, and *Contract*. The supplier element describes general information about a supplier (e.g., address, ordering methods). The index element describes the supplier's inventory (e.g., product description, part numbers, classification codes). The contract element describes the negotiation agreements between a buyer and a supplier on product attributes (e.g., price, quantity). Catalogs can be static or dynamic. In the cXML terminology a dynamic catalog is called a *punchout*.

At the business process level, the cXML approach is similar to OBI's (see Section 2.3.1.2). cXML defines a generic procurement protocol. This protocol consists of a number of commonly agreed upon online procurement activities (e.g., product selection, order request, order approval, order transmission, order routing). E-commerce hubs provide means for catalog and purchase order management (e.g, catalog publishing and subscription, automated purchase order routing and tracking).

cXML offers similar properties to those in OBI, namely, heterogeneity, autonomy, and adaptability. cXML appears to rate higher than OBI with regard to scalability because the integration cost in an XML-based approach tends to be less significant than other approaches. cXML addresses security by including authentication information message headers. One advantage of cXML approach is economy of scale and ease of managing business relationships. Both suppliers and buyers only need to manage relationships with the trusted intermediary rather than with all their business partners.

2.4.4.3 RosettaNet

RosettaNet [48] aims at standardizing product descriptions and business processes in information technology supply chain applications. RosettaNet's supply chain include information technology products (e.g., boards, systems, peripherals, finished systems) and electronic components (e.g., chips, connectors). RosettaNet focuses on three key areas of standardization to automate Web-based interactions. First, the vocabulary needs to be aligned. The *RosettaNet Business Dictionary* contains vocabulary that can be used to describe business properties (e.g., business name, address, tax identifier). The *RosettaNet Technical Dictionary* contains properties that can be used to describe characteristics of products (e.g., computer parts) and services (e.g., purchase order). Second, the way in which business messages are wrapped and transported must be specified. The *RosettaNet Implementation Framework* specifies content of messages, transport protocols (HTTP, CGI, email, SSL) for communication and common security mechanism (digital certificates, digital signatures). Third, the business process governing the interchange of the business messages themselves must be harmonized and specified. *RosettaNet*'s PIPs (*Partner Interface Processes*) are pre-defined XML-based *conversations*. A *conversation* consists of a set of business documents (e.g., purchase order, purchase order acknowledgment) and message exchange logic (e.g., the sequencing of the actions that take place during a product quote request). A PIP is defined using a combination of textual and graphical (UML-based state machine) representations.

At the communication layer, common Internet transport protocols are supported. At the content layer, RosettaNet uses an XML-based schema as document content model. The use of a vertical ontology (i.e, common vocabulary with information technology supply chain domain) contributes to solving the problem of semantic heterogeneity. At the business process layer, RosettaNet focuses on providing a common basis for public interactions via PIPs. The integration of PIPs with internal business processes is performed by partners. RosettaNet does not provide means to define arbitrary global business processes. RosettaNet offers similar properties as OBI with regards to security.

It offers similar properties as eCO with regard to autonomy, adaptability, scalability, coupling, and external manageability.

2.5 Deployment Platforms for Web-based Interactions

Major software vendors (*IBM*, *Microsoft*, *Sun Microsystems*, *HP*, *Oracle*, *BEA systems*, etc) are currently working on implementing Web service platforms. The purpose of this section is not to compare commercial products but to overview their main features. Because there are a large number of products, this section does not attempt to cover all of them. Instead, we focus on the major players in this arena. Our coverage is based on user manuals and white papers since there are few or no published technical papers detailing commercial products. Additionally, existing products are at various development stages and operate at different levels of disclosure.

Microsoft .NET [155] – *.NET* embraces the concept of Web services to enable B2B interaction. It consists of three key elements: *.NET Framework and tools*, *.NET Enterprise Servers*, and *.NET Service Building Blocks*. *.NET Framework and tools* provides the standard-based tools for SOAP, WSDL, and UDDI. *.NET Enterprise Servers* provides the core components for building Web services. These include database like *SQL Server 2000*, messaging software like *Exchange 2000 Server*, business process technology like *BizTalk Server 2000*, and *Internet Security and Acceleration Server*. *.NET Service Building Blocks* contains pre-defined Web services created using the *.NET* infrastructure (e.g., *Passport* and *HailStorm*).

SOAP is used as the main transport protocol in the communication layer. Interoperability at the communication layer is also supported by *Microsoft Message Queue* (MSMQ) supplemented with gateways for sending and receiving documents in various formats from trading partners. *Microsoft Host Integration Server* is used to support connection to proprietary systems like IBM mainframes. Heterogeneity at the content layer is addressed by adhering to open standards (XML and WSDL) and the wrapping of applications as *.NET Managed Components*. Building business processes (called *Orchestration*) is done through *BizTalk Server*. Developers use the *Biztalk Orchestration Designer* to create *Biztalk processes*. These are compiled into *XLANG schedules* which are executed by the *Biztalk Scheduler Engine*.

WebSphere [104] – *WebSphere* is a family of IBM products for B2B interactions. The *application server* is the cornerstone of *WebSphere*. It aims at providing database and backend integration as well as security and performance capability (e.g. workload management). The *WebSphere application server Advanced Edition* adds support for J2EE specification. It also extends J2EE with direct access to advanced CORBA services for greater flexibility and improved interoperability. The advanced edition integrates support for key Web service standards such as SOAP, UDDI, and WSDL. Additionally, it provides distributed transaction support for major database systems including *IBM*'s *DB2*, *Oracle*, *Sybase*, and *Informix*. Other products make up the *WebSphere* platform. These include *WebSphere Business Components*, *WebSphere Commerce*, and *WebSphere MQ Family*. The *WebSphere Business Components* provides pre–built, tested, and "plug and play" components for building new applications or extending existing ones. *WebSphere Commerce* provides mechanisms for building B2B sites including catalog creation and payment processing. *WebSphere MQ Family*, formerly known as as *MQSeries*, is a family of message-oriented middleware products that enable communication between applications running on different hardware platforms.

Sun ONE (*Sun Open Net Environment*) [157] – *Sun ONE* is a platform for Web services developed by *Sun*. Two main product lines make up the *Sun ONE* platform: *Forte tools* and *iPlanet*. *Forte tools* offer *Integrated Development Environment* (IDE) for the Java, C, C++, and Fortran languages. It enables developers to access the plug-ins they need and hence speed the development of Web services. *iPlanet* is the core of *Sun ONE* platform. It includes a stack of products that allow the creation, deployment, and execution of Web services. Examples of such products are the *iPlanet Portal Server*, *iPlanet Application Server*, and *iPlanet Integration Server*. The *iPlanet Portal Server* is the representation layer of *iPlanet*. It delivers services to end-users by aggregating content and providing security, personalization, and knowledge management. The *iPlanet Application Server* enables access to legacy applications and databases. It also provides a J2EE execution environment for Web services. The *iPlanet Integration Server* is a workflow-based engine that enables businesses to define workflows across legacy applications and create services.

Sun ONE uses workflows to ensure interoperability at the business process layer. However, it is not clear how services are composed using the *iPlanet Application Server*. *Sun ONE* supports the emerging Web service standards such as SOAP, WSDL, and UDDI. The *iPlanet Portal Server* enables the integration of any HTML or XML encoded content and heterogeneous applications that run on major operating systems such as *Microsoft Windows*, and *Unix*. Complementary packages provide additional functionality including secure communications. *iPlanet* addresses scalability by offering built-in services such as load balancing.

Vitria BusinessWare [214] – *Vitria BusinessWare* emphasizes on business process management and automation. It adopts *UML* and *WfMC reference model* for modeling business processes. The exchange of information between trading partners is done using XML. However, *BusinessWare* assumes that those partners will agree upon a common standard XML DTD to describe the documents to be exchanged. *BusinessWare* also requires businesses to agree on the semantics of business processes' activities. *BusinessWare*'s processes are divided into two types: *public* and *private.* A placement of purchase order described in RosettaNet PIPs is an example of public process. The way that different companies deal with an incoming order from a customer is an example of private process. The separation between private and public process allows trading partners to change their private process without affecting the cross-organization public business process.

BusinessWare is composed of four modules: *Business process management*, *Business-to-Business communications*, *Enterprise application integration*, and *Real-time analysis.* The *Business process management* controls and coordinates the flow of information between internal and external process systems. Both private and public processes can be defined using the graphical modeling tool. The *Business-to-Business communications* is responsible for interactions with trading partners using multiple protocols (HTTP-S, FTP, IIOP, SOAP, EDI, fax and email) and data formats (XML, IDL, EDI, RosettaNet). The *Enterprise application integration* provides connectors for major databases, messaging systems, and packaged applications. The *Real-time analysis* enables the gathering and analysis of process information. It allows businesses to identify processing bottlenecks and react to fast-changing business conditions.

Oracle Integration Server [169] – *Oracle Integration Server* is one of the products of *Oracle Application Server* which is based on J2EE and emerging Web service standards. It supports transport protocols such as SOAP, HTTP-S, SMTP, FTP/S, IIOP, and various messaging systems (JMS, IBM MQSeries, TIBCO/Rendezvous). The *Integrator* has two main components. The first component provides an EJB container for executing the designed business process. The second component consists of the design and management tools which include *Integration Modeler*, *Business Process Monitor*, and *Business Intelligence.* The *Integration Modeler* offers a set of Web-based tools to model business process, map data sources from one form to another, and set up relationships with trading partners. The *Business Process Monitor* provides means for users to monitor, analyze, and drill down on the state of the business process (such as start, stop, resume). The *Business Process Intelligence* uses *Oracle* data warehousing facilities to analyze and gather information about the overall flow of business processes (i.e., the frequency of messages being sent/received).

HP NetAction [100] – The *HP NetAction* software suite includes the *HP NetAction Internet Operating Environment* (IOE), a platform for building B2B applications. The IOE includes the *HP Process Manager* and *HP Web Services Platform. HP Process Manager* (formerly called *ChangeEngine*) allows the graphical definition of business processes and provides an environment that automates the execution of those processes. It has a component-based architecture based on J2EE. *HP Process Manager* also provides an audit logger that can be used to read information in XML format from a JMS (*Java Message Service*) queue. It allows the definition of audit nodes within a business process to indicate the points in the process at which audit information should be collected. *HP Web Services Platform* is a standards-based architecture for developing Web services. Key components of the *HP Web Services Platform* include *HP-SOAP 2.0*, *HP Service Composer* (a graphical tool for creating and mapping WSDL interfaces), *HP Registry Composer* (a graphical tool for registering and discovering Web services in UDDI registries). HP announced in July 2002 it was discontinuing its development and support of *NetAction*.

BEA WebLogic Integrator [14] – *BEA WebLogic Integrator* is the cornerstone of *BEA WebLogic E-Business* Platform. It is built on top of a J2EE compliant application server and J2EE connector architecture. It supports current Web service standards such as SOAP, UDDI, and WSDL. The *Integrator* is composed of four major modules: *Application server*, *Application integration*, *Business process management*, and *B2B integration*. The *Application server* provides the infrastructure and functionalities for developing and deploying multi-tiers distributed applications as EJB components. The *Application integration* leverages the J2EE connector architecture to simplify integration with existing enterprise applications such as SAP R/3 and PeopleSoft. The *Business process management* provides a design tool and execution engine for business processes. The *B2B integration* manages interactions with external business processes. A separate module called *B2B integration/collaboration* is used to manage different B2B protocols (such as RosettaNet PIPs, BEA's eXtensible Open Collaboration Protocol) and *Quality of Service* (QoS) of the trading partners.

WebMethods [220] – *WebMethods* is composed of three modules: *WebMethods Enterprise Server*, *WebMethods Enterprise Adaptor* and *WebMethods Enterprise Rule Agent*. The *Rule Agent* is used to set up specific business rules that are required for integrating business processes across different enterprises. The *adaptors* connect information sources to *WebMethods Enterprise Server* and provide bi-directional mapping of information between the native format and the server's. Several adaptors are provided to allow the mapping of XML messages to industry-adopted message types (RossettaNet, cXML, OBI, EDI). The hub of the system is *WebMethods Enterprise Server* which acts as the central control and storage point. It uses XML for exchanging messages between trading partners. The server supports multiple transport protocols such as SOAP, HTTP, HTTP-S, RMI-IIOP, SMTP and FTP. It also defines a process-oriented language called *Flow* to visually compose services.

TIBCO ActiveEnterprise [206] – *ActiveEnterprise* uses a set of products to enable B2B interactions. *TIBCO InConcert* is a tool for defining and managing dynamic workflows. *TIBCO IntegrationManager* defines and manages automated business processes that span multiple applications and transactions. *TIBCO MessageBroker* performs rule-based transformation and mapping of messages between different messaging softwares. *TIBCO Hawk* is a sophisticated tool for administrating and monitoring of system behaviors within *ActiveEnterprise*. *TIBCO Rendezvous* is an advanced messaging system that supports publish/subscribe, request/reply, synchronous/asynchronous, certified and transactional messaging paradigms. *ActiveEnterprise* supports other messaging protocols such as JMS, HTTP/S, COM, CORBA and MQSeries. At the content layer, *ActiveEnterprise* supports various vertical and horizontal industry standards such as cXML, RosettaNet, EDI, and HealthCare standards.

In Table 2.4, commercial Web service platforms are summarized using the following set of parameters: major modules, communication standards, content and business process standards, and key technologies. For example, BEA Weblogic Integrator includes an application server, application integration, business process management, and B2B Integration. The communication standards supported in BEA Weblogic Integrator are SOAP, JMS and IIOP. BEA Weblogic Integrator supports WSDL, XML, RosettaNet-PIP, and BEA-XOCP as content and business process standards. The key technologies that are supported include components (J2EE), XML, workflows, and Web services. Note that all deployment platforms support HTTP as a communication protocol. Additionally, the list of supported standards (communication, content, and B2B protocol) is non-exhaustive as new standards are constantly being added.

2.6 Research Prototypes for Web Service Composition

In this section, we overview research prototypes that support Web service composition. Note that the list of prototypes described in this section is not exhaustive. We focus on a representative set of such prototypes.

CMI (*Collaboration Management Infrastructure*) [190, 82] – CMI provides an architecture for inter-enterprise workflows. The main components of CMI engine includes the *CORE*, *coordination* and the *awareness engines*. The *CORE engine* provides basic primitives used by the coordination and awareness engines. These primitives include constructs for defining resources, roles, and generic state machines. CMI's *coordination model* extends the traditional workflow coordination primitives with advanced primitives such as *placeholder*. The concept of placeholder enables the dynamic establish-

	Major Modules	*Communication Standards*	*Content and Business Process Standards*	*Key Technologies*
IBM WebSphere	Application Server, MQSeries, Business Components, WebSphere Commerce	MQSeries, JMS, IIOP, SOAP, HTTP	WSDL, XML, RosettaNet-PIP, cXML, EDI	Components (J2EE), XML, Web Services
Sun ONE	Forte tools and iPlanet	JMS, SOAP, LDAP, WAP, IIOP, HTTP	EDI, XML, WSDL	Components (J2EE), XML, Web services and Workflow
Oracle Integration Server	Integration Modeler, System Monitoring and Administration, Business Process Monitor, Business Intelligence	Oracle Queue, JMS, SOAP, IIOP, MQSeries, TIBCO/rendezvous, HTTP	XML, WSDL, EDI, RosettaNet-PIP, ebXML	Components (J2EE), workflow, XML, data mining, Web services
HP NetAction	HP Opencall, HP Chat, HP NetAction Internet Operating Environment	SOAP, JMS, IIOP, HTTP	XML, WSDL	Components (J2EE), XML, workflow (ChangeEngine), Web services
Microsoft .NET	.NET Framework and Tools, .NET Enterprise Servers, .NET Service Building Blocks	MSMQ, SOAP, Microsoft Host Integration Server, HTTP	XML, WSDL, RosettaNet-PIP, XLANG from BizTalk Server	DCOM, MSMQ, Web services, XML, BizTalk Orchestration Engine
BEA WebLogic Integrator	Application Server, Application Integration, Business Process Management, B2B Integration	SOAP, JMS, IIOP, HTTP	WSDL, XML, RosettaNet-PIP, BEA-XOCP	Components (J2EE), XML, workflow, Web services
WebMethods	Enterprise Server, Enterprise Adaptor, and Enterprise Rule Agent	SOAP, IIOP, JMS, HTTP	WSDL, XML, EDI, RosettaNet-PIP, ebXML, cXML, OBI	Components, workflow, Web services and Agents
Vitria Business Ware	Business Process Management, B2B Communications, Enterprise Application Integration and Real-Time Analysis	SOAP, IIOP, JMS, HTTP	XML, EDI, RosettaNet-PIP, ebXML, xCBL, cXML	Components, XML, workflow, process model, process analysis
TIBCO Active Enterprise	InConcert, IntegrationManager, MessageBroker, Hawk, and Rendezvous	SOAP, JMS, IIOP, MQSeries, HTTP	WSDL, XML, HL7, EDI, RosettaNet-PIP, BizTalk, ebXML, cXML, xCBL	Messaging software, XML, workflow, Web services

Table 2.4 Deployment Platforms

ment of trading relationships. A placeholder activity is replaced at runtime with a concrete activity having the same input and output as those defined as part of the placeholder. A selection policy is specified to indicate the activity that should be executed. If multiple providers offer implementations for an activity interface, the selection policy may use a broker to choose the implementation that offers the "best" quality of service. CMI's *awareness model* captures information that is closely related to a specific role and situation of a process participant. Awareness information is specified by process/awareness designers using *awareness specifications*.

eFlow [37] – *eFlow* is a platform that supports the specification, enactment, and management of composite services. A composite service is described as a process schema that combines basic or composite services. A composite service is modeled by a graph that defines the order of execution among the nodes in the process. It may include *service*, *decision*, and *event* nodes. Service nodes represent the invocation of a basic or composite service. The definition of a service node contains a *search recipe* represented in a query language. When a service node is invoked, a search recipe is executed to select a reference to a specific service. Decision nodes specify the alternatives and rules controlling the execution flow. Event nodes enable service processes to send and receive several types of events. A *service process instance* is an enactment of a process schema. To support heterogeneity of services, eFlow provides adapters for services that support various B2B interaction protocols such as OBI and RosettaNet.

WISE (*Workflow based Internet SErvices*) [189, 118] – WISE aims at providing an infrastructure for the support of cross-organizational business processes in *virtual enterprises*. WISE architecture is organized into four components: process *definition*, *enactment*, *monitoring* and *coordination*. The *process definition* component allows *Virtual Business Process* (VBPs) to be defined using as building blocks the entries of a catalog where companies within a trading community (TC) can post their services. The *process enactment* component compiles the description of the VBP into a representation suitable for enactment and controls the execution of the process by invoking the corresponding services of the TC. The *process monitoring* component keeps track of the progress made in the execution of the VBP. The information produced by this tool is used to create an awareness model used for load balancing, routing, quality of service, and analysis purposes. The *process coordination* component supports multimedia conferencing and cooperative browsing of relevant information between all participants in the TC.

CrossFlow [127] – The main contribution of CrossFlow is in using the concept of *contracts* as a basic tool for cooperation. Businesses specify their interactions through *contracts* (e.g., purchase and employment contracts).

When a provider wants to advertise a service, it uses its contract manager to send a contract template to a *trader* or *matchmaking engine*. When a consumer wants to outsource a service, it uses a contract template to search for relevant providers via the trader. If a matching is found between consumer's requirements and provider's offer, an electronic contract is made by filling in the template. Based on the specifications in the contract, a dynamic contract and service enactment infrastructure are set up. The symmetrical infrastructure in provider's and consumer's sides contains proxy gateways that control their interactions. The dynamically created modules can be removed after contract completion.

Mentor-Lite [222] – Mentor-Lite addresses the problem of distributing the execution of workflows. The idea is to partition the overall workflow specification into several sub-workflows, each encompassing all the activities that are to be executed by a given entity within an organization. The basic building block of Mentor-Lite is an interpreter for workflow based on state charts. Two other modules are integrated with the workflow interpreter defining the workflow engine: *communication manager* and *log manager*. The *communication manager* is responsible for sending and receiving synchronization messages between the engines. It uses the *Transaction Processing* (TP) monitor *Tuxedo* for delivering synchronization messages within queued transactions. The *log manager* provides logging and recovery facilities. A separate workflow log is used at each site where a workflow engine is running.

XL (XML Language) [74, 75] – XL defines an XML language for the specification of Web services. An XL service specification contains *local declarations*, *declarative clauses*, and *operation specifications*. Two kinds of local variables can be declared in XL. The first kind of variable represents the internal state of the service. The second kind of variable represents the internal state of a particular conversation in which the service is involved (e.g., session ID). Declarative clauses include variables that control the Web service global state. In particular, the *history* and *on change* clauses address the issue of external manageability and adaptability. If the *history* clause is specified, all operation invocations are automatically logged. The *on change* clause uses triggers to detect changes in variables declared in the Web services' local declarations.

SELF-SERV (compoSing wEb accessibLe inFormation and buSiness sERvices) [16, 192] – SELF-SERV proposes a process-based language for composing Web services based on *state charts*. It also defines a *peer-to-peer* Web service execution model in which the responsibility of coordinating the execution of a composite service is distributed across several peer components called *coordinators*. The coordinator is a lightweight scheduler which determines when a state within a state chart should be entered and what should be done when the state is entered. It also determines when should a state be exited and what should be done after the state is exited. The knowledge needed by a coordinator to answer these questions at runtime is statically extracted from the state chart describing the composite service operations and represented in the form of routing tables.

The aforementioned prototypes are compared in Table 2.5 using key interaction layers. For example, eFlow uses RMI at the communication layer. At the content layer, eFlow provides adapters to support different interaction protocols such as OBI and RosettaNet. Interoperability at the business layer is enabled through a process description model based on state machines.

	Communication	*Content*	*Business Process*
CMI	Transport protocols (e.g., HTTP, CORBA) must *a priori* be agreed upon	Message format (e.g., XML, EDI) must *a priori* be agreed upon	State machine based model for process description
WISE	Coordination and communication module	Not Addressed	Virtual business processes
Cross Flow	Java RMI	Contract in XML	Contracts
Mentor-Lite	Transaction Processing (TP) monitor (Tuxedo)	Not Addressed	Business processes expressed as state and activity charts
eFlow	Java RMI	Provides adapters to support different protocols such as OBI and RosettaNet	State machine based model for process description
XL	SOAP	XML Schema	Little or no statements for inter-service business processes
SELF-SERV	SOAP	Not Addressed	State charts

Table 2.5 Prototypes vs. Interaction Layers

The same prototypes are compared in Table 2.6 using key interaction dimensions. For example, eFlow allows loose coupling among participants. In terms of autonomy, trading partners do not need to reveal how their services are implemented. Heterogeneous interaction protocols are supported through adapters. External manageability and adaptability are possible via event tracking and process templates respectively. Security, however is not addressed. Scalability is accommodated using distributed service enactment engines.

	Coupling	*Autonomy*	*Het.*	*Ext. Manag.*	*Adapt.*	*Security*	*Scal.*
CMI	Tight and long term	External systems only need to reveal the state they are in after they accomplish a task, not how they accomplish the task	Use of object-oriented proxies	State dependent control flow and use of awareness events	Primitives such as *optional* and *inhibitor* can be used for coping with some unforeseen events	Role	Distributed and parallel engines for execution
WISE	Tight and long term	Partners must advertise services in encapsulated objects	Object-based middleware	Process monitoring and analysis module	Execution guarantee	Not Addressed	Distributed architecture
Cross Flow	Loose and transient	Partners must agree on service contract definition	Partners must install service contract run time environment	Quality of Service (QoS) module provides monitoring facilities	Primitives for flexible execution are restricted to those provided by traditional workflows	Not Addressed	Cost of entry: participants must locally install contract run time environment
Mentor-Lite	Tight and long term	Participants do not need to reveal how services are implemented	Application programs are connected to the workflow engine by specific wrappers	Not Addressed	Not Addressed	Not Addressed	Workflows are partitioned into several subworkflows and distributed
eFlow	Loose and long term	External systems need to describe their services not their implementation	Provides adapters for different protocols and platforms such as OBI, RosettaNet, and e-speak	Event tracking	Provides process templates, service nodes, and service data repositories for reuse	Not Addressed	Distributed service enactment engines
XL	Loose and transient	Participants do not need to reveal how services are implemented	Web services can be written in XL, Java, or other languages	History clauses	Change clauses	Security features of J2EE	Not Addressed
SELF-SERV	Loose and transient	Participants do not need to reveal how services are implemented	Service wrappers	Not Addressed	Not Addressed	Not Addressed	Peer-to-peer execution model

Table 2.6 Prototypes vs. Interaction Dimensions

2.7 Summary and Discussion

In this section, we compare the different approaches to interactions on the pre-Semantic Web and Semantic Web eras. We discuss the commonalities and differences between Web services and related technologies such as components, agents, and workflows. Finally, we illustrate the role of Web services on the Semantic Web.

2.7.1 Comparison of Semantic Web Interaction Technologies

We identify two sets of parameters that together exhaustively define how applications interact on the Web. The first set (applicable to enabling technologies and prototypes) consists of the following parameters: communication layer, content layer, and business process layer. The second set (applicable to enabling technologies and prototypes) consists of the following parameters: coupling, autonomy, heterogeneity, external manageability, adaptability, security, and scalability.

In Table 2.7, enabling technologies technologies for the pre Semantic Web era are compared using the most important architectural layers. For example, communications in EDI are conducted through VANs. The content layer is supported through ANSI X12 and EDIFACT formatted documents. Interactions at the business process layer are limited to pre-defined business processes. In Table 2.8, key Semantic Web technologies are compared using the most important architectural layers. For example, *Web Services*' communication layer is typically provided by SOAP. The content layer is supported by using WSDL language. However, WSDL currently provides little support for semantic description of business documents. One of the current trends to support semantic interoperability is the use of ontologies (e.g., DAML-S). WSFL, XLANG, and BPEL4WS languages provide support for interactions at the business process layer. However, these languages are still at their early stage.

In Table 2.9, enabling technologies For the pre Semantic Web era are now compared using salient interaction parameters (dimensions). For example, *EJB-based* B2B's coupling is tight and long term. Autonomy is provided by separating the interface and the implementation using the EJB remote interface. Heterogeneity is supported at the platform levels (e.g., Unix and Windows) but only Java is supported. The use of event services provides support for external manageability. Adaptability is partially addressed through the separation between contracts and business logic. Security is provided through the EJB container. Scalability is not much of a concern for intra-enterprise applications. In Table 2.10, Semantic Web interaction technologies

	Communication	*Content*	*Business Process*
EDI	VANs	ANSI X12 and EDIFACT formatted documents	Pre-defined business processes
EDIINT	SMTP (for EDIINT AS1) and HTTP (for EDIINT AS2)	ANSI X12 and EDIFACT formatted documents	Pre-defined business processes
OBI	HTTP	ANSI X12 formatted documents	Pre-defined protocol for Internet procurement
CORBA	ORBs and IIOP	Not Addressed	Ad hoc: hand-coded programming of the integration logic
DCOM	DCOM runtime environment	Not Addressed	Ad hoc: hand-coded programming of the integration logic
EJB	RMI/JMS	Not Addressed	Ad hoc: hand-coded programming of the integration logic
Workflows	Not Addressed	Not Addressed	Inter-enterprise business processes (public and private)

Table 2.7 Pre Semantic Web Technologies vs. Interaction Layers

	Communication	*Content*	*Business Process*
Ontologies	Not Addressed	Shared Conceptualization	Not Addressed
Web Services	SOAP and REST	WSDL focuses on syntactic interoperability. Semantic Web service frameworks provide support for semantic interoperability	BPEL4WS and ebXML's business process specification
Agents	Agent Communication Language	Common Ontology	Not Addressed
eCO	HTTP	xCBL	Not Addressed
cXML	HTTP and URL form encoding	XML DTDs	Pre-defined protocol for Internet procurement
RosettaNet	HTTP, E-mail, etc.	RosettaNet Business Dictionary and RosettaNet Technical Dictionary	Partner Interface Processes (PIPs). Pre-defined protocol for Internet procurement

Table 2.8 Semantic Technologies vs. Interaction Layers

are compared using the same parameters. For example, Web services support both transient and long-term as well as loose relationships. The separation between WSDL interface and implementation definition caters for the autonomy of participants. WSDL descriptions allow the wrapping of heterogeneous applications. The issues of external manageability and adaptability are currently not addressed. Research efforts are still on-going to provide security mechanisms for Web services.

2.7.2 Web Services and Related Technologies

Web services share some features with the component, agent, and workflow-based approaches. However, several characteristics differentiate Web services from components, agents, and workflows.
Web Services and Components – Web services use document-based communication. This in in contrast with component-based frameworks which use object-based communication, thereby yielding systems where the coupling between components is tight [213]. Additionally, by using HTTP as a communication protocol, Web services enables much more firewall-friendly computing than component-based systems. For example there is no standard port for IIOP, so it normally does not traverse firewalls easily. Although a specification has been submitted to OMG to dealing with IIOP firewall traversal, ORB implementations are still using their own proprietary solutions such as *VisiBroker's GateKeeper* and *IONA's WonderWall.*

Web Services and Agents – As in Web services, agent-based systems provide "directories" where an agent advertise their distinct functionalities and other agents search to locate it [101]. However, agents are inherently communicative, whereas Web services are passive until invoked. Web services use XML formatted message over ubiquitous protocols such as HTTP to interact with each other. However, agents use ACL language to format their messages. As discussed in Section 2.4, agents are loosely coupled while agents are tightly coupled. All these reasons make Web service suitable for enabling cross-organizational interactions. Agents generally provide alerts and updates when new events become available.

Web Services and Workflows – Service composition shares some features with workflows. For example, to define a composite service, the provider needs to specify the flow of service invocations (i.e., services to be invoked, their input and output data, and their execution dependencies). Similarly, in a workflow, the designer must specify the flow of work (i.e., work items to be invoked, their input and output data, and their execution dependencies). However, several features distinguish between composite services and workflows. We list below the main differences:

- Distributed workflow systems require that each participating enterprise deploys a full-fledged execution engine, capable of interpreting the workflow definition. The same workflow model must be adopted by all the participants in the global workflow. They assume a tight coupling among the distributed sub-workflows. Modifications to sub-workflows need to be coordinated. Hence, distributed workflow systems are appropriate for the development of business processes within a single enterprise.
- In workflows, input and output data are typically specified by a set of variable names [38]. The values of the input variables are passed to a

selected resource at the time an activity is started. Activity execution results are inserted into the output variables. Communications between the workflow system and resources is done through *adapters* which deal with data mapping issues. However, the development of adaptors is a difficult and tedious task [38]. In contrast, Web services interact by exchanging messages, thereby avoiding the need for adapters.

- A number of XML-based interaction standards (e.g., RosettaNet, cXML) are being defined to support B2B interactions. Many applications that support such standards are being or have been developed. It is likely that composite services will interact with services that follow one of these standards [38]. However, many workflow systems do not support such standards, although some vendors are moving in this direction [38].

2.7.3 The Role of Web Services in the Semantic Web Landscape

The current technologies for Web-based interactions may be viewed as complementary. In Figure 2.9, we summarize these technologies and the way they co–exist in a Semantic Web interactions framework. Component middleware, workflows, Web services, and agents define the building blocks for developing Semantic Web applications. Ontologies, EDI, OBI, and XML-based standards (eCO, RosettaNet, etc.) focus on defining the semantics of interactions among businesses. Component middleware (CORBA, DCOM, and EJB) are suitable for building robust and secure applications *within* an enterprise. Intra-enterprise business processes are managed using systems such as ERPs (e.g., *SAP/R3*) and workflows (e.g., IBM's *MQSeries*). Inter-enterprise workflows mostly focus on interactions at the business process layer. Their aim is to automate business processes that span the boundaries of disparate enterprises.

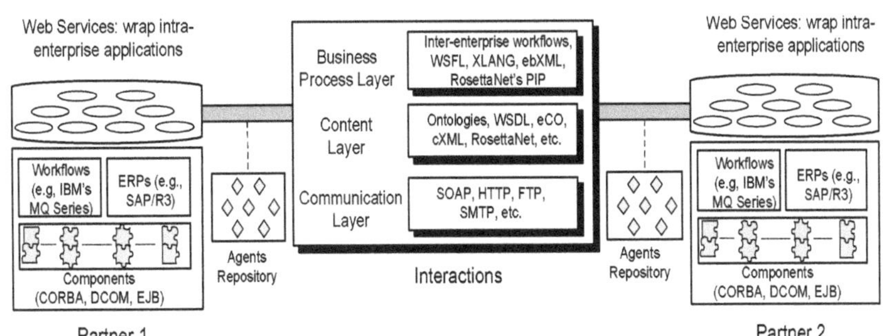

Fig. 2.9 Technologies in a Semantic Web Interaction Framework

Web services take components a step further by enabling inter-enterprise interactions. They define the entry points to enterprises' internal systems. Web services may wrap intra-enterprise components to provide connectivity between autonomous and heterogeneous inter-enterprise applications. They may also wrap other applications developed, for example, in Java or Visual Basic. Agents may be used add new functions to Web services (e.g., change monitoring) or customize existing functions based on operating conditions or observations on users' behavior. Web services may use a workflow-based approach or service composition techniques and standards (e.g., BPEL4WS) to support inter-enterprise business processes. Web services adopt ontologies and XML-based standards to capture the semantics of documents and business processes. For example, Web services may use *RosettaNet* or *cXML* to carry out interactions among businesses according to these frameworks. *EDI* and *OBI* standards may also be used to enable interactions at the content layer. However, they provide little support in terms of expanding the set of supported document types.

	Coupling	*Auto.*	*Het.*	*Ext. Manag.*	*Adapt.*	*Security*	*Scal.*
EDI	Loose and long term	New documents must be approved by EDI guideline committees	Support of heterogeneous applications thanks to translator software	Not Addressed	Impact of local changes limited. New documents must be approved	Private VANs	Expensive networks. Need to agree on implementation conventions
EDIINT	Loose and long term	New documents must be approved by EDI guideline committees	Support of heterogeneous applications thanks to translator software	Not Addressed	Impact of local changes limited. New documents must be approved	RFC 1847, MIME security with PGP, etc.	Lower entry-cost than EDI (Internet-based)
OBI	Loose and long term	Higher than EDI (document extensibility is not an important requirement)	Support of heterogeneous applications thanks to translator software	Not Addressed	Higher than EDI (document extensibility is not an important requirement)	SSL/HTTP, digital signatures, and digital credentials	Lower entry-cost than EDI (Internet-based)
CORBA	Tight and long term	Separation between interface and implementation (IDL)	Different languages (e.g., Java, C++) and platforms (Unix, Windows)	Event service	Not Addressed	Supported by CORBA security service	Suitable for intra-enterprise applications. Participants need to have a stub for each component server
DCOM	Tight and long term	Separation between interface and implementation (IDL)	Different languages (e.g., Microsoft J++, C++) but Windows platform	Event service	Not Addressed	Based on Windows NT security model	Suitable for intra-enterprise applications. Proxies needed at client side
EJB	Tight and long term	Separation between interface and implementation (EJB remote interface)	Java language and different platforms (Unix, windows)	Event service	Contracts can be changed independently of the business logic	Security features provided in EJB container	Suitable for intra-enterprise applications. Participants must define a remote interface for each bean
Workf.	System-specific	Separation between public and private business processes	Different workflow engines	Adding appl-specific states	Process wrappers and adapters help localize changes	Not Addressed	May require creation of new process wrappers and adapters

Table 2.9 Pre Semantic Web Technologies vs. Interaction Dimensions

	Coupling	*Auto.*	*Het.*	*Ext. Manag.*	*Adapt.*	*Security*	*Scal.*
Ontology	Loose and long-term	Participants bound to concepts defined within the ontology	Participants bound to concepts defined within the ontology	Not Addressed	Not Addressed	Not Addressed	Participants need to describe their applications according to a given ontology
Web Services	Loose, transient, and long-term	Separation between WSDL interface and implementation definitions	WSDL descriptions to wrap underlying applications	Not Addressed	Not Addressed	On-going efforts (e.g., XML digital signatures, S-HTTP)	Availability of development tools. XML tags increase the volume of information. Replicated registries must exchange data to maintain coherence
Agents	Tight and long-term	Participants must adhere to concepts defined within a common ontology	Agents may be used to wrap heterogeneous applications	Events and monitoring agents	Not Addressed	Not Addressed	Agents need to formulate requests based on the common ontology. They must have a way of matching requests with their known ontologies
eCO	Loose, transient, and long term	Separation between description and implementation. Marketplaces may hinder autonomy	XML Schemas. Marketplaces may help addressing semantic heterogeneity.	Not Addressed	Impact of local changes limited. Support of extensibility documents	Optional	Establishment of a relationship with a partner does not require additional work from this partner
cXML	Loose, transient, and long term	Higher than EDI because document extensibility is not an important requirement	XML DTDs	Not Addressed	Impact of local changes limited. Extensibility of documents is not required	Authentication information. Trusted intermediaries	Cost of entry is lower than in OBI thanks to the use of XML
Rosetta Net	Loose and long term	Separation between description and implementation. Marketplaces may hinder autonomy	RosettaNet business and technical dictionaries. Use of vertical technology	Not Addressed	Impact of local changes limited. Support of extensibility documents	SSL/HTTP Digital certificates and signatures	Establishment of a relationship with a partner does not require additional work from this partner

Table 2.10 Semantic Web Technologies vs. Interaction Dimensions

Chapter 3
Describing and Organizing Semantic Web Services

The semantic organization and description of Web services is an important requirement for enabling the automatic composition of Web services. The number of Web services available on the Web is large and continuously changing. Additionally, service providers may be located in different places over the world. Finally, the large scale, dynamics, and heterogeneity of Web services may hinder any attempt for "understanding" their semantics and hence outsourcing them. This calls for techniques to organize Web services in a way they can be efficiently "understood" and outsourced.

In this chapter, we propose a community centered framework for organizing and describing semantic Web services [139, 142, 149, 17, 5]. We introduce the concept of *community* to cater for an ontological organization and description of Web services. We develop an ontology, called *community ontology*, that serves as a "template" for describing communities and semantic Web services. We also propose a peer-to-peer approach for managing communities in highly dynamic environments. In particular, we present techniques for registering Web services with communities and coping with changes that occur in the Web service space.

This chapter is organized as follows. In Section 3.1, we give an overview of the proposed model for semantic Web services. In Section 3.2, we describe operational features of communities via *generic operations*. In Section 3.3, we present the technique used for registering Web services with a community. In Section 3.4, we propose algorithms for managing communities. We focus on dealing with changes issued by community and service providers.

3.1 The Proposed Model for Semantic Web Services

Ontologies are poised to play a central role to empower Web services with semantics. They are increasingly seen as key to enabling semantics-driven data

B. Medjahed and A. Bouguettaya, *Service Composition for the Semantic Web*,
DOI 10.1007/978-1-4419-8465-4_3,

access and processing. In this section, we give an overview of the proposed model for organizing and describing Web services on the Semantic Web.

3.1.1 Ontological Support for Communities

Combining the emerging Semantic Web concepts of Web services and ontology are at the core of the proposed model. To cater for an ontological organization and description of Web services, we propose the concept of *community*. A *community* is a "container" that clusters Web services based on a specific area of interest (e.g., disability, adoption). All Web services that belong to a given community share the same area of interest. Communities provide descriptions of desired services (e.g., providing interfaces for insurance services) without referring to any actual service.

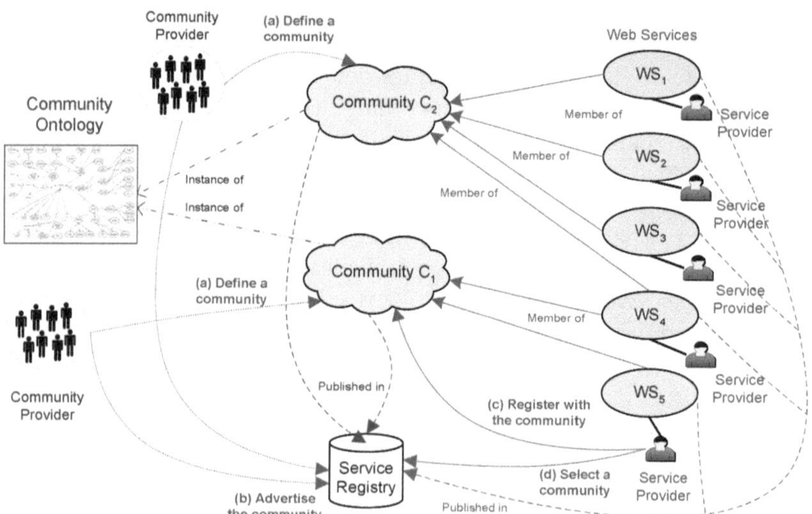

Fig. 3.1 The Proposed Model for Semantic Web Services

We define a *metadata* ontology, called *community ontology*, for creating communities of Web services. *Metadata* ontologies provide concepts that allow the description of other concepts [71]. Figure 5.2 summarizes the proposed model for semantic Web services. Communities are instances of the community ontology. They are created by *community providers* which use the *community ontology* as a template. Community providers are generally groups of government agencies, non-profit organizations, and businesses that share a common domain of interest. For example, the Department for the Aging and other related agencies, such as the Department of Health, would define a community that provides healthcare benefits for senior citizens. A community is itself a service that is created, advertised, discovered, and invoked in the same way "regular" Web services are. The providers of a community assign values to the attributes and concepts of the community ontology (Figure 5.2 - step a). Communities are published in a registry (e.g., UDDI) so that they can be discovered by service providers (Figure 5.2 - step b). *Service providers* (e.g., `medicare` provider) identify the community of interest (Figure 5.2 - step c) and register their services with it (Figure 5.2 - step d). A Web service may belong to different communities. For example a composite service (WS_4 in Figure 5.2) may outsource operations that have different domains of interest (e.g., "healthcare" and "elderly"). Since these operations belong to two different communities, the composite service is registered with the "healthcare" and "elderly" communities (C_1 and C_2 in Figure 5.2). End-users (e.g., case officers) select a community of interest and invoke its operations. Each invocation of a community operation is translated into the invocation of a community member's operation.

3.1.2 Structure of a Community

A community C_i is formally defined by a tuple *(Identifier$_i$, Category$_i$, G-operation$_i$, Members$_i$)*. The *identifier$_i$* clause contains a unique *name* and a text *description* that summarizes C_i's features (Figure 3.2). *Category$_i$* describes the area of interest of the community. All Web services that belong to C_i have the same category as C_i's. C_i is accessible via a set of operations called *generic operations.* Those are specified in the *G-operation$_i$* clause. Generic operations are "abstract" operations that summarize the major functions needed by C_i's members. Community providers define generic operations based on their expertise on the corresponding area of interest that is, C_i's category. The term "abstract" means that no implementation is provided for generic operations. Community providers only define an interface for each generic operation op_{ik}. This interface could subsequently be used and implemented by community members (i.e., actual Web services) interested in offering op_{ik}. We say that those members *support* or *import* op_{ik}. The execution of op_{ik} hence refers to the execution of an actual operation offered by a member that support op_{ik}. The *Members$_i$* clause refers to the list of C_i's members. By being members of C_i, Web service providers "promise" that they will be*supporting* one or several of C_i's generic operations. In this section, we focus on describing the category clause and community ontology.

The *category* of a community C_i is formally defined by a tuple *(Domain$_i$, Synonyms$_i$, Specialization$_i$,*Overlapping$_i$*)*. *Domain$_i$* gives the area of interest of the community (e.g., "healthcare"). It takes its value from a taxonomy for domain names. For flexibility purposes, different communities may adopt different taxonomies to specify their category. We use XML namespaces to prefix categories with the taxonomy in which they are defined. Simply put, XML

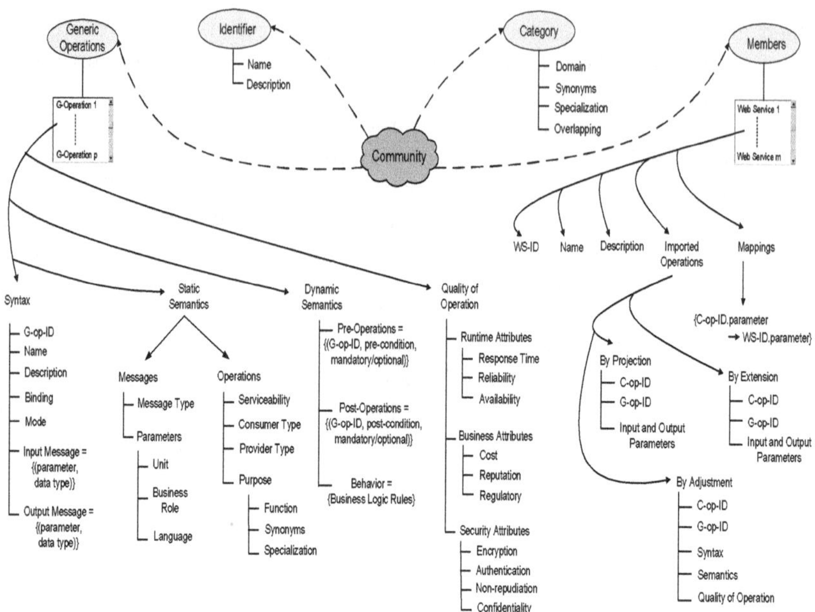

Fig. 3.2 The General Structure of a Community

namespaces provide a method for qualifying element and attribute names used in XML documents by associating them with URI references. $Synonyms_i$ contains a set of alternative domain names for C_i. For example "medical" is a synonym of "healthcare". Values assigned to this attribute are taken from the same taxonomy as the one used for domains.$Specialization_i$ is a set of characteristics of the C_i's domain.For example, "insurance" and "children" are specialization of "healthcare". This means that C_i provides health insurance services for children. Communities are generally not independent. They are linked to each other via *inter-ontology* relationships. These relationships are specified in the $Overlapping_i$ attribute. $Overlapping_i$ contains the list of categories that *overlap* with C_i's category. It is used to provide a peer-to-peer topology for connecting communities with "overlapping" categories. We say that $category_i$ and $category_j$ *overlap* if they are related to each other. For example, an operation that belongs to a community whose domain is *family* may be combined with another operation that belong to a community whose domain is *insurance*. This would enable providing health insurance for needy families. It should be noted that it is the responsibility of the community providers to identify related categories and assign them to the overlapping attribute.

3.1.3 Generic Operations

A generic operation is defined by a set of *functional* and *non-functional* attributes. *Functional* attributes describe *syntactic* and *semantic*features of generic operations. *Syntactic* attributes represent the structure of a generic operation.An example of syntactic attribute is the list of input and output parameters that define the operation's messages. *Semantic* attributes refer to the meaning of the operation or its messages. We consider two types of semantic attributes: *static* and *dynamic* semantic attributes. *Static* semantic attributes (or simply static attributes) describe non-computational features of generic operations. Those are semantic attributes that are generally independent of the execution of the operation. An example of static attribute is the operation's category. *Dynamic* semantic attributes (or simply dynamic attributes) describe computational features of generic operations. They generally refer to the way and constraints under which the operation is executed. An example of dynamic attribute is the business logic of the operation i.e., the results returned by the operation given certain parameters and conditions.

Non-functional attributes, also called *qualitative* attributes, include a set of metrics that measure the quality of the operation.Examples of such attributes include time, availability, and cost. Two services providers that support the same generic operation may have different values for their qualitative attributes. Non-functional attributes model in fact the competitive advantage that Web services may have on each other.

While defining a community, community providers assign values to part of the attributes of their generic operations. The rest of the attributes are assigned either by service providers or third parties during the registration of Web services with C_i. Table 3.1 summarizes the different attributes and mentions the parties that are responsible of assigning their values (using the $\surd$ symbol). For example the types of input and output messages (e.g., purchase order, registration confirmation) are define by community providers. The cost (dollar amount) of executing an operation is service-specific and hence defined by the service provider. The other qualitative attributes (e.g., response time, availability) are assigned by third parties (e.g., trusted parties). The way those parties determine the values to be assigned (e.g., via monitoring) is out of the scope of this book. It is worth noting that the values of some attributes may be assigned by both community and service providers. For example, the content of input/output messages is given by community providers. However, service providers may modify this content by adding and/or removing parameters to input and output messages.

Group	Sub-Group	Attribute	Comm. Prov.	Service Prov.	Third Party
Syntax	Message	Input	√	√	
		Output	√	√	
		Num. of param.	√	√	
	Operation	G-op-ID	√		
		Name	√		
		Description	√		
		Mode	√		
		Binding		√	
Static Semantics	Message	Message Type	√		
		Business Role	√		
		Unit	√	√	
		Language	√	√	
	Operation	Serviceability	√		
		Consumer Type	√		
		Provider Type	√		
		Purpose	√		
		Category	√		
Dynamic Semantics	Inter-operation	Pre-operations	√	√	
		Post-operations	√	√	
	Intra-operation	Behavior	√	√	
Quality of Operation	Run-time	Response Time			√
		Reliability			√
		Availability			√
	Business	Cost		√	
		Reputation			√
		Regulatory			√
	Security/Privacy	Encryption			√
		Authentication			√
		Non-repudiation			√
		Confidentiality			√

Table 3.1 Assigning Values to Generic Operation Attributes

3.1.4 Community Members

Service providers can, at any time, select a community of interest (based on categories) and register their services with it. The registration process requires giving an *identifier* (*WS-ID*), *name*, and *description* for the Web service. The *identifier* takes the form of a unique UUID. The *description* summarizes the main features of the Web service. Service providers specify the list of generic operations supported by their service through the *imported* attribute. We define three techniques for importing generic operations: *projection*, *extension*, and *adjustment*. Details about these techniques are given in the remainder of this chapter. The invocation of an imported operation is translated into the invocation of an "actual" service operation. The correspondence between imported and "actual" operations is done through the *mapping* attribute. For each imported operation, the provider gives the ID of the corresponding "actual" operation. It also defines a one-to-one mapping between the imported operation's parameters and "actual" operation's parameters. Defining mappings between parameters enables the support of "legacy" Web services. Providers do not need to change the message parameters in their actual service codes.

Assume that a service provider *SP* offers a given operation *op*. The following three cases are then possible: (i) If there is a community C_i that contains a generic operation op_{ik} similar to *op*, *SP* would import op_{ik} "as is"; (ii) If there is a community C_i that contains a generic operation op_{ik} "closely" similar to *op* (e.g., *op* has less input parameters than defined in op_{ik}), *SP* would import op_{ik} using *projection*, *extension*, and/or *adjustment* technique; (iii) If no community has an operation similar or "closely" similar to *op*, *SP* would define a new community C_j that has *op* as a generic operation and *SP*'s service as a member. The latter case is similar to the "traditional" WSDL/UDDI/SOAP model where service providers create descriptions for their services. The difference is that *SP* instantiates the attributes and concepts of the community ontology while in the "traditional" model, providers define their service descriptions from scratch.

3.2 Operational Description of Communities via Generic Operations

As mentioned previously, a generic operation is described at four different levels: *syntactic*, *static semantic*, *dynamic semantic* and *qualitative* levels. In this section, we give a detailed description of generic operation attributes for each of those levels.

3.2.1 Syntactic Attributes

We identify two levels for syntactically describing a generic operation: *operation* and *message* levels. The operation level contains attributes that describe the operation (e.g., *name*, *description* of the operation). The message levels caters for the syntactic description of messages exchanged by the operation (e.g., *name*, and *data type* of a message parameter).

3.2.1.1 Operation Syntax

A generic operation has a unique identifier called *G-op-ID*. It takes the form of a *Universally Unique ID* (UUID). A UUID is an identifier that is unique across both space and time [7]. The operation also has a *name* and a text *description* thatsummarizes the operation's features. The *binding* defines the message formats and protocols used to interact with the operation. An operation may be accessible using several bindings such as *SOAP/HTTP*, and *SOAP/MIME*. The binding of an operation is assigned by the service provider. This is in contrast to the rest of syntactic attributes whose values are pre-defined by community providers. Indeed, the binding attribute is dependent on the way the generic operation is implemented at the service provider side. A provider may offer SOAP/HTTP access to a generic operation supported by its Web service while another provider may prefer to use SOAP/MIME for the same operation.

The *mode* of an operation refers to the order according to which its input and output messages messages are sent and received. It states whether the operation initiates interactions or simply replies to invocations from other services. We define two operation modes: *In/Out* or *Out/In*. One of this values is assigned by community providers to each operation. *In/Out* operation first receives an input message by a client, process it (locally or forward it to another service), and then returns an output message to the client. *Out/In* first sends an output message to a server and receives an input message as a result. An example of *In/Out* operation is `checkEligibilityWIC` which checks citizen's eligibility for a nutrition program for pregnant women (WIC or Women Infant and Children). As specified in WSDL standard, some operations may be limited to an input or an output message [7]. For example, `expirationWIC` is an operation that automatically notifies citizens about the termination of their eligibility period for WIC programs. This operation obviously does not require any input message. However, such operations may be considered as *In/Out* or *Out/In* operations where the input or output message is empty. Hence, without loss of generality, we focus in the proposed framework on the aforementioned operation modes.

3.2.1.2 Message Syntax

Each input or output message contains one or more parameters. A parameter has a *name* and *data type*. We use the set *In-Out(G-op-ID)* to refer to the list of input and output parameters' names. The data type gives the range of values that may be assigned to the parameter. We use XML Schema's *built-in* data types as the typing system. *Built-in* types are pre-defined in the XML schema specification. They can be either *primitive* or *derived*. Unlike *primitive* types (e.g., `string`, `decimal`), *derived* types are defined in terms of other types. For example, `integer` is derived from the `decimal` primitive type. Although message parameters are predefined by community providers, service providers have the ability to add new parameters, remove some, or change the content (e.g., data type) of pre-defined parameters.

3.2.2 Static Semantic Attributes

The static semantics of a generic operation refers to a set of attributes whose content is independent of the execution of the operation. It should not only specify the semantics of the operation itself (e.g., what does the operation do) but also the semantics of all messages handled by the operation. In the rest of this section, we define static semantics at two levels: the message parameter and operation levels.

3.2.2.1 Operation Semantics

The static semantic of an operation is defined by the following attributes: *serviceability, provider type, consumer type, purpose*, and *category. Serviceability* gives the type of assistance provided by the operation. Examples of values for this attribute are "cash", "in-kind", "informational", and "educational". TANF (Temporary Assistance for Needy Families) is an example of welfare program that provides financial support to needy families.A food stamp is an example of in-kind support available to indigent citizens. Returning the list of senior activity centers is an example of informational support. Enhancing communication skills of visuallyimpaired people is an example of educational support. Other types of support may bementioned by assigning the value "other"to this attribute.

A generic operation may be supported viaone or several *provider types.* A provider may be governmental("federal", "state", "local", and "tribal") or non-governmental("non-profit" and "business") agencies. For example, `nursingHome` may be provided by the Department of Aging (government agency) and Red Cross (non-profit). The *consumer type* property specifies the group of citizens (e.g., children, pregnant women) that are eligible to the operation's welfare program. Different groups may be eligible for the same benefit. For example, WIC (Women, Infant, and Children) is a program for pregnant women, lactating mothers, and children.

Each generic operation performs a certain functionality for a specific area of interest. This is specified through the *purpose* and *category* attributes respectively. An operation inherits the category of the community in which it is defined. Hence, all operations that belong to the same community share the same category. The *purpose* attribute describes the goal of the operation. It is defined by three attributes: *function, synonyms*, and *specialization.* The *function* describes the businessfunctionality offered by the operation. Examples of functionsare "eligibility" and "registration". *Synonyms* and *specialization* attributes work as they do for categories.

3.2.2.2 Message Semantics

Messages must be semantically described so that they can be "correctly" interpreted by service providers and consumers. We associate a *message type* $\mathcal{MT}$ to each message. $\mathcal{MT}$ gives a general description of the content represented by the message. For example, a message may represent a purchase order or an invoice. *Vertical* ontologies are the ideal concept to describe the type of message. *Vertical* ontologies capture the knowledge valid for a particular domain such as medical, mechanic, chemistry, and electronic [71]. An example of such ontology is *RosettaNet's PIPs* (*Partner Interface Processes*) [32].

The message type does not capture the whole semantics of a message. Indeed, it is important to describe the semantics of each parameter belonging to that message. Message parameters are so far represented through their name and data type. While data types are an important feature of message parameters, they do not capture their semantics. For example, an `eligibility period` parameter may be specified in days, weeks, or months. We identify three attributes to model the semantics of message parameters: *business role*, *unit*, and *language*. These attributes are pre-defined by community providers. The *business role* gives the type of information conveyed by the message parameter. For example, an `address` parameter may refer to the first (street address and unit number) or second (city and zip code) line of an address. Another example is that of a `price` parameter. It may represent a total price or price without taxes. Business roles take their values from a pre-defined taxonomy. Every parameter would have a well-defined meaning according to that taxonomy. An example of such taxonomy is *RosettaNet*'s business dictionary [32]. It contains a common vocabulary that can be used to describe business properties. For example, if the `price` parameter has an "extendedPrice" role (defined in *RosettaNet*), then it represents a "total price for a product quantity". For flexibility purposes, different community providers may adopt different taxonomies to specify their parameters' business roles. As for categories, we use XML namespaces to prefix business roles with the taxonomy according to which they are defined.

The *unit* attribute refers to the measurement units in which the parameter's content is provided. For example, a `weight` parameter may be expressed in "Kilograms" or "Pounds". A `price` parameter may be in "US Dollars" or "Euro". We use standard measurement units (length, area, weight, money code, etc.) to assign values to parameters' units. If a parameter does not have a unit (e.g., `address`), its unit is equal to "none". The content of a message parameter may be specified in different languages. For example, a `profession` parameter may be expressed in English or Spanish. A `translation` operation make take as input, an English word (input parameter) and returns as output, its translation in Urdu (output parameter). We adopt the standard taxonomy for languages to specify the value of this attribute. In contrast to the business role whose content is handled only by community providers, the unit and language attributes may changed by service providers. Service providers should have the flexibility to support more units and languages than those specified by community providers. For example, a service provider may decide to support a *weight* parameter in both "Kilograms" and "Pounds" although the community providers specified "Pounds" as the only measurement unit for this parameter. Formally, a message parameter P is defined as a tuple $(\mathcal{T},\mathcal{R},\mathcal{U},\mathcal{L})$ where $\mathcal{T}$ is the parameter's data type (in XML Schema),

$\mathcal{R}$ is its business role taken from a taxonomy for business roles, $\mathcal{U}$ gives P's unit of measurement, and $\mathcal{L}$ is the set of languages according to which P may be expressed.

3.2.3 Dynamic Semantics

Dynamic semantics allows the description of attributes related to the execution of generic operations. Those attributes may relate the execution of an operation op_{ik} to the execution of other operations (*inter-operation* attributes) or describe features inherent to the execution of op_{ik} (*intra-operation* attributes). The execution of an operation op_{ik} generally goes through four major observable states (Figure 3.3): *Ready*, *Start*, *Active*, and *end*. The execution of op_{ik} is in the *Ready* state if the request for executing op_{ik} has not been made yet. The *Start* state means that op_{ik} execution has been initiated. It refers to one of the following events: (i) an input message is sent to op_{ik} if op_{ik}'s mode is *In/Out*; or (ii) an output message has been sent from op_{ik} if op_{ik}'s mode is *Out/In*. We say that op_{ik} is in the *Active* state if op_{ik} has already been initiated and the corresponding request is being processed. After processing the request, the operation reaches the *End* state during which results are returned. It refers to one of the following events: (i) an output message is sent to the client if op_{ik}'s mode is *In/Out*; or (ii) an input message is received from the server if op_{ik}'s mode is *Out/In*. We define a precedence relationship between states, noted $\longrightarrow_t$, as follows: $S_1 \longrightarrow_t S_2$ if S_1 occurs before S_2.

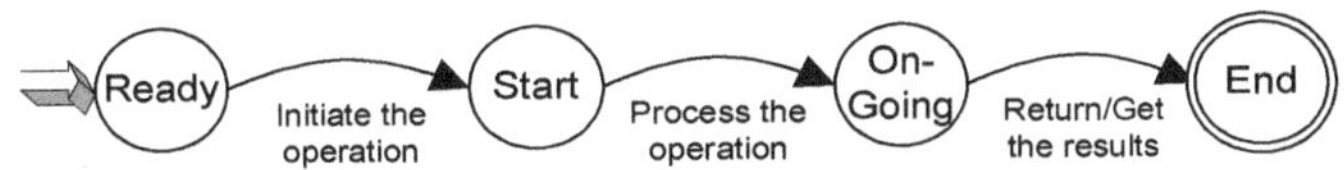

Fig. 3.3 Operation Execution States

3.2.3.1 Pre-Operations

Executing a Web service operation may require going through a pre-defined process that involvesthe execution of several operations called *pre-operations*.This pre-defined process may be dictated by government regulations. For example, senior citizens must first register with a an Area Agency on Aging via `checkRegistration` operation before applying for any welfare program. They may also reflect the business logic of the Web service. For example, senior citizens must order a meal from a participating restaurant via the `orderMeal` operation before requesting its delivery through the `mealsOnWheels` operation.

Let us consider two generic operations $\mathrm{op}_{ik}$and op_{jl} that belong to the same or different communities. We say that op_{ik} is a *pre-operation* of op_{jl} if the invocation of op_{jl} is preceded by the execution of op_{ik}. We call op_{ik} and op_{jl} *source* and *target* operations respectively. An operation may have several pre-operations. It may also be the source (i.e., pre-operation) of several operations. Formally, op_{ik} is a *pre-operation*of op_{jl} if $End(\mathrm{op}_{ik}) \longrightarrow_t Ready(\mathrm{op}_{jl})$.

The definition of a pre-operation relationship includes a source operation op_{ik}, target operation op_{jl}, and the *condition* and *mandatory* attributes. The *condition* is a predicate over op_{ik}'s input and output parameters. op_{jl} can be invoked only if all its pre-operations reached their End state and their conditions are true. If no condition is specified for a given pre-operation then the default value is "true".For example, `mealsOnWheels` is executed only if the `orderMeal` operation has been approved. The *mandatory* attribute takes boolean values and specifies whether the executing the source operation is mandatory or optional. If this attribute is true then the relationship between op_{ik} and op_{jl} is obligatory. Otherwise, it is *recommended.* For example,senior citizens *must* have ordered meals from a restaurant before requesting home delivery from a volunteer center.However, it is recommended to get the list of participating (`participatingRestaurants`) restaurants before ordering a meal.Indeed, users can directly order a meal from a restaurant if they already know that restaurant's name.

3.2.3.2 Post-Operations

The execution of a given operation may trigger the invocation of other operations called *post-operations.* For example, a pregnant women that registers successfully for a food check program women (`registerFoodCheck`) is required to register for a nutritional counseling course (`registerNutritionCourse`). We say that op_{ik} is a *post-operation* of op_{jl} if the termination of op_{jl} precedes the invocation of op_{ik}. We call op_{jl} and op_{ik} *source* and *target* operations respectively. An operation may have several post-operations. It may also be the target (i.e., post-operation) of several operations. Note that if op_{ik} is a pre-operation of op_{jl} then op_{jl} is not necessarily a post-operation of op_{ik}. For example, `checkRegistration` is pre-operation of `orderMeal`. However, `orderMeal` is not a post-operation of `checkRegistration`. Indeed, users do not need to order meals whenever their registration with the Department on the Aging is checked. Formally, op_{ik} is a *post-operation*of op_{jl} if $End(\mathrm{op}_{jl}) \longrightarrow_t Ready(\mathrm{op}_{ik})$.

As for pre-conditions, we associate a *condition* and *mandatory* attribute to each post-operation relationship. A target operation enters the initiation states if *at least* one of its source operations has reached its End state and the corresponding condition is true.A post-operation may also bemandatory or optional. For example, a pregnantwomen that registers for a food check program women (`registerFoodCheck`) *must* also register for nutritional counseling course by invoking `registerNutritionCourse` (mandatory = true). The post-operation `register` is optional (mandatory = false). Indeed, citizens do not necessarily have to register with the Department on the Aging if they are not willing to do so.

3.2.3.3 Behavior

The *behavior* of a generic operation op_{ik} refers to the outcome expected after executing op_{ik} given a specific condition. It is defined by a set of *business logic rules* where each rule R_{ik}^{m} has the following format:

$$R_{ik}^{m} = \frac{(PreParameters_{ik}^{m}, PreCondition_{ik}^{m})}{(PostParameters_{ik}^{m}, PostCondition_{ik}^{m})}$$

$\text{PreParameters}_{ik}^{m}$ and $\text{PostParameters}_{ik}^{m}$ are sets of parameters. Each parameter is defined by name, data type, business role, unit, and language. The elements of $\text{PreParameters}_{ik}^{m}$ and $\text{PostParameters}_{ik}^{m}$ generally refer to op_{ik}'s input and output parameters. However, they may in some cases refer to parameters that are neither input nor output of op_{ik}. For example, assume that the *address* of every citizen registered with the Department on the Aging is stored in the department's database. In this case, this parameter should not be required as input for the `orderMeal` operation since its value could be retrieved from the database. $\text{PreCondition}_{ik}^{m}$ and $\text{PostCondition}_{ik}^{m}$ are predicates over the parameters in $\text{PreParameters}_{ik}^{m}$ and $\text{PostParameters}_{ik}^{m}$ respectively. The rule R_{ik}^{m} specifies that if $\text{PreCondition}_{ik}^{m}$ holds when the operation op_{ik} starts, then $\text{PostCondition}_{ik}^{m}$ holds after op_{ik} reaches its End state. If $\text{PreCondition}_{ik}^{m}$ does not hold, there are no guarantees about the behavior of the operation. Preconditions generally specify relationships between input values. Similarly, post-conditions generally specify relationships between the returned values. The following is an example of the pre and post condition of a rule associated with the operation `registerFoodCheck`:

PreCondition: *(income<22,090)* $\wedge$ *(familySize≥2)* $\wedge$ *(zipCode=22044)*
PostCondition: *(approved=true)* $\wedge$ *(duration=6)*

The rule uses the parameters *income* (unit = {year, US dollar}), *familySize*, and *zipcode* in the pre-condition. The attributes *approved* and *duration* (unit = {month}) are used in the post-condition. The rule specifies that citizens with a yearly income less than 22,090 US dollars and a minimum household size 2 are eligiblefor food checks and the eligibility period is 6 months.

3.2.4 Qualitative Properties

Multiple Web services that belong to the same community may import the same generic operation. It is hence important to define a set attributes that help select the "best" Web service supporting a given functionality. For this purpose, we define a *Quality of Operation* (QoP) model based on a set of *qualitative* attributes that are transversal to all operations such as the cost and response time.

The international quality standard ISO 8402 describes *quality* as "the totality of features and characteristics of a product or service that bear on its ability to satisfy stated or implied needs" [236, 181]. Wedefine QoP as a set of non-functional attributes that may impact the quality of the operations imported by a Web service. There are many QoP attributes important to Web services operations. We organize them into three groups of quantifiable attributes based on type of measurement performed by each attribute (Table 3.2): *run-time*, *business*, and *security*. Note that other attributes and groups may be added to the QoP model without altering the generality of the proposed framework.

QoP Group	QoP Attribute	Definition
Run-time	Response Time	$\text{Time}_{process}(op_{ik})$ + $\text{Time}_{results}(op_{ik})$ where $\text{Time}_{process}$ is the time to process op_{ik} and $\text{Time}_{results}$ is the time to transmit/receive the results
	Reliability	$\text{N}_{success}(op_{ik})/\text{N}_{invoked}(op_{ik})$ where $\text{N}_{success}$ is the number of times that op_{ik} has been successfully executed and $\text{N}_{invoked}$ is the total number of invocations
	Availability	$\text{UpTime}(op_{ik})/\text{TotalTime}(op_{ik})$ where UpTime is the time op_{ik} was accessible during the total measurement time TotalTime
Business	Cost	Dollar amount to execute the operation
	Reputation	$\sum_{u=1}^{n} Ranking_u(op_{ik})/n$, $1 \leq$ Reputation ≤ 10 where $Ranking_u$ is the ranking by user u and n is the number of the times op_{ik} has been ranked
	Regulatory	Compliance with government regulations, $1 \leq$ Regulatory ≤ 10
Security	Encryption	A boolean equal to *true* iff messages are encrypted
	Authentication	A boolean equal to *true* iff consumers are authenticated
	Non-repudiation	A boolean equal to *true* iff participants cannot deny requesting or delivering the service
	Confidentiality	List of parameters that are not divulged to external parties

Table 3.2 Quality of Operation Model

Run-time Attributes – These attributes enable the measurement of properties that are related to the execution of an operation op_{ik}. We identify three run-time attributes: *response time*, *reliability*, and *availability*. The *response time* measures the expected delay in seconds between the moment when op_{ik}) enters the Start state (i.e., op_{ik} is initiated) and reaches the End state (i.e., op_{ik} gets or sends the results). Time(op_{ik}) is computed using the expression $\text{Time}_{process}(op_{ik})$ + $\text{Time}_{results}(op_{ik})$. This means that the response time includes the time to process the operation ($\mathrm{Time}_{process}$) and the time to transmit or receive the results ($\mathrm{Time}_{results}$). The *reliability* of op_{ik} is the ability of the operation to be executed within the maximum expected time frame. Reliability(op_{ik}) is computed based on historical data about previous invocations of the operation using the expression $\mathrm{N}_{success}(op_{ik})/\mathrm{N}_{invoked}(op_{ik})$ where $\mathrm{N}_{success}(op_{ik})$ is the number of times that the operation has been successfully executed within maximum expected time frame and $\mathrm{N}_{invoked}(op_{ik})$ is the total number of invocations. The *availability* is the probability that the operation is accessible. Availability(op_{ik}) is measured by the expression UpTime(op_{ik})/TotalTime(op_{ik}) where UpTime is the time op_{ik} was accessible during the total measurement time TotalTime.

Business Attributes – These attributes allow the assessment of an operation op_{ik} froma business perspective. We identify three business attributes: *cost*, *reputation*, and *regulatory*. The *cost* gives the dollar amount required to execute op_{ik}. The *reputation* of $op_{ik}$is a measure of the operation's trustworthiness. It mainly dependson users' experiences on invoking op_{ik}. Users are givena range to rank Web service operations (e.g., between 1 and 10). The lowest value refer to the best ranking. Different users may have different opinions on the same operation. The reputation of op_{ik} is defined by the average ranking given by users to the operation. Reputation(op_{ik}) is computed by the expression $\sum_{u=1}^{n} Ranking_u(op_{ik})/n$, where $Ranking_u$ is the ranking by user u and n is the number of the times the operation has been ranked. The *regulatory* property is a measure of how well op_{ik} is aligned with government regulations. Regulatory(op_{ik}) is value within a range (e.g., between 1 and 10). The lowest value refer to an operation that is highly compliant with government regulations.

Security Attributes – These attributes describe whether the operation op_{ik} is compliant with security requirements. Indeed, service providers collect, store, process, and share information about millions of users who have different preferences regarding security of their information. We identify four properties related to security and privacy: *encryption*, *authentication*, *non-repudiation*, and *confidentiality*. *Encryption* is a boolean that indicates whether op_{ik}'s message aresecurely exchanged (using encryption techniques) between servers and clients. *Authentication*is a boolean that states whether op_{ik}'s consumers (users and other services)are authenticated (e.g., through passwords). *Non-repudiation* is a boolean that specifies whether participants (consumers and providers) can deny requesting or delivering the service after the fact. The *confidentiality* attribute indicates which parties are authorized to access the operation's input and output parameters. Confidentiality(op_{ik}) contains op_{ik}'sinput and output parameters that should not be divulged to external entities (i.e., other than the service provider). If a parameterdoes not belong to Confidentiality(op_{ik}), then no confidentiality constraint is specified on that parameter. Assume that *confidentiality(*op_{ik} = {`SSN`, `salary`} where

`SSN`, `salary` are two op_{ik}'s input parameters. The content of this attribute states that those two parameters are kept private by op_{ik}'s provider.

3.3 Registering Web Services With Communities

Registering A Web service with a community refers to the process of importing generic operations. The invocation of an imported operation is translated into the invocation of an "actual" service operation. The correspondence between imported and "actual" operations is done through the *mapping* attribute. For each imported operation, the provider gives the ID of the corresponding "actual" operation. It also defines a one-to-one mapping between the imported operation's parameters and "actual" operation's parameters. Defining mappings between parameters enables the support of "legacy" Web services. Providers do not need to modify the message parameters in their actual service codes.

3.3.1 The Web Service Registration Process

The registration process is handled by a network of software agents associated to service and community providers. *Member* and *community agents* (MA_j and CA_i) are attached to each service and community provider (SP_j and CP_i) respectively (Figure 3.4). MA_j handles the registration of SP_j's Web services with the community C_i. SP_j registers its service *WS-ID* using the following *registration statement*:

Register Service *WS-ID* **With Community** C_i
  Name *service-name*
  Description *service-description*
  [**Imported Generic** *G-op-ID*
    <importing statements>
    Mappings With Actual *Op-ID*
      [*G-op-ID.<parameter>* **Maps To** *Op–ID.<parameter>*]$^+$]$^+$

The clauses in the aforementioned statement correspond to the different attributes defined for service members within the community ontology. The *<importing statements>* is a sequence of statements for importing generic operation. A Web service may import several generic operations as stated by the "+" iteration symbol.

MA_j parses the registration statement and sends a registration message *SP_Register(WS-ID,name,desc,imported)* to CA_i (Figure 3.4, step (a)). The message includes the service ID (*WS-ID*), name, description, and the list of imported operations. The *imported* set is equal to {*(G-op-*

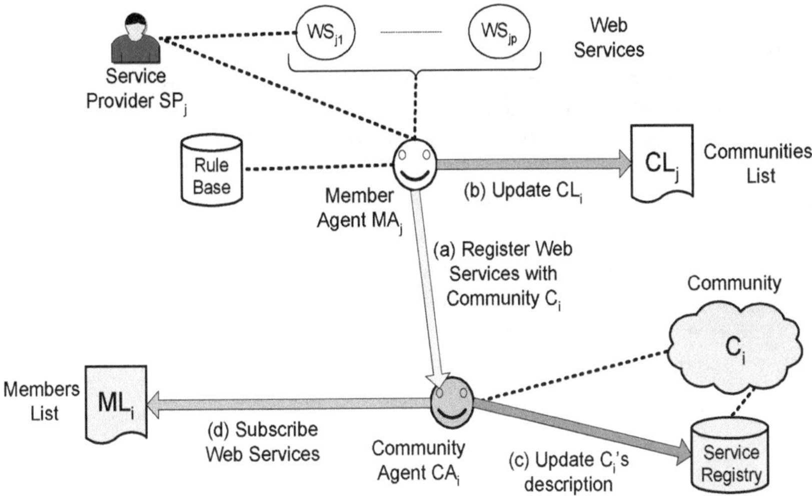

Fig. 3.4 The Web Service Registration Process

ID,mappings,AttSet,NotImpSet)}. It includes the mappings of G-op-ID (ID of the imported operation) with actual service operation. *AttSet* is the set of G-op-ID's attributes with their values as assigned by SP_j. It is defined by the set {*(attribute,value)*}. *NotImpSet* is the list of non-imported attributes. MA_j maintains a *Communities List* CL_j and *Rule Base* RB_j. CL_j is the list of communities with which SP_j's Web services are registered. Each entry in this list contains the G-op-ID of an imported operation, the WS-ID of the service that imported it, and the ID (CA-ID) of the community agent CA_i. To enable fast access to CL_j, we sort it on the G-op-ID column using *Counting Sort* algorithm [51]. RB_j contains a set of rules that enable MA_j to react to changes issued by community providers.

Upon reception of the registration message, CA_i updates the content of C_i's *members list* ML_i (Figure 3.4, steps (c) and (d)). Each entry in ML_i contains the ID of the imported operation (op-ID), the ID of the importing service (*WS-ID*), the ID of *WS-ID*'s agent (*MA-ID*), *WS-ID*'s *status* ("available ", "unavailable", or "unsubscribed"), and the list *NotImp* of *G-op-ID*'s attributes not imported by *WS-ID*. The *NotImp* column is assigned with the content of *NotImpSet* included in the registration message. We sort ML_i on the op-ID column using *Counting Sort* algorithm to enable fast access to ML_i [51].

Figure 3.5 gives the algorithm executed by a community agent CA_i and member agent MA during registration. SP_Register(WS-ID,name,desc,imported) describes the actions executed by CA_i as a reaction to a registration message sent by MA. The *Insert_Member()* function allows the insertion of a new member in C_i's description. *Insert_ML()* function allows the insertion of a new entry in the ML_i list for members.

```
Member Agent MA Algorithm {
Upon Reception of
 Register (WS-ID,name,desc,imported,C_i) statement From SP
  Parse the registration statement;
  Send SP_Register (WS-ID,name,desc,imported) To CA_i; }
```

```
Community Agent CA_i Algorithm {
Upon Reception of
 SP_Register (WS-ID,name,desc,imported) message From MA-ID
  Insert_Member (C_i,WS-ID,name,desc,imported);
  For each G-op-ID ∈ imported
   Do Insert_ML (G-op-ID,WS-ID,MA-ID,''available'',NotImpSet); }
```

Fig. 3.5 Service Registration: Member and Community Agent Algorithms

3.3.2 Importing Generic Operations

Service providers use generic operations as "templates" to define their operations. A Web service may offer all or some of the generic operations defined within a community. The provider specifies the G-op-IDs of the operations imported by its service. By adopting a generic operation, the service provider "promise" to abide by all attributes (syntactic, semantic, and behavioral) of that operation except those changed explicitly during importation. Providers may customize generic operations to best fit their capabilities via *importing statements*. Customization has the important advantage of enabling flexible and personalized Web service descriptions. It is important to note that customization process does not affect the description of generic operations. Two service providers may import the same generic operation in different ways.

We define three importing statements: *projection*, *extension*, *adjustment*. Importing statements are defined within member agents. Projection, extension, and adjustment may be combined to define imported operations. For example, a service provider may use projection and extension to remove existing parameters from a generic operation and add new ones.

Projection – A generic operation G-op-ID imported by *projection* uses a subset of the input/output parameters defined in G-op-ID. The rest of message parameters are not imported by the service and hence, are included in the *NotImpSet* sent by the member agent to the community agent. Assume that a `checkRegistrationAAA` operation includes `register` (boolean) and `registrationDate` (date) as output parameters. A service provider may customize this operation by keeping only the `register` parameter if it is not interested in returning citizen's registration date. In what follows, we give the general form of a *Project* statement. The input and output clauses give the subset of G-op-ID's parameters supported by the imported operation:

Project *G-op-ID*
  In <*list-of-parameter-names*>
  Out <*list-of-parameter-names*>

The *AttSet* submitted with the registration message takes the form {*(att,value)*} where *att* is a projected parameter and the content of *value* is "null" since no new value is assigned to the input or output parameter. We refer to *AttSet.Attributes* as the list of projected parameters. The list of not imported attributes *NotImpSet* is defined by the expression $(In(\text{op}_{ik}) \cap Out(\text{op}_{ik}))$ – *AttSet.Attributes.*

Extension – An imported operation defined by *extension* adds input and/or output parameters to the corresponding generic operation. The new parameters and their values are included in the registration messages sent by the member agent to the community agent. For example, a service provider (e.g., a volunteer center) may extend the `mealsOnWheels` operation by adding the deliverer's cell phone number as an output parameter. Service providers must assign values to the attributes of each new message parameters, namely data type, unit, business role, and language. Below is the general form of an extension statement:

Extend *G-op-ID*
  In [*(*<*name*>*,* <*data-type*>*,* <*unit*>*,* <*business-role*>*,* <*language*>*)*]*
  Out [*(*<*name*>*,* <*data-type*>*,* <*unit*>*,* <*business-role*>*,* <*language*>*)*]*

The *AttSet* submitted with the registration message takes the form {*(att,value)*} where *att* is a new attribute added by the extension statement and *value* = *(*<*name*>*,* <*data-type*>*,* <*unit*>*,* <*business-role*>*,* <*language*>*)*. The list of not imported attributes *NotImpSet* is empty since all message parameters are imported.

Adjustment – The aim of an adjustment statement is to modify the content of a generic operation's attributes. Service providers may assign values to attributes whose content is undefined (e.g., qualitative attributes) or change the content of previously assigned attributes (e.g., language attribute). Adjustment is done by adding a value to an attribute (Add clause) or deleting an existing value from it (Delete clause). For example, service providers may modify the language attribute if their operation supports a language different from the one specified by community providers. The Add and Delete clauses may be combined to remove and add values to an attributes. The new and deleted values are included in the registration messages sent by the member agent to the community agent. The general form of an adjustment statement is given below:

Adjust *G-op-ID*
  Add [<*value*> **To** <*attribute*>]*
  Delete [<*value*> **From** <*attribute*>]*

The *AttSet* submitted with the registration message takes the form {(att,["+"/"-"],value)} where *att* is an attribute modified by the adjustment statement. The *value* is preceded by a "+" or "-" symbol depending on whether that value is added or deleted from *att* respectively. The list of not imported attributes *NotImpSet* is empty since all message parameters are imported.

3.4 A Peer-to-Peer Approach for Managing Communities

Communities and their members operate in a highly dynamic environment where changes can be launched to adapt to actual business climate (e.g., economic, politic, organizational). Changes are initiated by community or service providers. At the community providers side, generic operations may be dynamically added, deleted, and modified. If a generic operation G-op-ID is deleted or modified, then all members that are supporting G-op-ID should be notified to ensure global consistency. At the service provider side, a Web service may cancel its membership with a community, make its operations temporarily unavailable, or modify the definition of its imported operations. The community provider should in this case be notified to avoid references to nonexistent or obsolete imported operations. All changes are introduced through member and community agents. Agents automatically interact with their peers to manage changes. We consider two types of changes based on the party that launched them: community or service providers.

3.4.1 Propagating Changes Initiated by Community Providers

Community providers (CPs) may modify the definition of their generic operations (Figure 3.6). For example, they may change the pre-operations attribute to reflect new government regulations. For this purpose, each CP_i executes a *Modify* statement defined in its CA_i agent (Figure 3.6, step 1). The statement includes the G-op-ID of the operation to be modified by CP_i and a *ModifySet* that contains the list of attributes to be modified along with their new content. *ModifySet* is defined by the set {(<attribute>,["+"/"-"],<value>)}. We use the notation *ModifySet.Att* to refer to the set of modified attributes. CA_i will then access the service registry and update C_i's description by changing the content of *ModifySet.Att*'s attributes (Figure 3.6, step 2). In the third step, CA_i accesses ML_i list to determine the list $\mathcal{L}$ of members *subscribed* with CP_i's changes. A member WS-ID is *subscribed* with CP_i's changes if WS-ID imports G-op-ID and at least one attribute in *ModifySet.Att* is imported by WS-ID. CA_i assigns the value "unavailable" to the *status* of each subscribed member. This prevents references to members that imported "obsolete" generic operations (Figure 3.6, step 3). Finally, CA_i sends a *CP-Modify(G-op-ID,* WS_j*,ModifySet)* notification to each subscribed member's MA_j (Figure 3.6, step 4). Formally, let C_i be a community and WS_j be a member that imported an operation op_{ik}. WS_j is *subscribed* with changes specified in *CP-Modify(G-op-ID,ModifySet)* if (i) G-op-ID = op_{ik} and (ii) $ModifySet.Att - ML_i[k].NotImp \neq \emptyset$ where k is the entry corresponding to G-op-ID and WS_j.

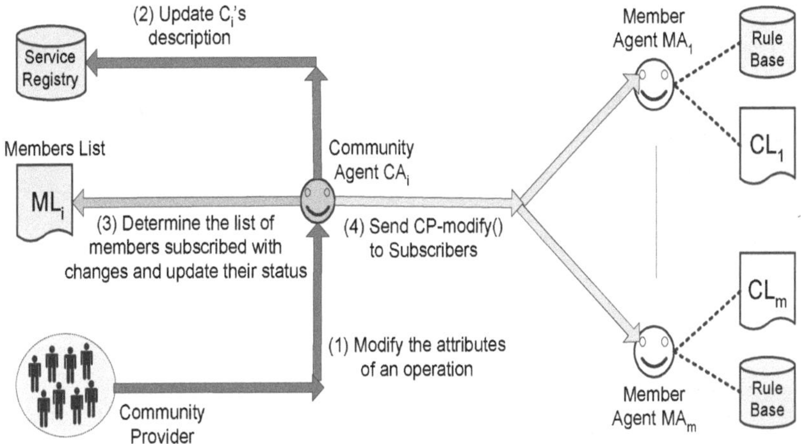

Fig. 3.6 Propagating Changes Initiated by a Community Provider to its Members

Because pre and post-operations for a given operation op_{ik} may belong to different communities, we associate two "dual" subscription lists $PPCS_i$ and $PPMS_i$ to each community agent CA_i. These lists are used to notify relevant parties (communities and members) about changes that are related to remote pre and post-operations. $PPCS_i$ (*Pre and Post-operation Community Subscription*) contains the list of communities C_j that use an operation op_{ik} of C_i as a remote pre or post-operation. Each entry in $PPCS_i$ contains the ID (op-ID) of op_{ik} and the ID of C_j's agent (CA-ID). Such entry is created at C_j's definition time; at that time, CA_j sends a *CP-PP-subscribe-CP(op-ID)* to CA_i (CP stands for Community Provider and PP for Pre/Post operation). $PPCS_i$ is used to notify C_j about changes that occur in op_{ik}. Each time CP_i executes a *Modify* statement on op_{ik}, CA_i accesses $PPCS_i$ list and sends a notification *CP-PP-Alert-CP(*op_{ik}*)* to each community agent CA_j that uses op_{ik} as a remote pre or post-operation (Figure 3.7). We sort $PPCS_i$ on the op-ID column using *Counting Sort* algorithm to enable fast access to the list [51]. Once the *CP-PP-Alert-CP(op_{ik})* message is received by CA_j, CA_j notifies C_j's members using the PPMS$_j$ list.

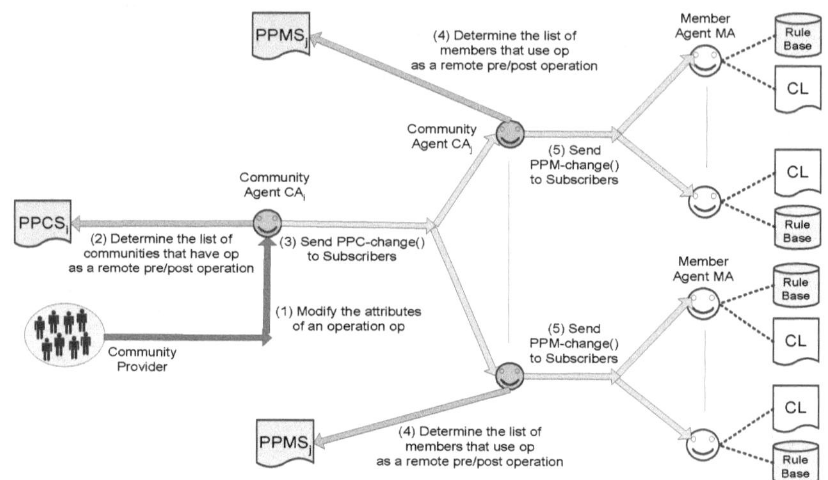

Fig. 3.7 Propagating Changes Initiated by Community Providers to their Peers

PPMS$_j$ (*Pre and Post-operation Member Subscription*) contains the list of C_j's members that use the operations op_{ik} of other communities C_i as remote pre or post-operations. This list is created at C_j's definition time. It is used to notify members about changes that occur in their pre and post-operations. Each entry in PPMS$_j$ contains the ID (CA-ID) of the community agent CA_i, the ID (PP-ID) of the remote pre or post-operation op_{ik}, and the ID (MA-ID) of the agent of a C_j's member that uses op_{ik} as a remote pre or post-operation. CA_j accesses the PPMS$_j$ list and sends a notification message *CP-PP-Alert-SP(op_{ik})* (SP stands for Service Provider) to each member agent MA-ID that uses op_{ik} as a remote pre-operation (Figure 3.7). We sort $PPMS_i$ on the CA-ID column using *Counting Sort* algorithm to enable fast access to the list [51]. To prevent references to members that imported "obsolete" generic operations, CA$_j$ assigns the value "unavailable" to the *status* of MA-ID entries in ML_j list. We only consider entries in which MA-ID imported operations that have op_{ik} as a remote pre or post-operation.

C$_j$'s provider may remove the remote pre/post operation op_{ik} from its generic operation definitions. To propagate this change, CA$_j$ removes from PPMS$_j$ the entry that corresponds to CA_i and op_{ik}. CA$_j$ also sends a *CP-PP-Remove-CP(op_{ik})* to CA_i. Upon reception of this message, CA_i removes from PPCS$_i$ the entry corresponding to CA_j and op_{ik}. CA_i will hence send no *CP-PP-Alert-CP(op_{ik})* messages to CA_j since C$_j$ does not use op$_{ik}$ as a remote pre or post operation. Figure 3.8 summarizes the algorithm executed by CA_i

```
Community Agent CA_i Algorithm {
Upon Reception of
 Modify (G-op-ID,ModifySet) From CP_i
  Update_Member (C_i,G-op-ID,ModifySet);
  For each ML_i[k].op-ID | (ML_i[k].op-ID=G-op-ID)
                          ∧(ModifySet-ML_i[k].NotImp≠∅)
   Do ML_i[k].status = "unavailable";
   Send CP_Modify(G-op-ID,ML_i[k].WS-ID,ModifySet) To ML_i[k].MA-ID;
  If ModifySet contains pre or post-operation attributes
   Then For each PPCS_i[k].op-ID | PPCS_i[k].op-ID==G-op-ID
    Do Send CP-PP-Alert-CP(G-op-ID) To PPCS_i[k].CA-ID;
 CP_PP_Alert_CP (G-op-ID) From CA_j
  For each PPMS_i[k] | PPCS_i[k].op-ID==G-op-ID
   Do Let p be the entry in ML_i | ML_i[p] has G-op-ID as pre/post-operation
    ML_i[p].status = "unavailable";
    Send CP-PP-Alert-SP(G-op-ID) To ML_i[p].MA-ID;
 CP_PP_Remove_CP (G-op-ID) From CA_j
  Let k be | PPCS_i[k].op-ID==G-op-ID ∧ PPCS_i[k].CA-ID==CA_j;
   remove entry k from PPCS_i; }
```

Fig. 3.8 Generic Operation Modification: Community Agent Algorithm

for managing the modification of generic operations. The *Update_Member()* function allows the update of the description of a community description within the service registry.

3.4.2 Propagating Changes Initiated by Service Providers

The provider of a Web service *WS-ID* may initiate changes that should be sent to their communities (Figure 3.9). A community C_i is notified about a change if the change is made on an operation imported from C_i. All changes are introduced through member agents and automatically forwarded to community agents which reflect those changes at the community level. We define the following service providers changes:

- *Modifying operations* – *WS-ID*'s provider may modify attributes (e.g., remove a message parameter) of a previously imported operation through modification statements defined in *WS-ID*'s agent *MA* (Figure 3.9, step 1). A modification statement includes the *G-op-ID* of the operation to be modified, *WS-ID* of the service that imported it, and the importing statement *I-statement* used to do the modification. Once *MA* gets a modification

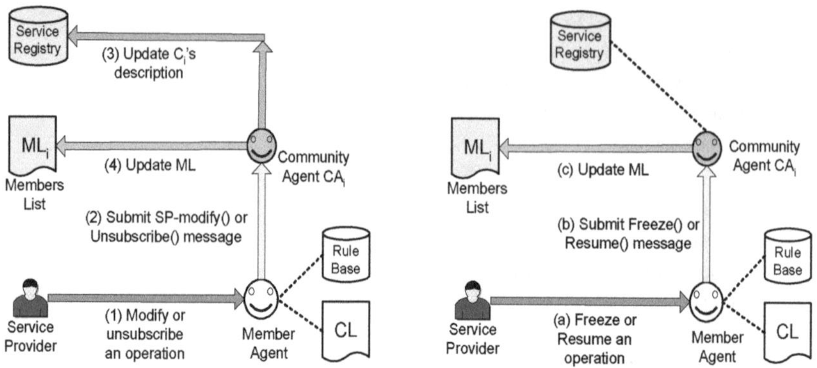

Fig. 3.9 Propagating Changes Initiated by Service Providers

statement, it sends an *SP-Modify(G-op-ID, WS-ID,IType,ModifySet)* message to C_i's agent CA_i (Figure 3.9, step 2). ModifySet is defined as in *CP-Modify()* messages. *IType* gives the type of I-statement ("projection", "extension", "adjust add", and "adjust delete"). Upon reception of the *SP-Modify()* message, CA_i updates C_i's description (Figure 3.9, step 3). If the message concerns a projection statement, CA_i updates the *NotImp* column in the ML_i 's entry that correspond to *G-op-ID* and *WS-ID* (Figure 3.9, step 4). It assigns the content of *ModifySet.Att* to this column. If the message concerns an "adjust delete" statement on a remote pre or post operation op_{jl}, then CA_i removes the entry in PPMS_i corresponding to CA_j, op_{jl}, and *WS-ID*'s agent. If the message concerns an "adjust add" statement on a remote pre or post operation op_{jl}, then CA_i adds a new entry in PPMS_i with the values CA_j, op_{jl}, and *WS-ID*'s agent *MA-ID.*

- *Freezing operations* – An imported operation may be "available", "unavailable" (e.g., due to network problem), or "unsubscribed". *WS-ID*'s provider may temporarily make an imported operation *G-op-ID* operation by executing the *Freeze* statement (Figure 3.9, step a) defined in *MA*. The statement includes the G-op-ID of the operation to be frozen and the WS-ID of the service that imported it. As a consequence, *MA* sends an *SP-Freeze(G-op-ID, WS-ID)* message to CA_i (Figure 3.9, step b). CA_i then assigns the "unavailable" value to the *status* column of the ML_i 's entry that correspond to *G-op-ID* and *WS-ID* (Figure 3.9, step c).
- *Resuming operations* – *WS-ID*'s provider may re-activate an operation G-op-ID that has previously been frozen through the *Resume* statement defined in n *MA*. The statement includes a reference to WS-ID and G-op-ID. As a consequence, *MA* sends an *SP-Freeze(G-op-ID, WS-ID)* to G-op-ID's community agent CA_i (Figure 3.9, step b). CA_i then assigns the "available" value to the *status* column of the ML_i 's entry that correspond to *G-op-ID* and *WS-ID* (Figure 3.9, step c).

```
Member Agent MA Algorithm {
Upon Reception of
 Modify (G-op-ID,WS-ID,I-Statement) From SP
  Parse the importing statement I-Statement;
  Get ModifySet From I-Statement;
  IType = type of the I-Statement;
  CA_i = Lookup_community(CL,G-op-ID);
  Send SP_Modify (G-op-ID,WS-ID,IsProjection,ModifySet) To CA_i;
 Freeze (G-op-ID,WS-ID) From SP
  CA_i = Lookup_community(CL,G-op-ID);
  Send SP_Freeze (G-op-ID,WS-ID) To CA_i;
 Resume (G-op-ID,WS-ID) From SP
  CA_i = Lookup_community(CL,G-op-ID);
  Send SP_Resume (G-op-ID,WS-ID) To CA_i;
 Unsubscribe (G-op-ID,WS-ID) From SP
  CA_i = Lookup_community(CL,G-op-ID);
  Send SP_Unsubscribe (G-op-ID,WS-ID) To CA_i; }
```

Fig. 3.10 Changes Issued by Service Providers: Member Agent Algorithm

```
Community Agent CA_i Algorithm {
Upon Reception of
 SP_Modify (G-op-ID,WS-ID,IType,ModifySet) From MA-ID
  Update (C_i,G-op-ID,ModifySet);
  Consider k | ML_i[k].op-ID==G-op-ID ∧ ML_i[k].WS-ID==WS-ID;
  Case IType
   "Projection": ML_i[k].NotImp = Parameters(G-op-ID) - ModifySet.Att;
   "Adjust Delete": If ModifySet contains pre or post-operations
            Then remove from PPMS_i the entry related to G-op-ID and MA-ID;
   "Adjust Add": If ModifySet contains pre or post-operations
            Then add to PPMS_i an entry for G-op-ID and MA-ID
 SP_Freeze (G-op-ID,WS-ID) From MA-ID
  Consider k | ML_i[k].op-ID==G-op-ID ∧ ML_i[k].WS-ID==WS-ID;
  ML_i[k].status = "unavailable";
 SP_Resume (G-op-ID,WS-ID) From MA-ID
  Consider k | ML_i[k].op-ID==G-op-ID ∧ ML_i[k].WS-ID==WS-ID;
  ML_i[k].status = "available";
 SP_Unsubscribe (G-op-ID,WS-ID) From MA-ID
  Consider k | ML_i[k].op-ID==G-op-ID ∧ ML_i[k].WS-ID==WS-ID;
  ML_i[k].status = "unsubscribed'; }
```

Fig. 3.11 Changes Issued by Service Providers: Community Agent Algorithm

- *Unsubscribing operations* – *WS-ID*'s provider may decide not to support an imported operation any more. For that purpose, it executes *MA*'s *Unsubscribe* statement (Figure 3.9, step 1). *MA* informs CA_i about this change (Figure 3.9, step 2) by sending an *Unsubscribe(G-op-ID, WS-ID)* message to it. CA_i then updates C_i's description (Figure 3.9, step 3). It also assigns the "unsubscribed" value to the *status* of the ML_i 's entry that correspond to *G-op-ID* and *WS-ID* (Figure 3.9, step 4). CA_i periodically checks the *status* column in ML_i and remove all entries associated with unsubscribed operations.

Figures 3.10 and 3.11 depict the algorithm executed by community and member agents for managing changes initiated by service providers. The *Lookup_Community()* function (lines 14) is executed on the communities list *CL*. It returns the CA_i's ID of the community C_i to which the operation G-op-ID belongs.

Each member's agent MA_j also needs to react to change notifications sent by a community agent via *CP-Modify(G-op-ID,* WS_j*,ModifySet)* or *CP-PP-Alert-SP(*op_{ik}*)* messages. The actions to be performed by MA_j as a result of change notification are captured using ECA (*Event Condition Action*) rules [46]. Briefly, the basic semantics of an ECA rule is as follows: when an event occurs, an action is executed if the corresponding condition is true. Event-driven systems are becoming the paradigm of choice for organizing many classes of loosely coupled and dynamic applications. Members react to changes using their own change control policies via local rule specified in their agent. Hence, the reaction to changes can be customized to the peculiarities of each member. Below is an example of ECA rule specified within a member agent:

Rule R_1
  Event CP-Modify(G-op-ID,WS_j,ModifySet)
  Condition Source $= C_1 \wedge$ *pre-operations* $\in$ *Modify.Att*
  Action <notify the provider to change its internal business logic>;
    send *Resume(G-op-ID,* WS_j*)* message to **source**

R_1 states that whenever the member receives a change notification issued by C_1's provider and if the change concerns the *pre-operations* attribute, the service provider should reflect the change by modifying its internal business logic. The member agent then sends a *Resume(G-op-ID,* WS_j*)* message to C_1's agent. The message is a confirmation that the member has locally reflected the changes done by CP_1. Figure 3.12 summarizes the change reaction algorithm executed by member agents.

```
Member Agent MA Algorithm {
Upon Reception of
 CP_Modify (G-op-ID,WS-ID,ModifySet)
  For each rule=(event,condition,actions) in the rule base RB
     | event==CP_Modify(G-op-ID,WS-ID,ModifySet) ∧ condition==.T
     Do Execute actions;
 CP_PP_Alert_SP(G-op-ID) From CA_i
  For each rule=(event,condition,actions) in the rule base RB
     | event== CP_PP_Alert_SP(G-op-ID) ∧ condition==.T
     Do Execute actions; }
```

Fig. 3.12 Reaction to Changes Issued by Community Providers: Member Agent Algorithm

Chapter 4
A Composability Framework for Semantic Web Services

Existing techniques for Web service composition generally require dealing with low level programming details, thus making the process of composing services demanding for composers [16, 36, 118, 160, 191]. Composers need to identify the way operations are interconnected, services are invoked, and messages are mapped to one another. To deal with this issue, we propose a model, called *composability model*, to check whether operations can be combined together, hence avoiding unexpected failures at run time. *Composability* refers to the process of checking if Web service operations to be composed can actually interact with each other [18].

The proposed model is defined by a set of rules called *composability rules*. Each rule compares a specific feature of interacting Web services. Since those features are relevant to different aspects of Web services (syntactic, semantic, behavioral, and qualitative), we organize composability rules into several *levels*. Each rule specifies the constraints and requirements for checking horizontal, vertical, and hybrid composability. We also define rules, called *business process composability* rules, to check whether a given composition of Web service operations provides a *value-added*.

Due to the sheer heterogeneity of Web services, it is not always possible to find services that are "fully" composable. Composers may, in this case, select services that are "partially" composable and then "adapt" their requests based on the results returned by the composability process. For that purpose, we introduce the notions of *composability degree* and *τ-composability* to cater for partial and total composability.

In this chapter, we give a detailed description of the proposed composability framework [152, 143]. The framework builds on the community-centric approach for semantic Web services presented in Chapter 3. In Section 4.1, we define the basic concepts of the model namely, composability *rule*, *level*, *degree*, and *τ-composability*. In Section 4.2, we describe syntactic composability rules. In Section 4.3 and 4.4, we define composability rules for comparing static and dynamic semantic features of Web services. Section 4.5 is devoted to composability rules related to quality of operation features. In Section 4.7,

B. Medjahed and A. Bouguettaya, *Service Composition for the Semantic Web*,
DOI 10.1007/978-1-4419-8465-4_4,

we describe business process composability. In Section 4.7, we propose algorithms for checking composability.

4.1 The Composability Model

The proposed model for composability contains rules organized into five levels (Figure 4.1). Each rule CR_{pq} at a level CL_p (p=0,5) compares a specific feature of services within CL_p. The first level CL_0 compares syntactic attributes such as the number of message parameters (CR_{00}). The second level CL_1 compares static semantic attributes. We define two groups of rules at this level. The first group compares the static semantics of messages. The second group compares the static semantics of operations. The third level CL_2 compares dynamic semantic attributes. The fourth level CL_3 focuses on quality of operation attributes. It contains three groups of rules. The first group compares security attributes. The second group checks business attributes. The third group deals with runtime attributes. The fifth level CL_4 deals with business process composability. It contains rules that check the *soundness* of a composite service, that is, whether that service provides a *value-added.*

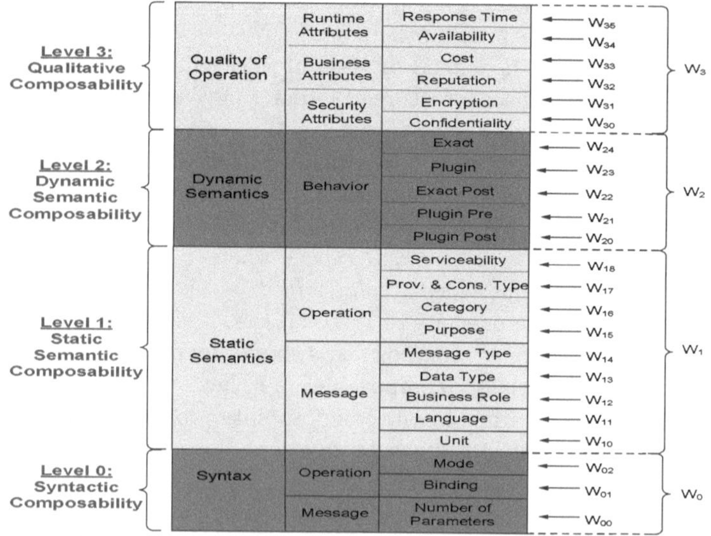

Fig. 4.1 Web Service Composability Stack

4.1.1 Horizontal and Vertical Composition

We define two ways of combining operations: *horizontal* and *vertical*. Each composability rule may be applicable to horizontal composition, vertical composition, or both.

Horizontal composition models a "supply chain"-like combination of operations (Figure 4.2). Let op_{ik} and op_{jl} be two operations that are horizontally composed. We call op_{ik} and op_{jl} *source* and *target* operations respectively. op_{ik} is first executed, followed by op_{jl}'s execution. op_{ik}'s messages are used to *feed* op_{jl}'s input message. Let $\mathcal{M}$ be a set of messages and $Input_{jl}$ the input message of op_{jl}. We say that $\mathcal{M}$ *feeds* $Input_{jl}$ if parameters in $\mathcal{M}$'s messages are used as $Input_{jl}$'s parameters. As depicted in Figure 4.2, In_{ik} and Out_{ik} messages feed In_{jl}. The precedence relationships between op_{ik}'s and op_{jl}'s states are given below:

- $Start_{ik} \longrightarrow_t Active_{ik} \longrightarrow_t End_{ik}$;
- $End_{ik} \longrightarrow_t Start_{jl} \longrightarrow_t Active_{jl} \longrightarrow_t End_{jl}$.

As example of the horizontal composition (case (a)), assume that op_{ik} provides translation from Chinese to English and op_{jl} provides translation from English to Urdu. The operations op_{ik} and op_{jl} may be horizontally composed to provide translation from Chinese to Urdu. In this case, the output of op_{ik} (English translation) is used as input by op_{jl}. The second case of horizontal composition (case (b)) refers to the situation where op_{ik} outsources from another operation (i.e., op_{ik} is vertically composed with a third operation). op_{ik} is then horizontally composed with op_{jl}. For example, a government agency may have a `get_directions` (Out/In) operation that is executed by outsourcing from other operations `People_Lookup` and `Direction-From-Address` (Figure 1.4). The `get_directions` operation is then horizontally composed with `Notify-Citizens` (In/Out operation).

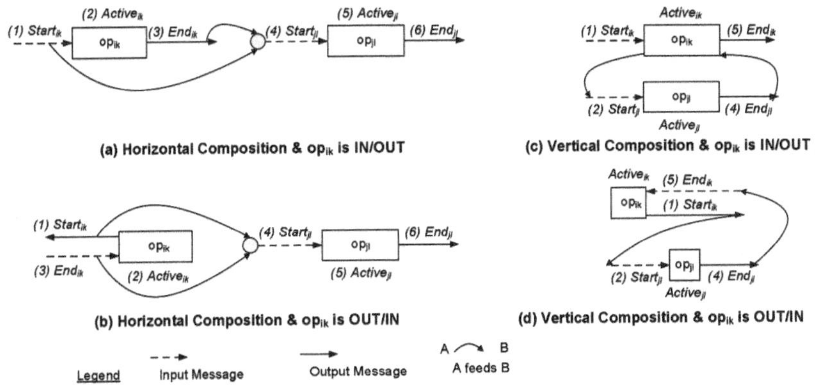

Fig. 4.2 Horizontal and Vertical Composition

Vertical Composition models the "subcontracting" of an operation op_{jl} by another operation op_{ik} (Figure 4.2). Let us consider the first case where op_{ik}'s mode is *In/Out*. Whenever op_{ik} is invoked, it transparently sends an input message to op_{jl}. op_{jl} then performs the requested function on behalf of op_{ik} and returns an output message to op_{ik}. op_{ik} will finally send the results to its invoker. Assume now that op_{ik}'s mode is *Out/In*. op_{ik} starts its execution by invoking op_{jl}. After op_{jl} terminates its execution, it sends results to op_{ik} which receives them as an input message. The precedence relationships between op_{ik}'s and op_{jl}'s are given below:

- $Start_{ik} \longrightarrow_t Start_{jl} \longrightarrow_t Active_{jl} \longrightarrow_t End_{jl} \longrightarrow_t End_{ik}$;
- $Start_{ik} \longrightarrow_t Active_{ik} \longrightarrow_t End_{ik}$.

An example of vertical composition is that of a personal computers (PC) reseller offering an operation `Request-Quotes` (case (c)). This operation allows customers to request quotes. The execution of `Request-Quotes` requires the invocation of another operation provided by a PC manufacturer to get the latest prices. The second case of vertical composition (case (d)) models "request-response" interactions. For example, let us consider an operation `Get-Immunization-Centers` (Out/In) provided by the Department for the Aging . Assume that the list of immunization centers is managed by the Health Department. To get up-to-date information about such centers, it would be more effective to outsource from a corresponding operation in the Health Department (In/Out), whenever `Get-Immunization-Centers` is invoked by a Department of Aging's officer.

4.1.2 Composability Degree

Composers may have different views on composability rules. One may, for example, give higher importance to syntactic composability while another may focus on semantic rules. To capture this aspect, we associate a *weight* W_p to each level CL_p. We also define a *weight* W_{pq} for each rule CR_{pq} in that level. A weight is an estimate of the significance of the corresponding level or rule from the composer's point of view. Composers assign a weight to each level and rule. The higher is a weight, the more important is the corresponding level or rule. W_p (≥ 0 and ≤ 1) compares CL_p to the other levels in terms of their importance. The total of weights assigned to the different levels equals 1. Similarly, W_{pq} (≥ 0 and ≤ 1) compares CR_{pq} to the other rules at level CL_p. The total of weights assigned to rules within a level equals 1. Formally, the different weights must respect the following constraints, where $|\mathrm{CL}_p|$ is the number of rules at level p:

1. $\forall$ p,q | $0 \leq p \leq 4$ and $0 \leq q \leq |\mathrm{CL}_p|-1$: $(0 \leq \mathrm{W}_p \leq 1) \wedge (0 \leq \mathrm{W}_{pq} \leq 1)$; and
2. $(\sum_{p=0}^{4} W_p = 1) \wedge (\forall$ p: $\sum_{q=0}^{|\mathrm{CL}_p|-1} W_{pq} = 1)$.

Due to the heterogeneity of Web services, it is not always possible to find operations that are fully composable with source operations. Composers may, in this case, select operations that are partially composable and then, adapt their operations based on the results returned by the composability process. For example, the composer may modify the data type of a parameter if it is not compatible with the data type of the corresponding target's parameter. For that purpose, we introduce the notion of composability *degree.*

The *degree* of op_{ik} and op_{jl} gives the ratio of composability rules that are satisfied between op_{ik} and op_{jl}. It takes its values from 0 to 1 (≥ 0 and ≤ 1). We define a function $satisfied_{pq}(op_{ik},op_{jl})$ that returns 1 if the rule CR_{pq} is satisfied between op_{ik} and op_{jl} and 0 otherwise. To reflect the composer's view on each rule CR_{pq}, we adjust the value returned by the function $satisfied_{pq}(op_{ik},op_{jl})$ with the weight W_{pq}. The degree at a given level CL_p is obtained by adding the adjusted values returned by the function *satisfied* applied on each CL_p's rule. Once the degree at CL_p is computed, we adjust it with the weight W_p assigned to CL_k. As specified below, the *degree* of op_{ik} and op_{jl} is obtained by summing composability degrees at all levels CL_p (p=0,4):

$$\text{Degree}(op_{ik},op_{jl}) = \sum_{p=0}^{4} \left(W_p \times \sum_{q=0}^{|CL_p|-1} \left(W_{pq} \times satisfied_{pq}(op_{ik},op_{jl}) \right) \right)$$

During a composition process, the composer assigns weights to each level and rule by providing a vector called *level weight* (LW) and matrix called *rule weight* (RW). The element LW_p (p=0,4) gives the weight assigned to level CL_p. The element CW_{pq} gives the weight assigned to rule CR_{pq}. If a rule CR_{pq} is undefined, then CW_{pq} is automatically assigned the value 0. Additionally, if the weight of a given level is equal to 0, then the weight of each rule within that level is also equal to 0. As an illustration, let us consider case study 1 (e-government). Let us assume that case officer *John* provides the weights given below to his source operation `scheduleTransportation`:

$$LW = \begin{pmatrix} 0.2 & 0.3 & 0.2 & 0.3 & 0.2 \end{pmatrix}$$

$$RW = \begin{pmatrix} 0.25 & 0.25 & 0.3 & 0 & 0 & 0 & 0 & 0 & 0 & 0 \\ 0.1 & 0.1 & 0.1 & 0.1 & 0.1 & 0.1 & 0.1 & 0.1 & 0.15 & 0.15 \\ 0.1 & 0.1 & 0.1 & 0.1 & 0.6 & 0 & 0 & 0 & 0 & 0 \\ 0.1 & 0.1 & 0.1 & 0.1 & 0 & 0 & 0 & 0 & 0 & 0 \\ 0 & 0.5 & 0.5 & 0 & 0 & 0 & 0 & 0 & 0 & 0 \end{pmatrix}$$

This example shows that the composer gives more importance to static semantic composability since the corresponding weight is greater than the other levels' weights. Among dynamic semantic properties, the composer gives higher priority to the *exact* behavioral rule. Assume now that `scheduleTransportation` is compared to `fasTransportation` using the composability model and that all composability rules are satisfied, except the ones that correspond to the following rules: CR_{00}, CR_{01}, CR_{02}, CR_{10}, CR_{15}, CR_{16}, CR_{20}, CR_{21}, CR_{22}, CR_{23}, CR_{24}, CR_{33}, CR_{35}, CR_{36}. The composability degree is computed as follows:

$$\begin{aligned}
&\mathit{Degree}\ (\texttt{scheduleTransportation,fasTransportation})\\
&\quad = 0.2 \times (0.25 + 0.25 + 0.3) + 0.3 \times (0.1 + 0.1 + 0.1) + 0.2\\
&\quad \times (0.1 + 0.1 + 0.1 + 0.1 + 0.6) + 0.1 \times (0.1 + 0.2 + 0.2)\\
&\quad = 0.57 = 57\%.
\end{aligned}$$

Based on the degree of op_{ik} and op_{jl}, we can decide about the composability of those operations. If *degree* = 0 then no rule is satisfied and the operations are *non composable*. If *degree* = 1 then all composability rules (with a positive level and rule weight) are satisfied and the operations are *fully* composable. Otherwise, a subset of rules are satisfied. In this case, op_{ik} and op_{jl} are *partially* composable:

If degree (op_{ik},op_{jl}) = 0
  Then op_{ik} and op_{jl} are non composable
  Else If degree (op_{ik},op_{jl}) = 1
    Then op_{ik} and op_{jl} are fully composable
    Else op_{ik} and op_{jl} are partially composable

4.1.3 τ-Composability

Composers may have different expectations about the composability degree of their operations. For that purpose, they provide a *composability threshold* τ ($0<\tau\leq1$) which gives the minimum value allowed for a composability degree. All operations op_{jl} so that *degree*(op_{ik},op_{jl}) $\geq \tau$ are candidates to be composed with op_{ik}. If the threshold is greater than degree(op_{ik},op_{jl}) then op_{ik} is not composable with op_{jl}. Based on the notions of degree and threshold, we introduce a "relaxed" definition of composability called τ-*composability*. τ-*composability* compares the composability degree and threshold to decide whether an operation is composable with another from composers' perspectives. op_{ik} is τ-*composable* with op_{jl} if *degree*(op_{ik},op_{jl}) $\geq \tau$.

The composability threshold is given by composers as part of their *profile*. Composers personalize the composability checking process via their profile. They assign values to the level weights vector (LW), rule weights matrix (RW), and τ. Other variables such as the maximum number of target operations can also be initialized. The way users create their profile depends on their level of expertise. We identify three types of users: *casual* (i.e., with minimal expertise), *expert* (i.e., with high expertise), and *regular* (i.e., with average expertise). *Casual* users may leave LW and RW unassigned in their profile. The system automatically distributes weights between levels and rules in a uniform way. The composability threshold will also be set to 1. In this case, full composability will be required. *Expert* users are knowledgable about the meaning of all operation and message attributes. They may customize the composability process by assigning the desired values to LW, RW, and τ. If the degree exceeds the threshold but not equals to 1, users change the specification of their operations based on the feedback returned by the system (e.g., which rules are not satisfied) to increase the degree. The third type of users, called *regular* users, includes those that have *some* knowledge about operation and message attributes. They may assign values to parts of LW and RW. In this case, the system automatically distributes weights between unassigned levels and rules. If τ was not assigned by a user, it is automatically set to 1 by the system.

4.1.4 Properties of a Composability Rule

Composability rules check whether two operations op_{ik} and op_{jl} are composable from different perspectives. We identify five *properties* that characterize composability rules: *level*, *granularity*, *attribute*, *symmetry*, and *composition type*.

Table 4.1 summarizes the different composability rules and their properties. We organize these rules into four *levels*: *syntactic*, *static semantic*, *dynamic semantic*, and *qualitative*. These levels check composability at the message and operation *granularity*. Each rule in a given level compares a specific pair of *attributes* of op_{ik} and op_{jl} (e.g., mode, binding, purpose, and cost). A rule is either *symmetric* or *asymmetric*. It is *symmetric* if the order in which it is checked (from op_{ik} to op_{jl} or op_{jl} to op_{ik}) is not important. This is in contrast with *asymmetric* rules; if an asymmetric rule is satisfied from op_{ik} to op_{jl} then it is not necessarily satisfied from op_{jl} to op_{ik}. Finally, a rule may be applicable for horizontal composition (e.g., *Plugin Prematch*), vertical composition (e.g., *Exact Postmach*), both (e.g., *purpose* and *category*), or hybrid (e.g., composition soundness).

4.2 Syntactic Composability Rules

We define two groups of syntactic composability rules. The first group contains rules that compare attributes at the operation granularity. Such rules

Level	Granularity	Attribute	Symmetry	Hor.	Vert.	Hybrid
Syntactic	Message	Number of Parameters	√	√	√	
	Operation	Binding	√	√	√	
		Mode		√	√	
Static Semantics	Message	Data type	√	√	√	
		Unit	√	√	√	
		Language	√	√	√	
		Business Role	√	√	√	
		Message Type	√		√	
	Operation	Purpose		√	√	
		Category		√	√	
		Prov. & Cons. Type		√	√	
		Serviceability	√		√	
Dynamic Semantics	Operation	Plugin Postmatch			√	
		Plugin Prematch		√		
		Exact Postmatch	√		√	
		Plugin			√	
		Exact	√		√	
Qualitative	Operation	Confidentiality			√	
		Non-repudiation	√		√	
		Authentication	√		√	
		Encryption	√		√	
		Regulatory			√	
		Reputation			√	
		Cost			√	
		Availability			√	
		Reliability			√	
		Response Time			√	
Business Process	Composite	Exact				√
		Loose				√
		Strong				√

√: The rule has the corresponding property.

Table 4.1 Composability Rules Properties

include *binding* and *mode* composability. The second group includes rules that check attributes at the message granularity. Such rules include *PN-Composability* which compares the number of parameters of operation messages.

4.2.1 Syntactic Composability at the Operation Granularity

The first syntactic attribute that needs to be checked is *binding*. Two operations op_{ik} and op_{jl} may support different binding protocols (e.g., SOAP/HTTP or SOAP/MIME). It is hence important to insure that they "understand" each other at the message format and protocol level. At least one of the protocols expected by an operation must be supported by the other. For example, it would be difficult for an operation that expects to receive messages in SOAP/MIME protocol to interact with another service that format its messages in SOAP/HTTP. Formally, op_{ik} and op_{jl} are *binding composable* if $Binding_{ik} \cap Binding_{jl} \neq \emptyset$.

Assume now that op_{ik} and op_{jl} are binding composable. For these operations to be "plugged" together, they must have "composable" modes. *Mode composability* depends on two criteria: the composition type (vertical or horizontal) and the source operation's mode $Mode_{ik}$. We consider the following possible cases:

1. *The composition is vertical and* Mode_{ik} = *"In/Out"* (Figure 4.2-(a)): the input of op_{ik} feeds op_{jl}'s input and the output of op_{jl} feeds op_{ik}'s output. Hence op_{jl} is an *In/Out* operation.
2. *The composition is vertical and* Mode_{ik} = *"Out/In"* (Figure 4.2-(b)): op_{ik} starts by sending an output message which should be received by op_{jl}. After processing the message, op_{jl} replies to op_{ik} through an output message. Hence op_{jl} is an *In/Out* operation.
3. *The composition is horizontal and* Mode_{ik} = *"In/Out"* (Figure 4.2-(a)): op_{ik}'s output message is the result returned by the execution of op_{ik}. It is used in part or whole to invoke op_{jl} by sending an input message to it. Hence op_{jl} is an *In/Out* operation.
4. *The composition is horizontal and* Mode_{ik} = *'Out/In"* (Figure 4.2-(b)): op_{ik}'s input message is the result of a subcontracting performed by op_{ik} (via vertical composition). It is used to invoke op_{jl} by sending an input message to it. Hence op_{jl} is an *In/Out* operation.

The target operation's mode $Mode_{jl}$ should be *In/Out*, independently of the composition type and the model of the source operation. We say that op_{ik} is *mode composable* with op_{jl} if $Mode_{jl}$ = *"In/Out"*.

4.2.2 Syntactic Composability at the Message Granularity

Syntactic composability also requires comparing op_{ik} and op_{jl} at the message level. There is a need to compare the input and output messages of both operations. For this purpose, we define a composability rule, called *Parameters Number Composability* (*PN-Composability*). *PN-Composability* compares the number of parameters in every pair of "plugged" messages. The definition of *PN-Composability* depends on the composition type and operations' modes. We identify the following four cases:

1. *The composition is vertical Composition and* Mode_{ik} = *"In/Out"*: In_{ik} is "plugged" with In_{jl} and Out_{jl} is "plugged" with Out_{ik} (Figure 4.2-(a)). In_{ik} (Out_{jl}) must provide at least as much information as expected by In_{jl}

(Out_{ik}). Hence, the number of parameters in In_{ik} (Out_{jl}) is at least equal to the number of parameters in In_{jl} (Out_{ik}).
2. *The composition is vertical and* Mode_{ik} = *"Out/In"*: Out_{ik} is "plugged" with In_{jl} and Out_{jl} is "plugged" with In_{ik} (Figure 4.2-(b)). The number of parameters in Out_{ik} (Out_{jl}) is at least equal to the number of parameters in In_{jl} (In_{ik}).
3. *The composition is horizontal and* Mode_{ik} = *"In/Out"*: in this case, In_{ik} and Out_{ik} are "plugged" with In_{jl} (Figure 4.2-(a)). Consequently, the total number of parameters in In_{ik} and Out_{ik} should be at least equal to In_{jl}'s.
4. *Horizontal Composition and* Mode_{ik} = *'Out/In"*: As illustrated in Figure 4.2-(b)), this case is similar to case (3).

Formally, we say that op_{ik} is *PN-composable* with op_{jl} if one of the following three conditions is true:

1. (i) the composition is vertical, (ii) $Mode_{ik}$ = "In/Out", (iii) $|\text{In}_{jl}| \leq |\text{In}_{ik}|$, and (iv) $|\text{Out}_{ik}| \leq |\text{Out}_{jl}|$.
2. (i) the composition is vertical, (i) $Mode_{ik}$ = "Out/In", (i) $|\text{In}_{jl}| \leq |\text{Out}_{ik}|$, and (iv) $|\text{In}_{ik}| \leq |\text{Out}_{jl}|$.
3. (i) the composition is horizontal and (ii) $|\text{In}_{jl}| \leq |\text{In}_{ik}| + |\text{Out}_{ik}|$.

4.3 Static Semantic Composability

For two operations op_{ik} and op_{jl} to be "plugged" together, they must be semantically "compliant". In this section, we present composability rules at the static level. We define each rule with regard to vertical and horizontal composability. We also consider composability at both operation and message granularities.

4.3.1 Static Semantic Composability of Operations

We summarize in Table 4.2 the static semantic rules at the operation granularity. The first rule compares op_{ik}'s and op_{jl}'s *serviceability*. Horizontal composition does not require comparing *serviceability* since no operation will "service" the other. However, the content of both attributes must be "similar" if op_{ik} and op_{jl} are vertically composed ($\text{serviceability}_{ik} = \text{serviceability}_{jl}$). For example, an operation providing cash support cannot "subcontract" in-kind operations. The "=" operator used here refers to one of the following two cases: (i) $\text{serviceability}_{ik}$ and $\text{serviceability}_{jl}$ have the same content if the attributes use the same vertical ontology; or (ii) $\text{serviceability}_{ik}$ and $\text{serviceability}_{jl}$ have "mappable" content if the attributes use different vertical ontologies.

$CR(op_{ik}, op_{jl})$	*Vertical Composition*	*Horizontal Composition*
Serviceability	$\text{serviceability}_{ik} = \text{serviceability}_{jl}$	Not Applicable
Provider - Consumer	$\text{provider}_{ik} \cap \text{provider}_{jl} \neq \emptyset$ and $\text{consumer}_{ik} \cap \text{consumer}_{jl} \neq \emptyset$	$\text{provider}_{ik} \cap \text{consumer}_{jl} \neq \emptyset$
Category	$\text{Spec}_{ik} \subseteq \text{Spec}_{jl}$; and $(\text{Dom}_{ik} = \text{Dom}_{jl})$ or $(\text{Dom}_{ik} \in \text{Syn}_{jl})$ or $(\text{Dom}_{jl} \in \text{Syn}_{ik})$ or $(\text{Syn}_{ik} \cap \text{Syn}_{jl} \neq \emptyset)$	$\text{category}_{jl} \in \text{Overlap}_{ik}$
Purpose	$\text{Spec}_{ik} \subseteq \text{Spec}_{jl}$; and $(\text{Func}_{ik} = \text{Func}_{jl})$ or $(\text{Func}_{ik} \in \text{Syn}_{jl})$ or $(\text{Func}_{jl} \in \text{Syn}_{ik})$ or $(\text{Syn}_{ik} \cap \text{Syn}_{jl} \neq \emptyset)$	$\text{purpose}_{jl} \in \text{Overlap}_{ik}$

Table 4.2 Static Semantic Rules for Operations

The second rule compares op_{ik}'s and op_{jl}'s *provider* and *consumer types.* If the composition is vertical, op_{ik} and op_{jl} must have at least one common provider type and one common consumer type. For example, if op_{ik} expects to outsource from a federal agency's operation then op_{jl}'s agency should include the type "federal". Additionally, if op_{ik} provides benefits for children and pregnant women then op_{jl} should provide benefits for at least those two groups. If op_{ik} is horizontally composed with op_{jl}, then it should be viewed as a consumer of op_{jl}. Hence, op_{jl}'s consumer type should include at least one value from op_{ik}'s provider types.

The third rule compares operations' *categories.* Assume that op_{ik} is vertically composed with op_{jl}. Since op_{ik} is meant to "replace" op_{jl}, the following two conditions should be true: (i) op_{ik}'s and op_{jl}'s domains of interest are similar or synonyms, and (ii) all characteristics (i.e., elements of the "spec" attribute) of op_{ik}'s category are provided by op_{jl}'s. For example, assume that op_{ik}'s category provides health insurance for children (i.e., Dom_{ik}="healthcare" and Spec_{ik}={"children", "insurance"}). The operation op_{jl} should not only deal with healthcare but also *at least* provide insurance for children as well. Assume now that op_{ik} is horizontally composed with op_{jl}. Category_{ik} and category_{jl} should be defined so that op_{ik} and op_{jl} "can" be combined. This is captured by the *Overlap* attribute of a category. Hence, category_{ik} is composable with category_{jl} if Overlap_{ik} contains category_{jl}.

The last rule compares operations' *purposes.* The *purpose composability* rule is defined in the same way as *category composability* where Dom is replaced by Func.

4.3.2 Static Semantic Composability for Messages

Table 4.3 summarizes the static semantic rules at the message granularity. The first rule compares op_{ik}'s and op_{jl}'s message types. This rule is applicable only to vertical composition since horizontal composition does not involve replacing op_{ik}'s messages with op_{jl}'s or vice versa. Assume that op_{ik} is vertically composed with op_{jl}. As depicted in Figure 4.2, we identify two cases based on the mode of op_{ik}. If op_{ik}'s mode is *In/Out*, then In_{ik}'s (resp. Out_{ik}'s) and In_{jl}'s (Out_{jl}'s) types should be similar. If op_{ik}'s mode is *Out/In*, then Out_{ik}'s (resp. In_{ik}'s) and In_{jl}'s (Out_{jl}'s) types should be similar.

CR(op_{ik}, op_{jl})	*Vertical Composition and $Mode_{ik}$ = In/Out*	*Vertical Composition and $Mode_{ik}$ = Out/In*	*Horizontal Composition*
Message Type	$\mathcal{MT}(In_{ik}) = \mathcal{MT}(In_{jl})$; and $\mathcal{MT}(Out_{ik}) = \mathcal{MT}(Out_{jl})$	$\mathcal{MT}(Out_{ik}) = \mathcal{MT}(In_{jl})$; and $\mathcal{MT}(Out_{jl}) = \mathcal{MT}(In_{ik})$	Not Applicable
Data Type	$\forall$ $p \in In_{jl}$ $\exists$ $p' \in In_{ik}$ | compatible(p',p); and $\forall$ $p \in Out_{ik}$ $\exists$ $p' \in Out_{jl}$ | compatible(p',p).	$\forall$ $p \in In_{jl}$ $\exists$ $p' \in Out_{ik}$ | compatible(p',p); and $\forall$ $p \in In_{ik}$ $\exists$ $p' \in Out_{jl}$ | compatible(p',p).	$\forall$ $p \in In_{jl}$ $\exists$ $p' \in In_{ik} \cup Out_{ik}$ | compatible(p',p)
Role	$\forall$ $p \in In_{jl}$ $\exists$ $p' \in In_{ik}$ | role(p') = role(p); and $\forall$ $p \in Out_{ik}$ $\exists$ $p' \in Out_{jl}$ | role(p') = role(p).	$\forall$ $p \in In_{jl}$ $\exists$ $p' \in Out_{ik}$ | role(p') = role(p); and $\forall$ $p \in In_{ik}$ $\exists$ $p' \in Out_{jl}$ | role(p') = role(p).	$\forall$ $p \in In_{jl}$ $\exists$ $p' \in In_{ik} \cup Out_{ik}$ | role(p') = role(p)
Language	$\forall$ $p \in In_{jl}$ $\exists$ $p' \in In_{ik}$ | lang(p') = lang(p); and $\forall$ $p \in Out_{ik}$ $\exists$ $p' \in Out_{jl}$ | lang(p') = lang(p).	$\forall$ $p \in In_{jl}$ $\exists$ $p' \in Out_{ik}$ | lang(p') = lang(p); and $\forall$ $p \in In_{ik}$ $\exists$ $p' \in Out_{jl}$ | lang(p') = lang(p).	$\forall$ $p \in In_{jl}$ $\exists$ $p' \in In_{ik} \cup Out_{ik}$ | lang(p') = lang(p)
Unit	$\forall$ $p \in In_{jl}$ $\exists$ $p' \in In_{ik}$ | unit(p') = unit(p); and $\forall$ $p \in Out_{ik}$ $\exists$ $p' \in Out_{jl}$ | unit(p') = unit(p).	$\forall$ $p \in In_{jl}$ $\exists$ $p' \in Out_{ik}$ | unit(p') = unit(p); and $\forall$ $p \in In_{ik}$ $\exists$ $p' \in Out_{jl}$ | unit(p') = unit(p).	$\forall$ $p \in In_{jl}$ $\exists$ $p' \in In_{ik} \cup Out_{ik}$ | unit(p') = unit(p)

Table 4.3 Static Semantic Rules for Messages

The second composability rule compares parameters' data types. It is based on the notion of *compatibility* between data types (XML Schema). Two parameters are *data type compatible* if they have the same built-in type. Compatibility of derived types and complex data types can also be adopted. However, these issues are out of the scope of this book. A discussion about typing in XML can be found in [115].

Data type composability depends on the composition type (horizontal or vertical) and operations' modes. As depicted in Figure 4.2, we identify the following four cases. If op_{ik} is vertically composed with op_{jl} and $Mode_{ik}$ =

"In/Out", then In_{ik} is "plugged" with In_{jl} and Out_{jl} is "plugged" with Out_{ik} (Figure 4.2-(c)). The data type of each parameter in In_{jl} (Out_{ik}) should be compatible with the data type of a corresponding parameter in In_{ik} (Out_{jl}). If op_{ik} is vertically composed with op_{jl} and $Mode_{ik}$ = *"Out/In"*, then Out_{ik} is "plugged" with In_{jl} and Out_{jl} is "plugged" with In_{ik} (Figure 4.2-(d)). The data type of each parameter in In_{jl} (resp. In_{ik}) should be compatible with the data type of a corresponding parameter in Out_{ik} (Out_{jl}). If op_{ik} is horizontally composed with op_{jl}, then In_{ik} and Out_{ik} are "plugged" with In_{jl} independently of op_{ik}'s mode (Figure 4.2-(a) and (b)). The data type of each parameter in In_{jl} should be compatible with the data type of a corresponding parameter in In_{ik} or Out_{ik}.

The remaining three rules compare parameters' *business role*, *language*, and *unit* respectively. They are defined similarly to data type composability, except that the data type is replaced by *business role*, *language*, and *unit*, respectively.

4.4 Dynamic Semantic Composability

The *dynamic semantic* composability (or *B-Composability*) compares the business logic rules of source and target operations. Let us consider two rules R^n_{ik} =($PreC^n_{ik}$,$PostC^n_{ik}$) and R^m_{jl} =($PreC^m_{jl}$,$PostC^m_{jl}$) that belong to op_i and op_j respectively. B-composability relates $PreC^n_{ik}$ to $PreC^m_{jl}$ and $PostC^n_{ik}$ to $PostC^m_{jl}$. We define several forms of B-composability depending on the relationships between post- and pre-conditions. Each form is an instantiation of the general form of B-composability, called *generic B-composability*. We say that op_{ik} is *Generically B-composable* with op_{jl} if:

$$\forall\ R^n_{ik} \in Rules(\text{op}_{ik})\ \exists\ R^m_{jl} \in Rules(\text{op}_{jl})\ |$$
$$(\widetilde{PreC}_{ikn}\ \mathcal{R}_1\ PreC^m_{jl}) \wedge (PostC^m_{jl}\ \mathcal{R}_2\ PostC^n_{ik})$$

The relations $\mathcal{R}_1$ and $\mathcal{R}_2$ relate preconditions and postconditions, respectively. Each relation is either equivalence ($\Leftrightarrow$), implication ($\Rightarrow$), or *nil* (meaning that the corresponding term is dropped). As illustrated in this section, we may need to include information about the postcondition in the precondition clause. To allow this flexibility, we define $\widetilde{PreC}_{ikn}$ as either $PreC^n_{ik}$ or $PreC^n_{ik} \wedge PostC^n_{ik}$ in the generic B-composability rule. Note that techniques for comparing pre and post-conditions have been presented in [235]. However, these techniques deal with component-based environments *not* Web services.

Figure 4.3 depicts the different forms of B-Composability rules. We first give the strongest rule and then weaken the rules by relaxing $\mathcal{R}_1$ and $\mathcal{R}_2$ from $\Leftrightarrow$ to $\Rightarrow$, and *nil*. We also vary $\widetilde{PreC}_{ikn}$ from $PreC^n_{ik}$ to $PreC^n_{ik} \wedge PostC^n_{ik}$.

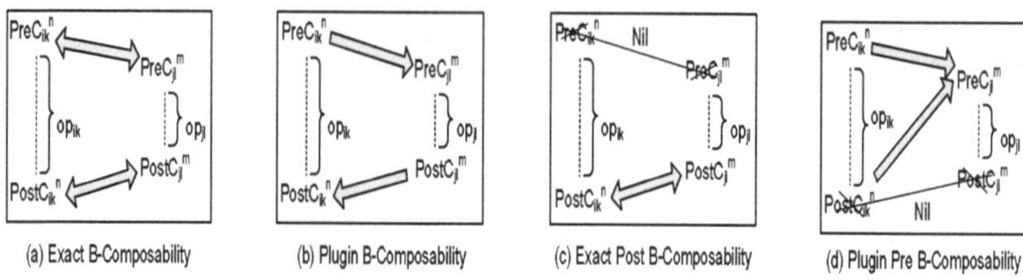

Fig. 4.3 B-Composability Rules

Relaxing the rules enables the comparison of less closely related operations.

Exact – Exact B-composability instantiates $\mathcal{R}_1$ and $\mathcal{R}_2$ to $\Leftrightarrow$ and $\widetilde{PreC}_{ikn}$ to $PreC_{ik}^n$ (Figure 4.3.a). If two operations are exactly B-composable, then their business logics are equivalent. Hence, whenever one operation is used, it could be replaced by the other with no change in observable business logic. This rule is suitable for vertical composition since op_{ik} and op_{jl} are in their *active* state simultaneously.

Plugin – This rule relaxes both $\mathcal{R}_1$ and $\mathcal{R}_2$ from $\Leftrightarrow$ to $\Rightarrow$. It also instantiates $\widetilde{PreC}_{ikn}$ to $PreC_{ik}^n$. The rule R_{ik}^n is matched by any rule R_{jl}^m whose precondition is weaker to allow *at least* all of the conditions that R_{ik}^n allows. The post-condition of R_{jl}^m is stronger than R_{ik}^n's to provide a condition *at least* as strong as R_{ik}^n's. As depicted in Figure 4.3.b, this rule is suitable for vertical composition since op_{ik} and op_{jl} are in their *active* state simultaneously.

Exact Post – In some cases, composers are concerned only with the effects of operations. For example, a composer may be interested in an operation that provides a social benefit independently of any precondition of that operation. Thus, a useful relaxation of the exact B-composability is to consider only the postcondition part of the conjunction. *Exact post* is also an instance of the generic B-composability, with $\mathcal{R}_2$ instantiated to $\Leftrightarrow$ and dropping both $\widetilde{PreC}_{ikn}$ and $PreC_{jl}^m$ (Figure 4.3.c). Since only equivalence relationship is used, the exact post is symmetric. Because $op_{ik}$and op_{jl} are in their *active* state simultaneously (Figure 4.3.c), this rule is suitable for vertical composition.

Plugin Pre – Plugin Pre includes information about op_i's postcondition in the precondition and drops the relationship between postconditions. It is an instantiation of generic B-composability where $\mathcal{R}_1$ is instantiated to $\Rightarrow$, $\mathcal{R}_2$ to *nil*, and $\widetilde{PreC}_{ikn}$ to $PreC_{ik}^n \wedge PostC_{ik}^n$. This rule is particularly useful to check horizontal composability that is, whether the execution of op_i can be followed by the execution of op_j. Figure 4.3.d shows that op_{ik} and op_{jl} enter their *active* states sequentially ($Active_{ik} \longrightarrow_t Active_{jl}$). Since op_i is executed (according to R_{ik}^n) before op_j, $PreC_{ik}^n$ and $PostC_{kl}$ are by definition true. In order for op_j to be executable according to R_{jl}^m, its precondition $PreC_{jl}^m$ should be true. One way to ensure this is to check that the implication $PreC_{ik}^n \wedge PostC_{ik}^n \Rightarrow PreC_{jl}^m$ is true.

4.5 Qualitative Composability

Composers have generally preferences regarding the quality of operations they would like to compose. For that purpose, we define a set of composability rules, called *qualitative rules*, to compare qualitative features of interacting operations. Assume that op_{ik} and op_{jl} are vertically composed. Since op_{ik} "subcontracts" op_{jl}, it is important to make sure that op_{jl}'s quality is at least "similar" to op_{ik}'s quality. However, if op_{ik} and op_{jl} are horizontally composed, then their quality are independent. Hence, qualitative rules are applicable for vertical composition.

Each rule compares the content of a given qualitative attribute (noted *Q-attribute*) in op_{ik} and op_{jl}. Each rule has the general form $\mathcal{R}$(*Q-attribute*$_{ik}$,*Q-attribute*$_{jl}$) where $\mathcal{R}$ is a relationship between *Q-attribute*$_{ik}$ to *Q-attribute*$_{jl}$ (e.g., $=$, $\subseteq$, $\leq$, $\geq$). The definition of $\mathcal{R}$ differs from one rule to another. The first qualitative rule compares the *encryption* attribute. It guarantees that either both op_{ik} and op_{jl} encrypt their messages or none of them does. *Authentication* and *Non-repudiation* attributes are compared in the same way. The last security-related rule compares the *confidentiality* attribute. The privacy preferences of op_{ik} should be preserved by the privacy features exposed by op_{jl}. If op_{ik}'s provider does not want a parameter p to be divulged (i.e., $p \in$ *confidentiality*$_{ik}$) then p should also belong to *confidentiality*$_{jl}$. We say that the security attributes of op_{ik} are composable with op_{jl}'s security attributes if:

- $\mathrm{Encryption}_{ik} = \mathrm{Encryption}_{jl}$; and
- $\mathrm{Authentication}_{ik} = \mathrm{Authentication}_{jl}$; and
- $\mathrm{Non\text{-}repudiation}_{ik} = \mathrm{Non\text{-}repudiation}_{jl}$; and
- $\mathrm{Privacy}_{ik} \subseteq \mathrm{Privacy}_{jl}$.

The second subset of qualitative rules compare op_{ik}'s and op_{jl}'s business attributes (*cost, reputation*, and *regulatory*). Since op_{ik} subcontracts from op_{jl}, then the cost of executing op_{jl} should at most be equal to op_{ik}. Similarly, the ranking of op_{jl} in terms of its *reputation* and *regulatory* features should be at least as good as op_{ik}'s ranking. We say that the business attributes of op_{ik} are composable with op_{jl}'s business attributes if:

- $\mathrm{Cost}_{ik} \geq \mathrm{Cost}_{jl}$; and
- $\mathrm{Reputation}_{ik} \geq \mathrm{Reputation}_{jl}$; and
- $\mathrm{Regulatory}_{ik} \geq \mathrm{Regulatory}_{jl}$.

The last subset of qualitative rules compare run-time attributes: *response time*, *reliability*, and *availability*. The time to executed a subcontracted operation op_{jl} should be less or equal to the response time expected expected by op_{ik}. Additionally, op_{jl} should be at least as reliable and available than op_{ik}. We say that the run-time attributes of op_{ik} are composable with op_{jl}'s run-time attributes if:

- $\mathrm{Time}_{ik} \geq \mathrm{Time}_{jl}$; and
- $\mathrm{Reliability}_{ik} \leq \mathrm{Reliability}_{jl}$; and
- $\mathrm{Availability}_{ik} \leq \mathrm{Availability}_{jl}$.

4.6 Business Process Composability

Service composition involves combining a set of generic operations in a specific way. One important issue to consider is whether such combination provides an added value. To address this issue, we define a rule, called *composition soundness*, to check whether a given composition of generic operations is *sound*. By *sound*, we mean that the way operations are combined provides an added value.

4.6.1 Composition and Stored Templates

The definition of *composition soundness* is based on the notions of *composition* and *stored templates* defined below. A *composition template* is built for each composite service *CS* and gives its general structure. It is modeled by a directed graph *(V, E)* where *V* is a set of generic operation IDs (G-op-IDs) and *E* is a set of edges. If an operation *op* is vertically composed with another operation *op'* in CS, then *op* and *op'* represent the same node in *V* since the execution of *op* is "replaced" by the execution of *op'*. Edges in *E* model horizontal composition relationships between *E*'s operations. An edge $(\mathrm{op}_{ik}, \mathrm{op}_{jl})$ belongs to E if op_{ik} is horizontally composed with op_{jl}. Figure 4.4 shows an example of composition template for a composite service CS that collects social benefits for senior citizens. CS uses four operations `lookupSACenter`, `findTransportation`, `loookupMealsProviders`, and `mealsOnWheels`. CS first looks for senior activity center. Then, based on the location of that center, it provides for transportation from citizen's residence to the center. It also looks for a participant restaurant around the center and then, arranges for a delivery from the restaurant to center location. The template shows that `lookupSACenter` is horizontally composed with `findTransportation` and `loookupMealsProviders`. The `loookupMealsProviders` operation is horizontally composed with `mealsOnWheels`.

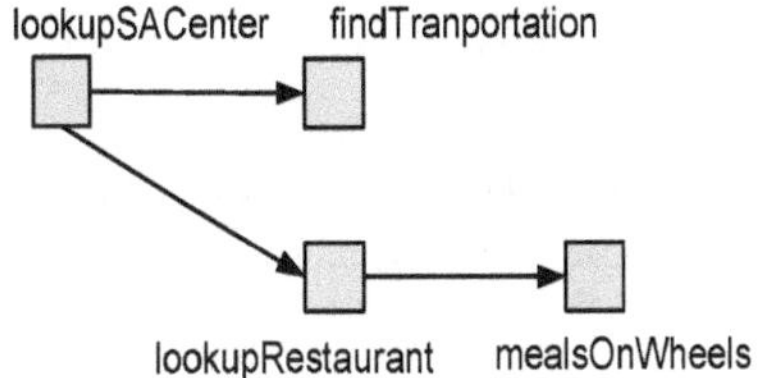

Fig. 4.4 Example of Composition Template

Stored templates are defined by directed graphs similar to those used for composition templates. The difference between stored and composition templates is twofold. First, stored templates are saved in a *stored template repository* (*ST-repository*) while composition are computed for each composite service and then discarded. Second, the interpretation given to composition and stored templates are different. Composition templates model actual composite services as defined by users. Hence they may or may not provide added values. Stored template model "potential" composite services. They are generally pre-defined by domain experts (i.e, community providers). Hence, they inherently provide added values. For example, government agencies dealing with social services would agree that one composite service that collects benefits for senior citizens would combine the following operations: `lookupSACenter`, `findTransportation`, `loookupMealsProviders`, `mealsOnWheels`, `registerInsurance`, and `registerLegalAid` (Figure 4.5). Stored templates may also be "learned" by the system. Each time a composite service is defined by a user, the system saves the corresponding composition template in the *ST-repository* if the template does not already exist in the repository.

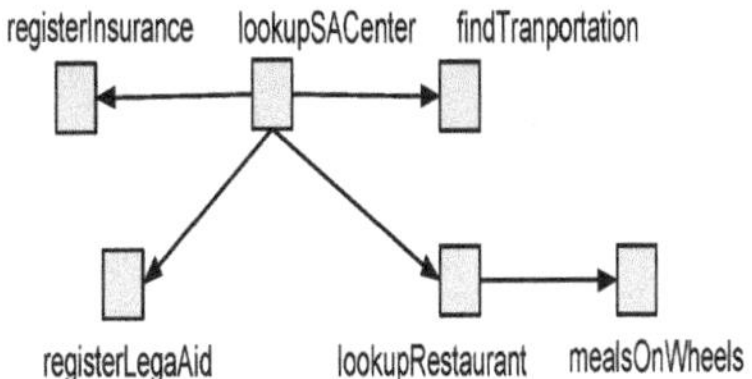

Fig. 4.5 Example of Stored Template

4.6.2 Composition Soundness

Because stored templates intrinsically provide added values, they can prove or disprove the soundness of a composite service *CS*. The idea is to compare the composition template of *CS* (*template(CS)*) with the existing stored templates. The following four cases are then possible:

1. *Case 1:* If *template(CS)* is equal to a given stored template *ST*, then *CS* provides *exactly* the same functionalities as the functionalities modeled by *ST*. We say that *CS* is *exactly sound* with respect to *ST*.
2. *Case 2:* If *template(CS)* is a *subgraph* of a given stored template *ST*, then *CS* provides a subset of the functionalities modeled by *ST*. For example, the composition template depicted in Figure 4.4 is a subgraph of the stored templates depicted in Figure 4.5. We say that *CS* is *loosely sound* with respect to *ST*.
3. *Case 3:* If a given stored template *ST* is a *subgraph* of *template(CS)*, then *CS* provides all the functionalities modeled by *ST*. *CS* also provides functionalities not offered by *ST*. We say that *CS* is *strongly sound* with respect to *ST*.
4. *Case 4:* If none of the previous cases is possible, then *CS* is not *sound*.

Formally, let *CS* be a composite service. We define three composition soundness rules as follows:

- *CS* is *exactly sound* if $\exists$ *ST* $\in$ ST-repository | *template(CS)* $=$ *ST*.
- *CS* is *loosely sound* if $\exists$ *ST* $\in$ ST-repository | *template(CS)* $\subset$ *ST*.
- *CS* is *strongly sound* if $\exists$ *ST* $\in$ ST-repository | *template(CS)* $\supset$ *ST*.

4.7 Checking Service Composability

We identify three avenues in the area of service composition that could benefit from checking composability: composition analysis, automatic composition, and operation outsourcing. In the first case, composability is checked *a posteriori*. Composers first specify their composite service (e.g., using BPEL4WS). The composition engine then checks the "correctness" of the composite service using composability rules. In the second case, the composition engine uses the composability rules to generate composite service descriptions from high-level specifications of composition requests. The engine needs to determine the set of participants relevant to the composition request while making sure that they are composable. In the third case, composability rules are used to "replace" an operation by a "compatible" one. This could be useful to enable the subcontracting of operations or substitutability of a participant by another. In this section, we propose two algorithms for checking composability in the case of operation outsourcing: *operation-centric* and *community-based* algorithms.

4.7.1 Operation-Centric Algorithm

The aim of this algorithm (Figure 4.6) is to determine the set of all operations within the service registry that could be outsourced by a given source operation SO. The target operation should be "similar enough" to the source operation so that it could be invoked instead of SO. We formulate this problem using the composability model as follows: "determine the set $\mathcal{T}$ of target operations op within the registry so that SO is vertically composable with op. The degree of similarity between SO and op is defined by τ.

Algorithm: *Operation_Centric_Composability_Checking*
Input: *SO, Registry, $\mathcal{T}$, Profile, nb_target*
Output: *List $\mathcal{T}$ of operations vertically composable with SO*

```
nb_target = 0;   degree = 0;   T = ∅;
  for each operation op ∈ Registry | (nb_target < max_target) do {
    syntactic(SO, op, degree)
    If degree > τ Then { T = T ∪ {op};
                         nb_target = nb_target + 1;
                         Continue; }
    static_semantics(SO, op, degree)
    If degree > τ Then { T = T ∪ {op};
                         nb_target = nb_target + 1;
                         Continue; }
    dynamic_semantics(SO, op, degree)
    If degree > τ Then { T = T ∪ {op};
                         nb_target = nb_target + 1;
                         Continue; }
    qualitative(SO, op, degree)
    If degree > τ Then { T = T ∪ {op};
                         nb_target = nb_target + 1;
                         Continue; }   }
```

Fig. 4.6 Operation-Centric Composability Algorithm

The algorithm browses the registry, checking the vertical composability of SO with every operation op in the registry (Figure 4.6). As the number of target operations may be large, users have the possibility to set in their profile the maximum number of target operations to be determined (*max_target* variable). Composability degree is computed after checking composability at each level and granularity. If the degree is greater or equal to τ, then *op* is a potential candidate to "replace" *SO*. In this case, *op* is added to $\mathcal{T}$. Users will be able to select the "best" operations to be outsourced via qualitative composability.

The syntactic, static semantic, and qualitative procedures are straightforward implementation of the corresponding vertical composability rules given in this chapter. The *dynamic_semantics()* procedure (Figure 4.7) compares *SO*'s business logic rules with *op*'s. Since B-composability rules are hierarchically organized, we adopt a bottom-up approach for checking these rules. For example, if the *Plugin Pre* rule is not satisfied, then the *Plugin* rule is necessarily not satisfied since *Plugin* $\Rightarrow$ *Plugin Pre*. A rule is checked if the corresponding weight is positive. For that purpose, we use a function *get_weightR(CR)* that returns the weight of the current rule *CR* from the RW matrix. We also use a function *get_weightL(CL)* that returns the weight of the current level *CL* from the LW vector.

Algorithm: *Dynamic_Semantics*

Input: *op, op', degree*

Output: *degree, are B-composability rules satisfied or not?*

```
d = 0;  /* d = degree for dynamic semantic composability */
        /* degree = total composability degree */
isExact = isExactPost = isPluginPre = isPlugin = false;
if get_weightR(CR) > 0
  then isPluginPre = check_plugin_pre(op,op');
if ¬isPluginPre
  then isPlugin = false
  else if get_weightR(CR) > 0
             then isPlugin = check_plugin(op,op');
if get_weightR(CR) > 0
  then isExactPost = check_exact_post(op,op');
if ¬isPlugin or ¬isExactPost
  then isExact = false
  else if get_weightR(CR) > 0
             then isExact = check_exact(op,op');
if isPluginPre then d = d + get_weightR(CR);
if isPlugin then d = d + get_weightR(CR);
if isExactPost then d = d + get_weightR(CR);
if isExact then d = d + get_weightR(CR);
degree = degree + d × get_weightL(CL);
```

Fig. 4.7 Business Logic Composability

B-composability rules are mainly based on proving implications between conditions (pre and post conditions) within a pair of business logic rules. However, proving theorems such as $Cond_1 \Rightarrow Cond_2$ is a NP-complete problem [186]. To deal with this issue we define an approximate solution for proving such theorems. The proposed solution (Figure 4.8) is based on the assumption that each condition is a conjunction of *terms*. Each *term* has the form x <r> v where x is parameter, v is a constant value, and <r> is a relational operator that belongs to $\{=,\neq,<,>,\leq,\geq\}$.

The theorem prover (Figure 4.8) first *unifies* the parameters in $Cond_1$ and $Cond_2$. The unification step works as follows: if there are parameters $\mathrm{x}_1^1,\ldots,\mathrm{x}_n^1$ in $Cond_1$ that are composable with parameters $\mathrm{x}_1^2,\ldots,\mathrm{x}_m^2$ in $Cond_2$, then replace $\mathrm{x}_1^1,\ldots,\mathrm{x}_n^1$ and $\mathrm{x}_1^2,\ldots,\mathrm{x}_m^2$ by the same parameter name (say x_1^2). Composability between parameters refers to the verification of composability rules between message parameters. The second step of the prover is to *match* each term t_{2p} of $Cond_2$ with a term t_{1q} in $Cond_1$. We say that t_{2p} *matches* with t_{1q} if $t_{1q} \Rightarrow t_{2p}$. Proving the matching between terms is done by applying one of the *inference rules* for relational operators. Note that the number of inference rules is finite. If a given term in $Cond_2$ matches with no term in $Cond_1$, then $Cond_1 \Rightarrow Cond_2$ is false. If all terms in $Cond_2$ are matched with a term in $Cond_1$, then $Cond_1 \Rightarrow Cond_2$ is true. We give below a summary of inference rules:

- $\frac{x>a \ \wedge \ a=b}{x>b}$; $\frac{x>a \ \wedge \ a>b}{x>b}$; $\frac{x>a \ \wedge \ a\geq b}{x\geq b}$; $\frac{x>b}{x\geq b}$.
- $\frac{x<a \ \wedge \ a=b}{x<b}$; $\frac{x<a \ \wedge \ a<b}{x<b}$; $\frac{x<a \ \wedge \ a\leq b}{x\leq b}$; $\frac{x<b}{x\leq b}$.
- $\frac{x\geq a \ \wedge \ a=b}{x\geq b}$; $\frac{x\geq a \ \wedge \ a>b}{x>b}$; $\frac{x\geq a \ \wedge \ a\geq b}{x\geq b}$.
- $\frac{x\leq a \ \wedge \ a=b}{x\leq b}$; $\frac{x\leq a \ \wedge \ a<b}{x<b}$; $\frac{x\leq a \ \wedge \ a\leq b}{x\leq b}$.
- $\frac{x\neq a \ \wedge \ a=b}{x\neq b}$.
- $\frac{x=a \ \wedge \ a=b}{x=b}$; $\frac{x=a}{x\geq a}$; $\frac{x=a}{x\leq a}$.
- $\frac{x=a \ \wedge \ a<b}{x<b}$; $\frac{x=a \ \wedge \ a>b}{x>b}$; $\frac{x=a \ \wedge \ a\leq b}{x\leq b}$; $\frac{x=a \ \wedge \ a\geq b}{x\geq b}$.

The composability algorithms return a boolean answer for whether operations are τ-composable (by comparing τ and the computed degree). However, a log containing details about which composability rules were not satisfied can also be returned. For example, a data type incompatibility between message parameters can be mentioned in the log by the `static_semantics_message` procedure. Composers have then the possibility to review that log and, if possible, modify the description of their outsourcing requests to increase the composability degree of their requests. For the sake of simplicity, we did not include such details in the algorithms.

Algorithm: *Prover*

Input: $Cond_1$, $Cond_2$

Output: *Test whether* $\mathrm{Cond}_1 \Rightarrow \mathrm{Cond}_2$

`while true do`
`If` $\exists\ x^1_1,...,x^1_n$ in $Cond_1$ composable with $x^2_1,...,x^2_m$ in $Cond_2$
`then replace` $x^1_1,...,x^1_n$ and $x^2_1,...,x^2_m$ by x^2_1
`else break`
for each term t_{2p} in $Cond_2$ `do`
`If` $\exists$ term t_{1q} in $Cond_1 \mid t_{1q} \Rightarrow t_{2p}$
`then return true`
`else return false`

Fig. 4.8 Theorem Prover

4.7.2 Community-based Algorithm

The *community-centric* algorithm for uses communities as a basis for selecting service operations. It browses "relevant" communities to determine all imported operations that could "replace" a given source operation *SO* *SR* (Figure 4.9). To accelerate the search process, the algorithm focuses on communities C_i whose category may be composed with *SO*'s category. The remaining communities and their imported operations are pruned from the service space. The algorithm then checks the vertical composability of *SO* with every imported operation op_{ik} in C_i. It considers imported operations instead of generic ones because imported operation are the actual operations offered by community members. Additionally, imported operations may change the description of generic operations (e.g., removing input/output parameters). Similarly to the operation-centric algorithm, the composability degree is computed after each composability rule. If the degree is greater or equal to τ-composability, then op_{ik} is a potential candidate to "replace" *SO*.

Algorithm: *Operation_Centric_Composability_Checking*

Input: *SO, Registry, $\mathcal{T}$, Profile, nb_target*

Output: *List $\mathcal{T}$ of operations vertically composable with SO*

```
nb_target = 0;   degree = 0;   T = ∅;
 for each community C_i ∈ Registry | category_composable(C_i, SO) and (nb_target < max_target) do {
   for each imported op_ik ∈ C_i | (nb_target < max_target) do {
    syntactic(SO, op, degree)
    If degree > τ Then { T = T ∪ {op};
                         nb_target = nb_target + 1;
                         Continue; }
    static_semantics(SO, op, degree)
    If degree > τ Then { T = T ∪ {op};
                         nb_target = nb_target + 1;
                         Continue; }
    dynamic_semantics(SO, op, degree)
    If degree > τ Then { T = T ∪ {op};
                         nb_target = nb_target + 1;
                         Continue; }
    qualitative(SO, op, degree)
    If degree > τ Then { T = T ∪ {op};
                         nb_target = nb_target + 1;
                         Continue; }  }
```

Fig. 4.9 Community-based Composability Algorithm

Chapter 5
Context-based Matching for Semantic Web Services

The process of composing Web services is far from trivial [7, 148]. To support users (or composers) in this effort, *composition engines* are being developed. Composition engines provide abstractions and mechanisms facilitating the definition and execution of composite services. They include mechanisms dealing with several issues such as orchestration, service matching, and composability [123]. This chapter focuses on *service matching.*

Service matching refers to the process of comparing Web services based on their capabilities. The aim is to determine whether a Web service "relates to" another Web service where "relates to" generically stands for "is equivalent to" and "is compatible with". We identify two scenarios where service matching can be used in a service composition engine: *substitution* and *dynamic composition. Substitution* aims at replacing a participant by another Web service. This may happen because of a network problem or if the original participant is made temporarily unavailable by its provider (e.g., for maintenance or upgrade). Such substitution should be done in a way that will not affect the business logic and behavior of the entire composite service. For instance, let us consider case study 2 (bioinformatics) depicted in Figure 1.3. Assume that the `curation` Web service used by BioPortal's composition engine is unavailable (e.g., because of network problems). To provide uninterrupted services to biologists, BioPortal needs to replace the existing `curation` service with another Web service that "matches" the former. Performing the matching process manually is tedious and time-consuming. *Dynamic composition* enables the specification of composite services without knowing *a priori* which participants will be actually used at run-time [139]. Composers give abstract specifications of their participants (e.g., by using the notion of generic service node defined in eFlow [39]). At run-time, the composition engine selects Web services that match participants' abstract specifications.

In this chapter, we provide a *context*-aware matching framework for service composition [138]. Simply put, a *context* is "*any information that can be used to characterize the situation of an entity. An entity is a person, place, or*

B. Medjahed and A. Bouguettaya, *Service Composition for the Semantic Web*,
DOI 10.1007/978-1-4419-8465-4_5, © Springer Science+Business Media, LLC 2011

object that is considered relevant to the interaction between a user and an application, including the user and the application themselves" [59]. Context has been used in several areas such as machine learning, computer vision, information retrieval, decision support, and pervasive computing [159]. We apply context to service matching. We view context as any client or provider-related information that enables interactions between service clients and providers.

An approach for matching non-functional properties of Web services represented using WS-Policy is defined in [212]. The definition of policy adopted in this book is however broader; it encompasses non-functional attributes, as well as other context-related specifications (functional, value-added, and domain). Additionally, we provide an end-to-end framework for processing service matching requests. A policy-based approach for Web service composition is proposed in [44]. The authors propose a classification of rules into syntactic, semantic and policy rules to discover and and compose Web services. The authors claim that the provision of rules with topic concepts allows the system to identify the relevant rules in a certain domain which are going to be used to select appropriate Web services for composition. Unlike the proposed model which is WS-Policy standard compliant, the policy specification used in [44] does not provide a uniform (policy-based) envelop for context specifications. Additionally, a policy as defined in this book is broader, encompassing contextual information such as functional, non-functional, value-added, and domain contexts. We also propose a peer-to-peer framework for matching context policies. A specification of Web service business rules based on WS-Policy framework is suggested in [200]. The policy assertions are modeled by the actions relating to the service and the conditions for performing them. [200] focuses on checking the policy of a Web Service against a service consumer's request. It does not provide a matching technique for Web service composition which could exploit such integration of context-related information in the policy assertions.

The rest of this chapter is organized as follows Section 5.1 describes the proposed context-aware Web service model. Section 5.2 describes our approach for organizing service contexts into communities. Section 5.3 gives details about the framework for matching Web services contexts. We will use case study 2 (bioinformatics) throughout this chapter to illustrate the proposed concepts and techniques.

5.1 A Context-Aware Web Service Model

In this section, we describe the main components of the proposed model for matching context-aware Web services. In Section 5.1.1, we give a context-oriented definition of Web services. In Section 5.1.2, we propose a categorization of Web service contexts using RDF ontology language. In Section 5.1.3, we define a two-level mechanism for modeling Web service contexts.

5.1.1 *Web Service* = {*Context Definitions*}

A variety of definitions of the Web service concept are given by different industry leaders, research groups, and Web service consortia. Existing definitions range from the very generic and all-inclusive to the very specific and restrictive [7]. They mostly focus on the rationale behind Web services (e.g., interoperation) and major technologies for interacting with Web services (e.g., XML, SOAP, WSDL). In this section, we give a *context-oriented* definition of a Web service, focusing on contextual information available to service clients and providers during their interactions.

Web services involve two major participants (Figure 5.1): *providers* and *clients*. Providers are the parties (e.g., businesses) that define and make services available on the Web. Clients are the entities that invoke those Web services. A client may be an end-user, software agent, another Web service, or a composition engine. Interactions between service providers and clients follow the producer-consumer model; providers offer Web service that are consumed by clients. Although a client and provider are involved in the same interaction, each participant has its own view on that interaction. From a client's perspective, interacting with providers depends on the situation, or *context*, of the current Web service. The *provider-related* context contains meta-data about the provider (and its service). Examples of such meta-data include service description, service security policy, and quality of service. From a provider's perspective, interacting with a client depends on the situation, or *context*, of that client. The *client-related* context contains meta-data about the client. Examples of such meta-data include the user's location, expertise level (e.g., expert, novice), and identity.

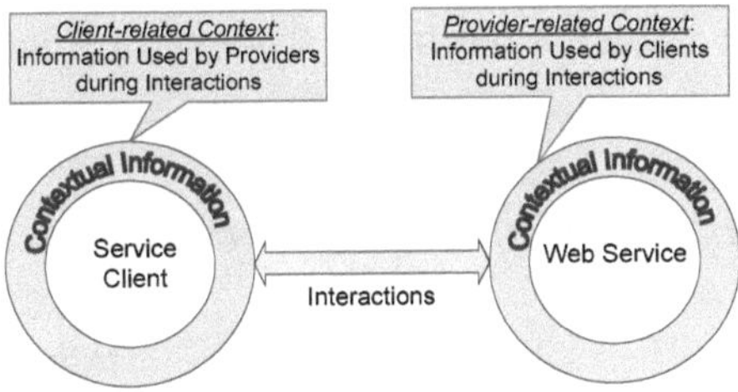

Fig. 5.1 Context-Aware Web Service Interactions

We adopt a broad definition of context for Web services, encompassing all information needed for enabling interactions between clients and providers. As depicted in Figure 5.1, we view a context as any information that can be used by (i) a Web service to interact with clients, and (ii) client to interact with Web services. Web services that use context, whether available to clients or providers, are called *context aware*. A *client-related* context includes information (about the client) used by the provider (or Web service) to interact with the client. The biologist's expertise level is an example of client-related context for the `curation` service (Figure 1.3). A *provider-related* context includes information (about the Web service or provider) used by the client to interact with the Web service (or provider). *Authentication* is an example of provider-related context for the `curation` service (Figure 1.3). This document, attached to the `curation` service, specifies the way service clients are authenticated. It may for instance state that the service supports the "Basic 256 RSA 15" or the "3DES RSA 15" security algorithm suites. Another example of provider-related context is a service description (e.g., in WSDL [7] or OWL-S [56]). This context describes the operational features of Web service (e.g., operation signature, messages, operation semantics). Details about the different categories of provider-related contexts are given in Section 5.1.2. In this chapter, we define a *context-aware* Web service *WS* as set of context definitions $\mathcal{C}(WS) = \mathcal{C}^C(WS) \cup \mathcal{C}^P(WS)$ where $\mathcal{C}^C(WS)$ and $\mathcal{C}^P(WS)$ are the sets of *client-related* and *provider-related* context definitions, respectively.

The definition above focuses on context relevant to matching capabilities for Web service composition. Other types of contexts geared toward the execution and deployment of composite Web services may also be defined. We refer to these contexts as *run-time* contexts. I-context and W-context defined in [129] are examples of run-time contexts. I-context gives information about a specific running instance of a participant Web service (e.g., whether the instance is in-progress, suspended, or terminated). W-context contains information about all running instances of a participant Web service (e.g., number of service instances that are currently running). Information included in run-time contexts may be used in the matching process. For example, a matching engine may decide to replace a participant service WS_1 by an "equivalent" one, if the execution status of WS_1 (defined in the I-context) is "aborted". Handling run-time contexts is out of the scope of this book.

5.1.2 Categorization of Web Service Contexts

The categorization of Web service contexts is important for the development of context-aware Web service environments. Despite the various attempts to develop a taxonomy for contexts, there is no generic context categorization. Relevant information differs from a domain to another and depends on the effective use of this information [159]. We propose a categorization of contextual information in Web service environments. Figure 5.2 depicts the categorization as an RDF ontology graph [71]. One or more context definitions are associated to a Web service. Each context definition belongs to a certain category which can be either *client-related* or *provider-related.*

Client-related context represents the provider's view on the client. It is obtained either *explicitly* or *implicitly* [59]. For example, end-users may explicitly feed a Web service with inputs (e.g., name, address) that identify them. A `tour guide` Web service may display different customized information on a hand-held computer based on the implicitly-obtained tourist location. Both implicit and explicit contexts may have subcategories. For example, implicit context may be sensed (e.g., acquired via physical or software sensors) or derived (e.g., time and date). Details about client-related contexts are out of the scope of this chapter. The *Provider-related* context models the client's view on the provider (or Web service). It is explicitly defined by the service provider. The provider of a Web service exposes a set of provider-related contexts to convey the conditions under which that service may be used or outsourced. Standards have so far been the key enablers for defining such contexts. For example, WSDL enables the specification of a service interface that includes the service operations, location, and protocols to access the service (e.g., SOAP/HTTP in RPC style). Clients use this context to decide whether or not to interact with a Web service.

We identify the following categories of provider-related contexts (Figure 5.2): *functional*, *non-functional*, *domain*, and *valued-added* contexts. *Functional* context describes the operational features of a Web service (e.g., in OWL-S language). Functional context attributes are of two types: syntactic and semantic. Examples of syntactic attributes include the list of input/output parameters that define an operation's messages, the data types of these parameters, and the protocol to be used for invoking the Web service (e.g., SOAP/HTTP, ebXML Messaging Service). Examples of semantic attributes include the pre-condition and effect of an operation execution [144]. For example, the `modeling` Web service (Figure 1.3) has a service description (i.e., functional context) that includes the SOAP/HTTP address to invoke the service. A *non-functional*, also called Quality of Service (QoS), context includes a set of metrics that measure the *quality* of a Web service. The international quality standard ISO 9000 describes *quality* as "the totality of features and characteristics of a product or service that bear on its ability to satisfy stated or implied needs" [181]. Examples of such characteristics include time, availability, reliability, and cost. Two providers that support the same service functionalities may have different values for their qualitative attributes. These attributes model in fact the competitive advantage that providers may have on each other. For example, the `homology search` Web service has a non-functional context that includes an estimated response time for homology search requests.

The *domain* context is organized into domain-dependent sub-categories. Each application domain has its own requirements for interacting with Web services in that domain [146, 141, 225]. Shipping and billing are examples of contexts in B2B E-commerce. A context in bio-informatics may refer to an experiment description in an experiment specification language [225]. For example, the `verification` Web Service (Figure 1.3) makes use of a range of biological contexts to elicit a target DNA sequence in hope of observing an expected phenotype. The *value-added* context brings "better" environments

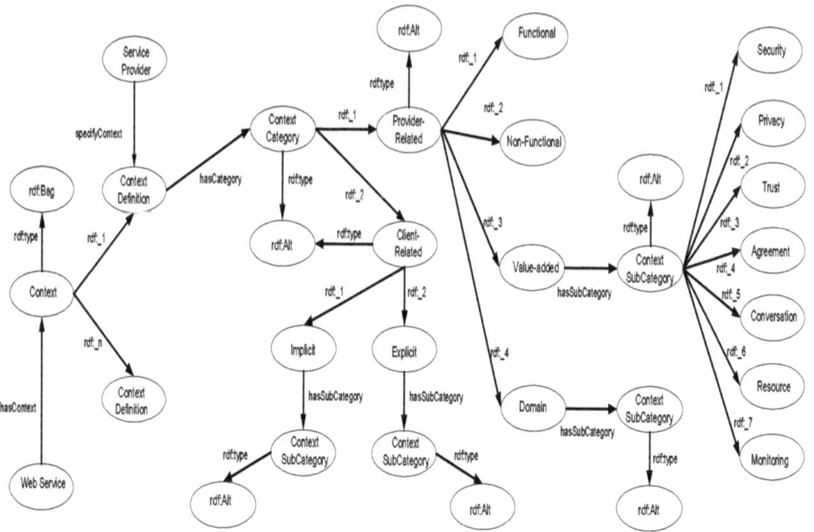

Fig. 5.2 RDF Ontology for Web Service Context Categories

for Web service interactions. It includes a set of specifications (or context definitions) for supporting optional (but important) requirements (e.g., security, privacy) useful while interacting with a Web service. We organize value-added contexts into the following sub-categories:

- *Security:* A *security context* states whether a Web service is compliant with security requirements such as encryption, authentication, non-repudiation, and reliability [21]. The `curation` Web service (Figure 1.3), for example, has an authentication context. Biologists need to be identified before storing their results in a curation database.
- *Privacy:* Providers indicate their privacy practices for a given Web service via *privacy contexts*. Examples of privacy practices include the list of external entities beyond the service provider where the collected data (e.g., input parameters) may be distributed and the purpose from collecting this data (e.g., marketing) [113]. Referring to Step 6 of the case study, the `curation` Web service may be restricted by the biologist's privacy requirements in revealing the undertaken DNA elicitation process.
- *Trust:* This context contains elements that are used to establish trust relationships between clients and providers [8]. In order to secure a client-provider communication, the two parties must exchange security credentials. However, each party needs to determine whether it can trust the asserted credentials of the other party. An illustration of this context is given by the `verification` Web service (Figure 1.3) where comparative experimental reactions are performed to determine whether there are pro-

teins whose matching contexts lead to similar biochemical evolution as the target. This step bears a certain level of trust requirement on the authority which provides the protein reactions' data.

- *Agreement (or Contracting):* Clients may require assurances or guarantees concerning the level and type of service being offered by the provider [207]. *Agreement contexts* enable the explicit specification of agreement terms between service providers and clients. For example, a disk storage service provider may specify the following agreement: "I guarantee 12 MB of memory to the client for one hour on weekdays. I have a high confidence (probability of 0.99) in meeting this guarantee. In the event, I am not able to meet this guarantee, I will pay a penalty of 50 US Dollars". Another example is the `homology search` Web service (Figure 1.3) which provides QoS assurance guarantee on the response time to accomplish the requested service.
- *Conversation:* Conversation refers to the sequences of operations (i.e., message exchanges) that could occur between a client and a Web service as part of the invocation of that service [7]. Using a particular Web service typically involves performing sequences of operations in a particular order. The *conversation context* specifies the set of correct conversations that a client should support to interact with a Web service. For example, The `curation` Web service (Figure 1.3) exposes a conversational context; biologists first provide authentication information. Then, they give information about their expertise level. Finally, they store their experiment data in the curation database.
- *Resource:* This context represents the computing means on which Web services operate. It gives the list of resources to be used while interacting with a Web service [76]. The *resource context* includes information about resources required from clients to invoke the Web service (e.g., wireless device). It also contains properties (e.g., number of blocks, block size, and manufacturers) of a resource (e.g., disk) used by a Web service (e.g., a disk storage service). The `visualization` Web service may, for example, require that the client graphical interface would have the capacity to perform at a certain resolution level.
- *Monitoring:* This context is required for a number of purposes, including status checking, troubleshooting, performance tuning, and debugging [207]. The *monitoring context* offers mechanisms that check the status of a service invocation. It also includes elements for inquiring about the "health" of a service in real time by detecting signs of failure. For example, the `alignment` Web service (Figure 1.3) may have a monitoring context that allows biologists to check the status of their alignment requests (e.g., estimated left time, current number of aligned sequences).

The domain category refers to *vertical* contexts that are valid in specific application domains such as B2B e-commerce, e-government, and bioinformatics. The other categories (i.e., functional, non-functional, and value-added) refer to *horizontal* contexts that are applicable across domains. The proposed ontology for Web service context categories is dynamic in the sense that new sub-categories may be added at any time. For example, negotiation may be added to the set of value-added contexts. Coordination and transaction sub-categories may be added under the conversation category. The security context may be organized into sub-categories encompassing contexts about authentication, encryption, non-repudiation, and reliability. New domain sub-categories may also be added at any time. The proposed technique for dynamically defining contexts is described in Section 5.3.3.

5.1.3 Modeling Contexts as Policies

Context modeling is an important issue that need to be addressed for enabling context-aware Web services. By context modeling, we refer to the language to be used for defining Web service contexts. The diversity of contextual information has led to several context modeling mechanisms such as *ConteXtML* [178], *contextual schemas* [209], *CxBR* (context-based reasoning) [85], and *CxG* (contextual graphs) [28]. These languages provide means for defining context is specific application domains such as pervasive computing, mobile computing, and robotics. They provide little or no support for defining context in Web service environments. In this section, we introduce an approach for context modeling suitable to service matching (Figure 5.3).

Figure 5.3 depicts an onion-like structure of the proposed mechanism for modeling Web service contexts. At the center is the *category* level surrounded by the *envelope* level. In the category level, providers create specifications (called *context specifications*) using appropriate Web service languages and standards. Each context belongs to a certain category (as stated in Figure 5.2). It is specified in a language related to that category. A *Type* attribute is associated to each context specification to state the language/standard used for that context. The use of a category level allows the leverage of existing Web service standards/languages for modeling contexts. It also ensures interoperability with "legacy" Web services; existing Web services may be exposed as context-aware. The proposed approach places no restrictions on the languages used in the category-specific level. Table 5.1 gives examples of standards/languages that may be adopted within each context category. For example, functional contexts may be specified in WSDL-S, DAML-S, or OWL-S languages. Languages for the agreement context include ebXML's Trading-Partner Agreement (TPA) and Collaboration-Protocol Agreement (CPA), WS-Agreement, and the Globus Toolkit's SLAs (Service Level Agreements). The way providers create context specifications is out of the scope of the matching framework. They may use appropriate tools for that purpose. For example, a WSDL editor (e.g., Eclipse WSDL Editor, Cape Clear WSDL Editor, XMLSpy WSDL editor) may be used to create a functional context specification of type WSDL.

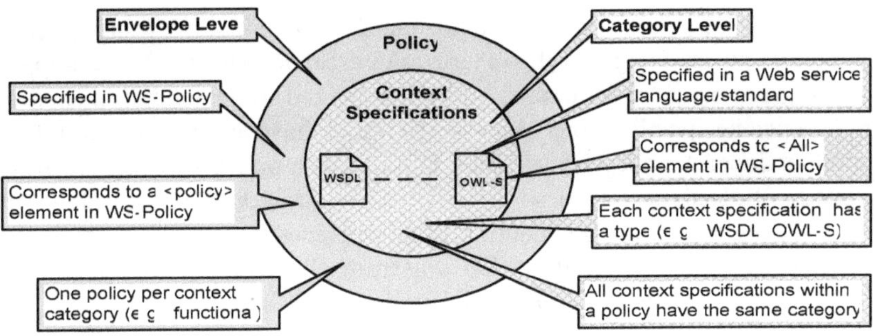

Fig. 5.3 Two-Level Approach for Modeling Web Service Contexts

A service provider may create one or more context specifications for a given context category. For example, she/he may define WSDL-S and OWL-S functional specifications for a given Web service. These specifications are exposed as (context) *policies* at the *envelope* level. A policy may refer not only to privacy and security features but also other service capabilities such as functional, non-functional (QoS), value-added, and domain capabilities. Each Web service has at most one context policy for each category; this policy envelops all context specifications corresponding to that category. We use the emerging WS-Policy standard for the definition of context policies [107]. The use of the envelope level enables the wrapping of context specifications in a uniform way. At a high level, all context specifications are seen as described in the same language (i.e., WS-Policy).

Category	*Category-specific Language*
Functional	WSDL-S, DAML-S, and OWL-S
Non-Functional	WSCL (Web Services Conversation Language) and HQML(Hierarchical QoS Markup Language)
Security	WS-SecurityPolicy and WS-SecureConversation
Privacy	P3P-like language
Trust	WS-Trust
Agreement	ebXML's TPA and CPA, WS-Agreement, and Globus Toolkit's SLAs (Service Level Agreement)
Conversation	RosettaNet PIP (Partner Interface Processes) and WSCI (Web Service Choreography Interface)
Resource	WS-Resource
Monitoring	The Globus Toolkit's Monitoring and Discovery service
Domain	B2B E-commerce (shipping and billing) and bio-informatics (experiment specification language)

Table 5.1 Examples of Category-specific Languages for Web Service Contexts

WS-Policy provides a general purpose model and syntax to describe and communicate the policies of a Web service. It defines a policy as a collection of *alternatives*, where each policy alternative is a collection of *assertions*.

A policy assertion represents a requirement, capability, or other property of a policy subject (e.g., Web service). Assertions indicate domain-specific (e.g., security, privacy) semantics and are expected to be defined in separate, domain-specific specifications. An assertion may have an arbitrary number of child assertions. A policy is described in XML as a policy *expression* through a number of constructs such as “Policy” tag to start and end a policy, “ExactlyOne” tag to contain a collection of alternatives, and “All” tag to include all assertions of an alternative. To illustrate the way context policies are specified, let us consider the following policy expression:

```
<wsp:Policy Name="mypolicy1">
 <wsp:ExactlyOne>
    <wsp:All>
       <context.ws:contextSpecification Type="WSDL-S">
           <!-- link to WSDL-S specification -->
       </context.ws:contextSpecification>
    </wsp:All>
    <wsp:All>
       <context.ws:contextSpecification Type="OWL-S">
           <!-- link to OWL-S specification -->
       </context.ws:contextSpecification>
    </wsp:All>
 </wsp:ExactlyOne>
<wsp:Policy>
```

The example above defines a policy for a functional context category. The way we associate a category to a policy expression is illustrated in Section 5.2. The “wsp” prefix refers to the WS-Policy XML namespace. The policy contains two alternatives, each alternative models a context specification. A context policy contains as many alternatives as the number of functional context specifications defined for the Web service. An alternative includes a “contextSpecification” assertion defined within the “context.ws” namespace. Each assertion has an attribute “Type”. A policy document does not contain more than one assertion of a certain type. For example, a Web service does not have more than one WSDL-S specification. Context specifications are given in separate XML documents. The URIs (Uniform Resource Identifier) of those documents (WSDL-S and OWL-S in the example) are given in the “contextSpecification” assertion.

5.1.4 Discussion

Several context-aware approaches have recently been proposed to enhance Web service discovery and composition mechanisms. [120] proposes a context-aware service discovery technique for mobile environments. It defines the context of a Web service as a set of attributes included in the service description. Examples of context attributes include user's location and network bandwidth. The discovery engine first lookups for Web services based on traditional criteria (e.g., service category in UDDI). Then, it reduces the qualified services to be returned to clients through context attribute evaluation. This approach uses contextual information for service discovery *not* for service composition. Additionally, it focuses on client-related contextual information. It does not seem to consider provider-related context which is important for Web service composition. Finally, the definition of context in [120] is limited to some attributes added to service descriptions. In this chapter, we adopt a more generic definition of Web service context through an ontology-based categorization of contextual information. [129] proposes an approach for Web service composition based on the use of agents and context. The suggested context model comprises three types of context: I-context refers to a Web service instance context, W-context is the Web service context that is defined by means of I-contexts, and C-context is the context of the composite service and is defined by the respective W-contexts. [129] focuses on run-time context which includes information related to the execution of composite Web services and their participants (e.g., number of current service instances and their status). We adopt a complementary approach by considering context needed for matching services in Web service composition. The approach presented in this chapter can be combined with the one presented in [129] to consider both run-time and provider/client-related context during service matching.

Contextualization is proposed at the Web service deployment, composition and conciliation or matching levels in [128]. The description of contexts is assumed to occur along three categories: profile, process model, and grounding. The profile describes the arguments and capabilities of context (what does the context require and provide). The process model suggests how context collects raw data from sensors and detects changes that need to be submitted to the Web service. Finally, the grounding defines the bindings (protocol, input/output messages, etc.) that make context accessible to a Web service. The authors did not however mention how relevant contexts are elicited in a service matchmaking process. A policy-based approach for developing context-oriented Web services is introduced in [131]. A Web service policy contains two elements: the resource element which identifies the computing means on which Web services operate, and the user element which identifies the personalization that Web services are subject to [130]. Context categorization described in this chapter is more generic than the one defined in [131]. Additionally, [131] does not consider the issue of service matching.

An approach for matching non-functional properties of Web services represented using WS-Policy is defined in [212]. The definition of policy adopted in this chapter is however broader; it encompasses non-functional attributes, as well as other context-related specifications (functional, value-added, and domain). Additionally, we provide an end-to-end framework for processing service matching requests. A policy-based approach for Web service composition is proposed in [44]. The authors propose a classification of rules into syntactic, semantic and policy rules to discover and and compose Web services. The authors claim that the provision of rules with topic concepts allows the system to identify the relevant rules in a certain domain which are going to be used to select appropriate Web services for composition. Unlike the proposed model which is WS-Policy standard compliant, the policy specification used in [44] does not provide a uniform (policy-based) envelop for context specifications. Additionally, a policy as defined in this chapter is broader, encompassing contextual information such as functional, non-functional, value-added, and domain contexts. A specification of Web service business rules based on WS-Policy framework is suggested in [200]. The policy assertions are modeled by the actions relating to the service and the conditions for performing them. [200] focuses on checking the policy of a Web Service against a service consumer's request. It does not provide a matching technique for Web service composition which could exploit such integration of context-related information in the policy assertions.

5.2 Organizing and Creating Service Contexts

In this section, we illustrate the way contexts are organized into communities based on their categories. We also introduce context-based policy assistants as means for facilitating the creation of contexts.

5.2.1 Context Communities

One or more context policies are associated to a Web service. Each policy is defined by the service provider and belongs to a certain category. We cluster context policies into *communities*; a *community* is a "container" that clumps together context policies related to the same category. A community is itself a Web service that is created and invoked similarly to "regular" Web services[1]. By defining communities as Web services, new context categories may be easily added to the framework. Introducing a new category is done by creating and deploying a new community service corresponding to that category. A community provider may, for example, be a grid service network administrator if the matching framework is to be used in grid environments. Another example of community provider is a domain-specific consortium such as a group of bioinformatics institutions contributing to the development of

[1] We use the terms community and community service interchangeably.

an experiment specification language. Details about creating communities are given in Section 5.3.3.

A community service oversees all context policies defined under a given category. It maintains two attributes: *category* and *members*. The *category* of a community is similar to category of its underlying context policies. The *members* attribute contains the list of context policies that fall into the community category. Each community member is defined by the couple (serviceID,policyID) where serviceID is a unique ID of a Web service (e.g., serviceKey in UDDI) that has the policy identified by policyID. As any "regular" Web service, the community service is accessed via operations. Details about community service operations are given in Section 5.3.2.

Each context policy file is attached to the *registration entry* of corresponding Web service. Registration allows providers to advertise general information about their Web services. This information is used by clients for discovering providers and Web services of interest. UDDI and ebXML Registry are examples of protocols that can be used for the registration of Web services [7]. In this chapter, we use UDDI as a registration repository. We adopt the mechanism introduced in WS-PolicyAttachment specification to attach policy expressions to UDDI [108]. We register context policies of a Web service as distinct tModels and then reference these tModels in the businessService entry defined for that service. tModel is a UDDI concept introduced for defining technical fingerprints (or specifications) of Web services [216]. We give below an example of tModel snippet for the previous policy expression:

```
<tModel tModelKey="uuid:...">
 ...
 <categoryBag>
  <keyedReference
    keyName="Reusable policy Expression"
    keyValue="policy"
    tModelKey="uuid:fa1d77dc-edf0-3a84-a99a-5972e434e993"/>
  <keyedReference
    keyName="Policy Expression for mypolicy1"
    keyValue="http://www.example.com/myservice/mypolicy1"
    tModelKey="uuid:a27078e4-fd38-320a-806f-6749e84f8005"/>
  <keyedReference
    tModelKey="uddi:uddi.org:categorization:general_keywords"
    keyName="context.ws:categorization"
    keyValue="functional"/>
 </categoryBag>
</tModel>
```

The tModelKey attribute in the tModel tag refers to a unique UUID (Universal Unique Identifier) generated by UDDI to refer to the tModel. UUIDs are 128-bit numbers used to uniquely identify an object or entity on the Internet. This UUID also represents the policyID of the context policy modeled by the tModel. The first keyedReference states that the tModel represents a policy expression by using the WS-Policy's built-in category "policy", which is its single valid value. This is necessary to enable UDDI inquiries for policy expressions in general. The second keyedReference designates the policy expression represented by the tModel. The tModelKey must match the fixed tModelKey from the Remote Policy Reference category system (i.e., "uuid:a27078e4-fd38-320a-806f-6749e84f8005"). The keyValue must be the URI that identifies the policy expression (i.e., "http://www.example.com/myservice/mypolicy1"). This keyedReference is necessary to enable UDDI inquiries for particular policy expressions based on their URI. The third keyedReference is a general keyword category. It consists of a namespace identifier (i.e., "context.ws:categorization") that refers to the context category, and a value within this category (i.e., "functional"). This keyedReference is necessary to enable UDDI inquiries for policy expressions based on their categories.

We define two techniques for updating the members attribute of a community service: *pull-based* and *push-based*. In the pull-based technique, the community service (of category C) periodically queries the UDDI registry to retrieve the list of context policies of category C and their Web service IDs. This is done through the `find_tModel` and `find_service` UDDI inquiries [7, 216]. The main issue of this technique is the frequency for refreshing the list of community members. A high frequency incurs a higher overhead for querying the UDDI registry. A low frequency has the disadvantage of using an obsolete list of community members. In the push-based technique, the members attribute of a community service is updated each time a new context policy with a category C is created. In this chapter, we adopt the push-based technique. Details about this technique are given in Section 5.3.2.

5.2.2 Context Policy Assistants

Service providers create context policies via *context policy assistants* (CPAs). Each service provider has a CPA attached to it. CPAs are *software agents* that facilitate interaction between (i) providers and the service registry (to store the context policies), and (ii) providers and community services (to update the list of community members). A *software agent* is a piece of software that autonomously acts to carry out tasks on behalf of users [223].

Service providers get their CPAs from a *CPA agent pool*. CPAs are mobile and hence have the capacity to migrate from the pool to service providers's sites. A service provider may create several context specifications (e.g., WSDL-S and WS-SecurityPolicy specifications) using context-specific languages such as those mentioned in Table 5.1. He/she first gives the URI and category of each context specification to his/her CPA. The CPA creates context policy documents (one document per category) as explained in Section 5.1.3. Then, it exposes each context policy as a tModel and attaches it to the Web service in the registry as explained in Section 5.2. Finally, the CPA notifies each community of category *C* about the creation of a new context policy with similar category. Each CPA has a list of available communities. An entry in the list contains the community ID (*C-ID*) and category. Details about the way this list is created and updated are given in Section 5.3.1.

5.3 Matching Web Service Contexts

In this section, we describe the context-based matching framework (Figure 5.4). Assume that the composition engine wants to replace a participant *WS* by another Web service. The composition engine sends a matching request `mrq = match-context(WS-ID)` to the Context-based Matching Engine (CME), where WS-ID is the (unique) service ID of *WS* (step 1). CME first retrieves *WS* context policies by submitting appropriate `find_tModel` and `find_service` inquiries to UDDI (step 2). Then, it decomposes the matching request `mrq` into sub-requests `sub-mrq(C,P)` based on the category *C* of each context policy *P* of *WS*. Each sub-request `sub-mrq(C,P)` is forwarded to the participating community service of category *C* (step 3). After processing its sub-request, the community service returns the list of candidate Web services with a context policy that matches *P* (step 4). CME finally gathers the results returned by all participating communities, determines the list of matched Web services, and returns it to the composition engine (step 5).

5.3.1 The Context Matching Engine

The Context Matching Engine (CME) is the cornerstone of the proposed framework. It receives matching requests from the composition engine and returns a list of *matched* Web services. CME is itself a Web service accessible through a set of operations. Defining CME as a Web service has three main advantages. First, CME can be integrated into existing service composition engines (e.g., BPEL engine) with minimal changes to the business logic and code of that composition engine. CME promotes significant decoupling with composition engines. It advertises an XML-based interface that can be used to invoke it. This reduces complexity, as composition engine designers do not have to worry about CME implementation details. Second, CME invocation may be included as part of composite service specifications. Composite services involve the orchestration of multiple participant Web services. Composers may specify the invocation of CME matching operation as part of their exception handling policy (e.g., in BPEL). Such exception handling policy may also be automatically inserted by the composite engine. CME will then be seen as any participant in a composite service specification. Third, defining CME as a Web service concords with the OGSA (Open Grid Services Architecture) approach where all grid resources (both logical and physical) are modeled as Web services [76]. CME would be a Web service in the second layer (Web services layer) of OGSA architecture.

CME Web service has four operations (Figure 5.5): `updateCommunityList`, `updateCPAList`, `notifyCPA`, and `matchWebService`. The first operation is invoked by community providers at the community creation time. The aim of this operation is to update CME's list of available communities. Each entry in *communityList* contains the community service ID (*C-ID*) and the community category. Each time a new CPA agent is deployed at a service provider's site (from the CPA agent pool), it invokes the `updateCPAList` of CME engine. CME maintains a list of all existing CPAs in CPAList. The CPA sends directions (e.g., URI of a CPA local database) about the way CME can notify it about important events (e.g., availability of a new community). CME returns as output the current *communityList*. This list is used subsequently by the CPA to register its context policies with communities. Whenever a community provider invokes the `updateCommunityList` operation (to report the creation of a new community), CME automatically sends notifications to existing CPAs via the *notifyCPA* operation. Each notification contains the newly created community service ID (*C-ID*) and its category.

The `matchWebService` operation returns a list of Web services (called *matched* Web services) from the registry whose context policies match the context policies of a given Web service (called *source* service). The composition engine invokes this operation by sending the unique ID of the source service. It is up to the composition engine's internal business logic to select one service from the list of matched Web services returned by CME. For example, a composition engine may select the Web service with the "best" quality of service. The selection process is out of the scope of the matching framework.

Figure 5.6 gives the algorithm executed by CME's `matchWebService` operation. The algorithm is composed of two phases: the *polling* phase and *decision* phase. In the polling phase (lines 1-10), CME sends matching requests to relevant community services. CME first gets the IDs of all context policies attached to the source service WS-ID (line 4). For that purpose, it submits a `find_tModel` inquiry to the UDDI registry. The inquiry uses as argument the tModelKey defined for WS-Policy expressions (see Section 5.2). It returns a list of policyIDs of the corresponding context policies. A `get_tModelDetail` inquiry is also executed to get the tModel policy document of each policyID. CME then determines the policyCategory of each tModel policy document (lines 5-6). To this end, it checks the general keyword category represented by the third keydReference in the tModel (see Section 5.2). CME gets the C-ID of the community that has policyCategory as a category by accessing

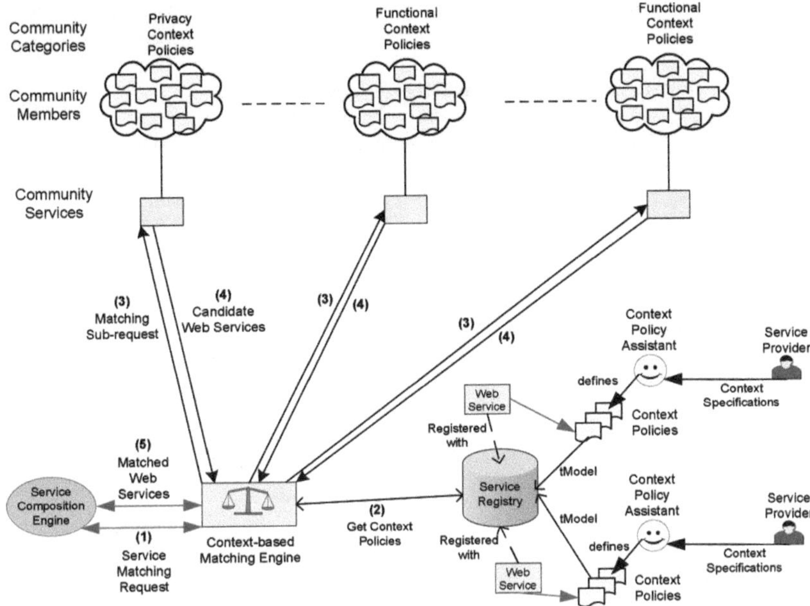

Fig. 5.4 Overview of the Matching Framework

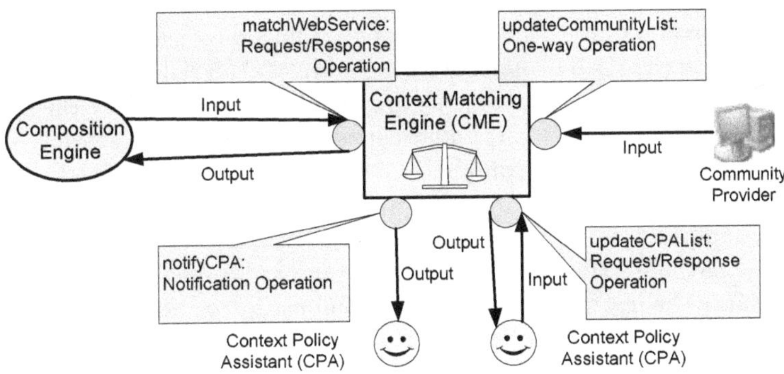

Fig. 5.5 CME Interface

the communityList table (line 7). It finally invokes the `matchContextPolicy` offered by the community service identified by C-ID (line 8). As the size of a policy document may be large (e.g., WSDL-S document with several XML elements), only policyID and WS-ID are forwarded to the community. Communities may retrieve context information via the registry. The previous steps (lines 6-8) are repeated for each context policy attached to the source service. The way community services process `matchContextPolicy` requests

```
(00) matchWebService Algorithm {    /* Executed by CME Engine */
(01) /* Phase 1 of the Algorithm: Polling Phase */
(02)   replies = 1;
(03)   Upon Invocation Of matchWebService (WS-ID) Do
(04)         all-policies = getAllPolicy (registry, WS-ID);
(05)         For Each policyID in all-policies Do
(06)               policyCategory = getCategory (policyID);
(07)               C-ID = getCommunityID (policyCategory, comunityList);
(08)               invoke matchContextPolicy (policyID, WS-ID) Of C-ID;
(09)         End Do
(10)   End Do
(11) /* Phase 2 of the Algorithm: Decision Phase */
(12)   Upon Reception Of (WS-ID, candidateWS) From C-ID Do
(13)         If replies == 1
(14)                 Then matchedWS = candidateWS
(15)                 Else matchedWS = matchedWS ∩ candidateWS;
(16)         If replies == |all-policies| Then Return (WS-ID, matchedWS);
(17)                                          Else replies = replies + 1;
(18)   End Do
(19) }
```

Fig. 5.6 Two-Phase Matching Algorithm

is community-dependent and done transparently to CME. Details about the `matchContextPolicy` operation are given in Section 5.3.2.

In the second phase (decision phase), CME consolidates the results received from communities involved in the polling phase (lines 11-19). Each community service C-ID replies with a candidateWS list. The list includes the IDs of services whose context policy matches (as defined by the community) the context policy (with similar category) of the source service. We use a variable "replies" which contains the number of votes received so far by CME. The variable is initialized and updated in lines 2 and 18 respectively. The decision phase terminates when CME receives the votes of all communities participating in the first phase (i.e., *replies* = |*all-policies*|). In this case, CME returns the list matchedWS to the composition engine (line 16). A Web service belongs to the matchedWS list if each context policy in the source service is matched by a corresponding context policy in that service. This is done by computing the intersection of candidateWS lists returned by all community services involved in the polling phase (lines 13-15).

5.3.2 Inside View of a Community Service

Community services provide a peer-to-peer topology for matching context policies. Each community handles context policies that belong to a specific category (i.e., the community's category). The interface exposed by a community service is composed of two operations (Figure 5.7): `updateCommunityMembers` and `matchContextPolicy`. The `updateCommunityMembers` operation enables interactions between communities and CPAs (context policy assistants). Service providers create context policies via their CPAs. At policy definition time, the CPA communicates with the corresponding community to update its members list. If a policy (identified by P-ID) of category C is created for a Web service WS-ID, then CPA invokes the `updateCommunityMembers` operation of the community of category C. This operation is one-way (i.e., has only an input message) and contains WS-ID and P-ID as input parameters.

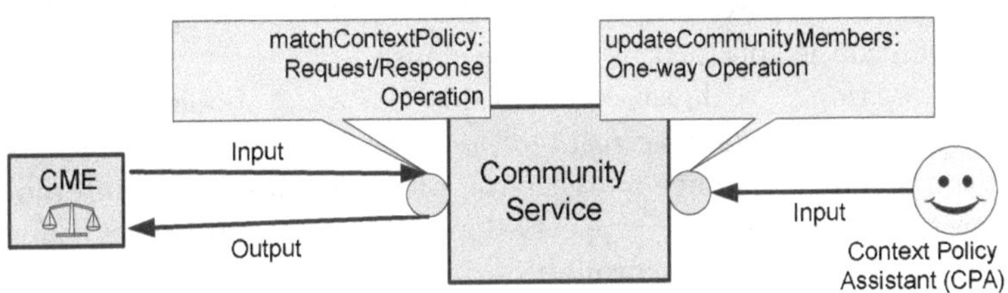

Fig. 5.7 Community Service Interface

The `matchContextPolicy` operation allows CME to send context matching requests to community services (Figure 5.6, line 8). It is an input/output operation; the input message is composed of the WS-ID of the source Web service (i.e, service to be matched) and a policyID of that service policy (called *source* policy). The operation compares the source policy with all policies (called *member* policies) that are members of the community. The output message contains the IDs of *candidate* Web services; a candidate is a Web service with a policy (called *candidate* policy) that matches the source policy.

The `matchContextPolicy` operation relies on *context rules* to decide whether a member policy matches a source policy. Each community has its own set of context rules stored in a *context rule base* (CxRB). The syntax of a context rule is given below:

Context Rule *rule-name*
 Context Property *property-name*
 Instances *source-instance, member-instance*
 Type *context-specification-type*
 Action *matchContextProperty(source-instance, member-instance)*

A context rule is identified by a name and corresponds to a specific *context property*. A *context property* is a matching criterion used by the community to decide whether a member policy matches the source policy. Several context properties may be associated to a given context category. For example, a non-functional context policy includes a set of quality of service parameters (e.g., response time) associated to the service. Each qualitative parameter is seen by the non-functional community service as a context property. This community has as many context rules as the number of qualitative parameters (e.g., cost, availability) defined in non-functional contexts. A property has a *source* and *member instance*; a source (member) instance is the value of the property in the source (member) policy. For example, the actual response time of the `homology search` Web service is the source instance of the *response time* property. As explained in Section 5.1.3, each policy may contain several context specifications of different types (e.g., WSDL-S, DAML-S, OWL-S). A rule deals with a context property as defined in a context specification type. This information is specified in the *type* clause.

The *action* clause contains a boolean function *matchContextProperty(source-instance,member-instance)* which returns *true* iff the member instance matches the source instance. The internal business logic of this function is property-dependent. It is up to the community provider to identify context properties and figure out the appropriate code associated to each property. Community providers may include the code of *matchContextProperty()* as part of the rule specification; they may also define that code as a stored procedure and provide a link to it within the rule specification. Below is an example of rule created for the *response time* property of a non-functional community:

Context Rule *rule-RT*
  Context Property *response time*
  Instances $time_S, time_M$
  Type HQML
  Action *matchContextProperty*($time_S, time_M$)
    { **If** $time_M \leq time_S$ **Then return** *true* **Else return** *false* }

The rule states that a member's response time matches a source's response time if the member's is at most equal to the source's (i.e., the response time of the member Web service is shorter or the same as the response time of the source). As specified in the *Type* clause, the rule compares *response time* property instances of HQML (Hierarchical QoS Markup Language) context specifications [90].

The `matchContextPolicy` operation uses three major components to determine candidate services (Figure 5.8): *context handler*, *rule validator*, and *property extractor*. The algorithm executed by the `matchContextPolicy` operation of a community C_i is summarized in Figure 5.9. Method calls that end with CH, RV, and PE are executed by the context handler, rule validator, and property extractor respectively. The context handler first retrieves the source policy document P_S (line 3). For each context specification C_S (modeled as an alternative in the policy document), it gets its type and URI (line 4-6). The context handler looks-up in C_i's members list for each policy

P_M that includes a context specification C_M of type similar to type-C_S and gets its URI (line 8-10). The *getURL-CH* (P_M, type-C_S) call return null if there is no context specification of type equal to type-C_S in P_M (line 11). If a service member already belongs to the list of candidate Web services, then it is skipped (line 8). There is no need to process the policy document of a member service if that service has already been selected by C_i as a candidate.

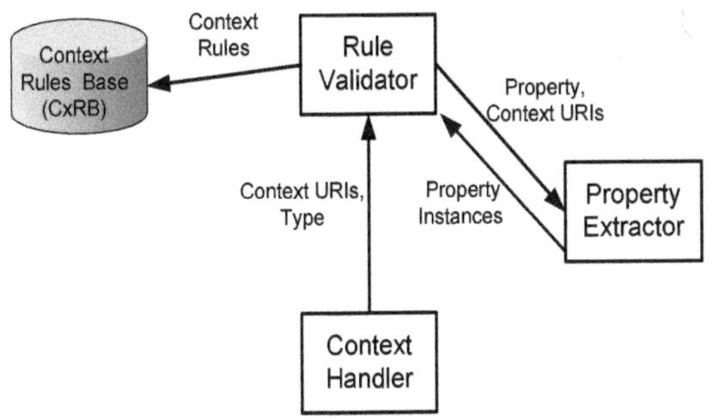

Fig. 5.8 Components of the matchContextPolicy Operation

As mentioned in Section 5.1.3, P_M contains at most one specification of type equal to type-s. P_M matches P_S if the following predicate is true: $\exists\ C_S \in P_S\ \exists\ C_M \in P_M \mid C_M$ *matches* C_S P_M matches P_S if there is a context specification in P_M that *matches* a context specification in P_S. Assume that a source service W_S has three context specifications WSDL-S, DAML-S, and OWL-S defined within its functional context policy P_S. The three specifications are alternatives advertised by W_S provider to describe its functional context. Clients (e.g. composition engine) may consider any of these alternatives as a functional specification of W_S. Hence, a service with policy P_M should have one specification that matches the WSDL-S *or* DAML-S *or* OWL-S specification of W_S. There is no need to find a match for the three specifications at the same time.

To check whether C_M *matches* C_S, the context handler forwards each tuple (P_S, uri-C_S, P_M, uri-C_M, type-C_S) to the rule validator. The rule validator retrieves from CxRB rule base the set $\mathcal{R}$ of all rules of type equal to type-C_S (line 7). The rule validator then gets the property name P_j of each rule R_j in $\mathcal{R}$ and passes P_i along with the URIs of C_S and C_M to the property extractor (lines 14-16). The property extractor parses the XML documents of C_S and C_M and returns the value of P_i in each document. Let I_S and I_M be the source's and member's instance respectively. The rule validator checks whether I_M matches I_S as defined in the *matchContextProperty* function of R_i (line 17). C_M matches C_S if the *matchContextProperty* function of each rule in $\mathcal{R}$ returns the boolean true (line 18). In this case, the WS-ID of the

```
(00)  matchContextPolicy (P_S-ID, source) Algorithm {
(01)     /* Executed by Community C_i */
(02)     candidateWS = ∅;
(03)     P_S = getPolicy-CH (registry, P_S-ID);
(04)     For each C_S ∈ P_S Do
(05)       type-C_S = getType-CH (P_S, C_S);
(06)       uri-C_S = getURL-CH (P_S, type-C_S);
(07)       R = getRules-RV (CxRB, type-C_S);
(08)      For Each (WS-ID, policyID) ∈ C_i.members | WS-ID ∉ candidateWS Do
(09)            P_M = getPolicy-CH (registry, policyID);
(10)            uri-C_M = getURL-CH (P_M, type-C_S);
(11)            If uri-C_M == null Then Continue;
(12)            match = true;
(13)                 For Each rule R_j ∈ R Do
(14)                   P_j = getProperty-RV (R_j);
(15)                   I_S = extractInstance-PE (P_j, uri-C_S);
(16)                   I_M = extractInstance-PE (P_j, uri-C_M);
(17)                   match = R_j.matchContextProperty-RV (I_S, I_M);
(18)                   If match == false Then Break;
(19)                 End Do
(20)            If match Then candidateWS = candidateWS ∪ {WS-ID};
(21)      End Do
(22)     End Do
(23)     Return (source, candidateWS);
(24)  }
```

Fig. 5.9 Matching Contexts in Communities

member service corresponding to P_M is added to the list of candidate Web services (line 20). Finally, the `matchContextPolicy` operation returns the source ID and list of candidates as a result (line 23).

The context matching algorithm depicted in Figure 5.9 compares context specifications that have the same type (see lines 6 and 10). Comparing context specifications that have different types within a community (e.g., DAML-S with WSDL-S) requires dealing with the issue of defining mappings between disparate languages or ontologies. This issue is out of the scope of this book. Techniques such as the ones described in [61, 69] may be adopted to deal with ontology mapping.

5.3.3 Community Factory

Web services operate in a highly dynamic environment where changes can occur to adapt to actual business climate (e.g., politic, economic, organizational). For example, new government regulations may require each Web service in the healthcare domain to expose its privacy practices. Generally speaking, changes are initiated by Web service providers or community providers.

At the Web service side, service providers may create a new context policy document of category C. For that purpose, the service provider's CPA invokes the `updateCommunityMembers` operation of the community of category C (see Section 5.3.2).

At the community side, community providers may create community services at any time. This happens when a new context category or subcategory is added to the context categorization ontology (Figure 5.2). Assume for example that a *negotiation* context is added to the set of value-added contexts. A community provider (e.g., consortium of companies developing a negotiation standard for Web services) would like then to create a new community for this category. We define a *design pattern* for the creation of community services. Design patterns are a powerful tool for designing flexible software [77]. They provide well-tested solutions to recurring software design problems. One such widely used pattern is the *Abstract Factory* pattern. This pattern provides an interface for creating families of related or dependent classes without having to specify the actual classes. The Abstract Factory uses *Factory Methods* to handle the actual creation of specific objects [77]. This is called a factory pattern because it is responsible for "manufacturing" objects.

We define an abstract factory design pattern for communities called *Community Abstract Factory*. This pattern's interface includes four methods: `matchContextPolicy`, `notifyCME`, `extractInstance`, and `createCxRB`. Community providers create concrete implementations of the abstract factory. Each concrete implementation represents a community service. The `matchContextPolicy` method enables communities to compare context policies as described in Figure 5.9. The `notifyCME` method allows community providers to notify CME engine whenever they create new communities. For that purpose, it invokes the `updateCommunityList` operation exposed by CME engine (Figure 5.5). The `extractInstance` method is used by a community's property extractor to retrieve the instance of a context property from a context specification corresponding to that community. The implementation of this method depends on the context category language. It is up to community providers to implement this method as needed. For example, the provider of a functional community should specify in `extractInstance` the way each qualitative parameter is retrieved from an HQML specification [90]. The `createCxRB` allows community providers to create CxRB rule bases and populate them with appropriate context rules. Community providers should identify the context property of each rule. They also need to specify the business logic of the *matchContextProperty()* function.

Chapter 6
Towards the Automatic Composition of Semantic Web Services

The *automatic* composition of Web services is a recent trend to unburden composers from the complexity of the composition process (e.g., checking composability, orchestrating Web services) [18, 134]. It is slated to play a major role in enabling the envisioned *Semantic Web Services* paradigm [221]. In this chapter, we present a Semantic Web centered approach for supporting the automatic composition of Web services [148, 145, 234, 151]. The proposed approach builds on the semantic description framework and composability model described in chapters 3 and 4 respectively. It consists of three conceptually separate phases (Figure 6.1): *specification*, *matchmaking*, and *generation*.

The *specification* phase (phase 1) enables high-level descriptions of composition requests. For that purpose, we define a *Composition Specification Language* (*CSL*). CSL extends *UML activity diagrams* [87] with an ontological description of the composition request. Using CSL, composers specify the *what* part of the desired composition but will not concern themselves with the *how* part. They are not required to be aware of the full technical details such as the list of participant services and the way they are executed and plugged together. The *matchmaking* phase (phase 2) uses the composability model to generate *composition plans* that conform to composers' specifications. One or several composition plans are generated for each composer's sub-request. By *composition plan*, we refer to the list of imported operations to be outsourced, their orchestration order, and the way they interact with each other (plugging operations, mapping messages, etc.) to "realize" the corresponding sub-request. In the *generation phase* (phase 3), detailed descriptions of the composite service are generated. We propose a *Quality of Composition* (*QoC*) model to assess the quality of the generated descriptions.

This chapter is organized as follows. In Section 6.1, we define the model and techniques used for the specification of composition requests. In Section 6.2, we propose a set of algorithms for checking composability and the automatic generation of composition plans. In Section 6.3, we illustrate the process of generating composite service descriptions.

B. Medjahed and A. Bouguettaya, *Service Composition for the Semantic Web*,
DOI 10.1007/978-1-4419-8465-4_6, © Springer Science+Business Media, LLC 2011

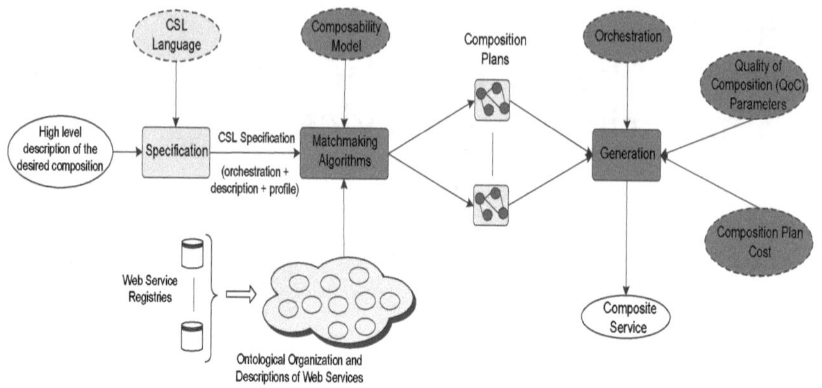

Fig. 6.1 Overview of the Proposed Approach for Service Composition

6.1 Specification of Composition Requests

The specification of a composition request requires dealing with two major issues: *orchestration* and *description*. A composer's request generally includes one or several *sub-requests*. For example, the request "visit a senior activity center" includes several sub-requests such as "lookup for senior activity center" and "set appointment with a senior activity center". The sub-requests should be executed in a specific order and if certain conditions are true (e.g., look for senior activity center *then* set up an appointment). Such order and conditions are specified through an *orchestration model*. Additionally, the automatic generation of composite services requires a clear and unambiguous *description* of the request and its sub-requests. For example, the composition engine should understand what "lookup for senior activity center" means. In this section, we define a language, called *Composition Specification Language* (*CSL*), for the specification of composition requests.

6.1.1 Orchestration Model

We define two types of orchestration: *composer-defined* and *system-generated* orchestration. *Composer-defined* is provided by the composer in the specification phase. It gives the execution order of the composition sub-requests. We refer to it as *inter-subrequest* orchestration since it represents the orchestration of sub-requests. *System-generated* orchestration is automatically generated by the composition engine. It gives the execution order of the participant services outsourced for each sub-request. We refer to it as *intra-subrequest* orchestration since it represents the orchestration within sub-requests. The orchestration model presented in this section deals with the first type. Details about system-generated orchestration are given in Section 6.2.

Several orchestration models have been proposed in the literature such as *UML activity diagrams*, *Petri-nets*, *statecharts*, and *π-calculus*. We adopt *UML activity diagrams* as an orchestration model [87]. Activity diagrams are the most widely used process modeling techniques both in conventional interaction technologies (e.g., workflows) and Web services [7]. The reason for their success is their ease-of-use and simplicity for modeling business processes. Several tools (e.g., *Rational Rose*) are available for designing business processes using activity diagrams. Additionally, the *Unified Modeling Language* (*UML*) has become the *de facto* standard for representing application architectures and design models. Finally, activity diagrams model orchestrations by specifying which actions should be performed, from the beginning of the execution to the end. This seems to be the most natural way in which users think of a process and developers code their applications [7].

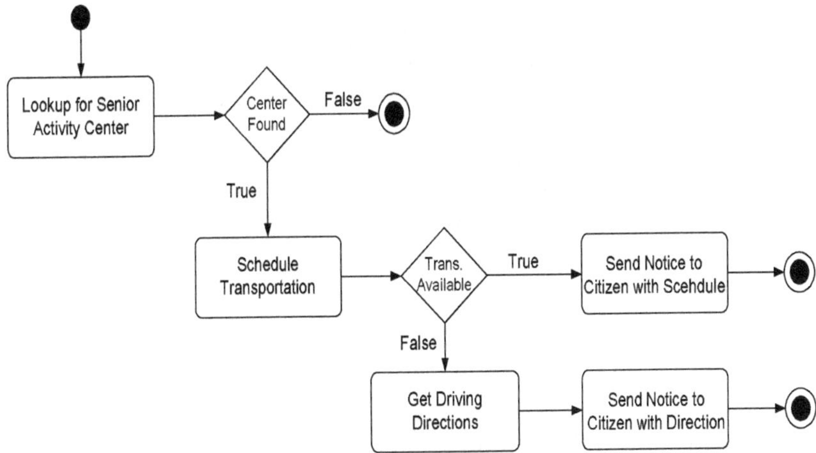

Fig. 6.2 Modeling Composition Request through Activity Diagrams

Activity diagrams show the flow of *activities* in a business process. Each activity represents a composition sub-request. A sub-request is modeled as a capsule (i.e., as a rectangle with rounded corners) with the sub-request name enclosed. We depict in Figure 6.2, an example of orchestration for a composition request within the e-government scenario. The case officer specify the composition request that is, "organizing a visit to a senior activity center" through an activity diagram. The filled circle is the starting point of the diagram. The filled circle with a border is the ending point. The composition request includes five sub-requests (e.g., `schedule transportation`). The case officer has also the possibility to indicate that one sub-request *conditionally* follows another. For example, the *diamond* labeled "Trans. Available" tests whether a government-funded transportation is available. In this case, a notification should be sent to the citizen with schedule. Otherwise, the case officer performs a `get driving directions` from the citizen's home to the activity center location. Activity diagrams may also model *parallelism* via *fork* and *join* constructs. A *fork* is represented by a black bar with one flow going into it and several leaving it. It denotes the beginning of parallel processing. A *join* is depicted by a black bar with several flows entering it and one leaving it. It denotes the end of parallel processing.

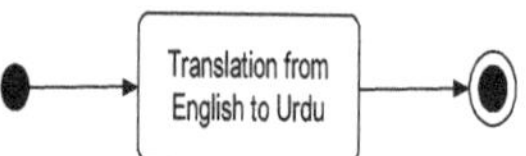

Fig. 6.3 Composition Request with one Single Sub-request

A composition request specification may consist of only one sub-request. For example, Figure 6.3 depicts a composition request that "provides translation from English to Urdu". The request contains one sub-request label `translation from English to Urdu`. It is important to note that, during the composite service generation process, each sub-request may be mapped to a set of Web service operations combined in a specific way. For example, the `translation from English to Urdu` sub-request would be mapped to the combination of Web service operations in the following order: `English-French` → `French-Chinese` → `Chinese-Urdu`.

6.1.2 Describing Composition Sub-Requests

Activity diagrams enable the specification of the execution order of the composition sub-requests. They provide no means for describing sub-requests. Such description concerns both syntactic and semantic features. To deal with this issue, we define an ontology for sub-requests called *sub-request ontology*. All sub-requests are described according to this ontology. Since a sub-request is meant to be mapped to one or several generic operations, we adopt the ontology defined for generic operations (Figure 3.2). Each sub-request is hence described by syntactic, static semantic, dynamic semantic, and qualitative attributes.

The ontology-based description of a request and its sub-requests produces an XML document. We give in Figure 6.4 the general form of this document. For the sake of clarity, we omit references to XML namespaces. The top element (*<request>*) contains the name of the request (*<name>* element), a text description (*<description>*) of the request, a *<parameters>* element, and several *<subRequest>* elements. The *<parameters>* element gives the input and output parameters used by composition sub-requests. Similarly to

```
<request>
    <name> ....... </name>
    <description>  ....... </description>
    <Parameters>  .......  <Parameters>
    <subRequest>
      <syntax> ....... </syntax>
      <staticSemantics> ....... </staticSemantics>
      <dynamicSemantics> ....... </dynamicSemantics>
      <quality> ....... </quality>
    </subRequest>
    .......
 </request>
```

Fig. 6.4 Description of a Composition Request in CSL

profile inputs, sub-request parameters (input and output) may be defined according to a specific taxonomy. The *<subRequest>* element contains six sub-elements. The first sub-element (*<syntax>*) includes syntactic attributes. The binding of a sub-request is similar to the binding of the composition request defined in the composer profile. The sub-elements *<staticSemantics>* and *<dynamicSemantics>* describe the static and dynamic semantics of the sub-request. The dynamic semantics of sub-request is limited to behavioral attributes. Pre-operations and post-operations represent pre-defined business processes given by community providers and are hence specific to generic operations. The *<quality>* sub-elements contains qualitative attributes of the sub-request. The *<input>* and *<output>* sub-elements describe the input and output parameters required by the sub-request. A sub-request may use as input/output, the parameters defined within the composer profile. It may also use the parameters defined within the *<parameters>* element. In both cases, the *<input>* and *<output>* sub-elements contain references to the parameters' names.

6.1.3 Customization via Composer Profiles

Customization is a key requirement of the automatic composition of Web services. Composers must be able to personalize the composition process according to their preferences. Such preferences make up the composer's *profile.* The general form of the profile definition construct is given below:

Define Profile
  Levels Assign <vector> **To** *LW*
  Rules Assign <matrix> **To** *RW*
  Degree Assign <value> **To** <τ-composability>
  Binding Assign <value> **To** <binding>

Plans Assign <value> **To** <max-plans>
Input [<parameter>]$^+$

As part of their profile definition, composers assign values to the level weights vector (LW) and rule weights matrix (RW). They also provide the τ-composability threshold and binding protocols supported by their composite services. Additionally, they give the maximum number of composition plans to be generated for each composition sub-request. They finally provide a list of input parameters (e.g., citizen's name, address) to be used during the execution of the generated composite service. Each parameter is defined by its name, data type, unit, business role, and language (Section 3). To facilitate the definition of such parameters, composers may use pre-defined parameters defined in any existing taxonomy. An example of such taxonomy is the *RosettaNet Technical Dictionary*. This dictionary contains properties that can be used to describe characteristics of a product or service [48].

6.2 Outsourcing Web Services in the Matchmaking Phase

Once a CSL specification (i.e., orchestration, profile, and description) is provided, the next step is to generate *composition plans* relevant to each sub-request using matchmaking algorithms. The general premise of such algorithms is to consider each sub-request as an *"abstract" operation.* Abstract operation would then be vertically composed with one or a combination of generic operations. Each vertical composition returns a set of composition plans. Let n be the number of sub-requests and *Nb_CP(r)* be the number of plans generated for the rth sub-request. The number of plans generated for the whole composition request would be $\sum_{r=1}^{n} Nb\_CP(r)$.

```
Matchmaking(Profile) {
for each sub-request SR_p do {
  Vert_Comp1:1(SR_p, Registry, Plans1:1[p], Profile, nb_plans);
  if nb_plans ≤ Profile.max_plans
     then Vert_Comp1:N(SR_p, Registry, Plans1:n[p], Profile, nb_plans);
} }
```

Fig. 6.5 Main Matchmaking Algorithm

The generation of composition plans is based on checking composability rules between each sub-request and the imported operations. The main matchmaking algorithm is depicted in Figure 6.5. For each sub-request, the algorithm first tries to vertically compose it with one generic operation. We refer to such composition as a *one-to-one* (1:1) composition. We use the operation-centric and community-based algorithm proposed in the previous chapter for enabling (1:1) composition. Each entry *Plans1:1[p]* contains the list of composition plans generated for sub-request SR_p. If the number of generated plans is less or equal to the maximum number of plan per request, then the algorithm tries to vertically compose the sub-request with a combination of generic operations. We refer to such composition as a *one-to-many* (1:N) composition.

The one-to-many vertical composition algorithm determines the set of imported operations (belonging to a community) which, combined in certain way, could be vertically composed with a sub-request. For example, the `English-Urdu` sub-request is composable with the combination of three operations: `English-French`, `French-Chinese`, and `Chinese-Urdu`. To support 1:N vertical composition, we introduce the notion of *flow graph*. The *flow graph* links together all operations that are *horizontally composable*. The nodes of this graph are of two types: *operation* and *compound* nodes (Figure 6.6). Arrows in this graph relate nodes of different types. Operation nodes may be linked to compound nodes and vice versa. However, no operation node is linked with another operation node. Similarly, no compound node is linked to another compound node.

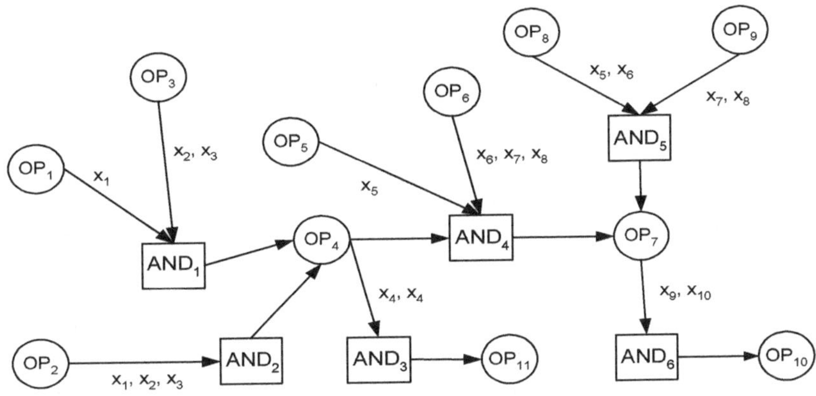

Fig. 6.6 The Flow Graph

Each compound node *And* in the flow graph has one predecessor op_i and one successor op_j (e.g. And_2). This situation models the fact that op_i is horizontally composable with op_j. This means that op_j can be invoked after the execution of op_i. The arrow $op_i \rightarrow And$ is labeled with op_i's outputs that could be used as op_j's inputs. op_j is labeled with its output parameters. The compound node *And* is labeled with op_i's inputs. If the same op_i's output occurs m times on the arrow, then op_i should be executed m times before invoking op_j (e.g., x_4 in op_4). Each compound node is labeled with all input parameters defined in its predecessors (i.e., operations).

The flow graph is built in an incremental fashion, each time an operation *op* is imported (Figure 6.7). This assumes that all operations in the service registry are already modeled in the flow graph. To update this graph, we compare *op* with each operation node op_i in the graph. If *op* is horizontally composable with op_i, then a new operation node is created for *op*. A new compound node And_k is also inserted in the graph. Horizontal composability is checked by evaluating the conditions defined in Chapter 4 for horizontal composition. The procedure *composable_horizontal()* returns the set of parameters $\mathcal{P}$ of *op* that are horizontally composable with op_i's parameters. The nodes *op*, And_k, and op_i are then linked by the following edges: $op \rightarrow \text{And}_k \rightarrow op_i$. The edge $op \rightarrow \text{And}_k$ is labeled with $\mathcal{P}$. The operation node *op* is labeled with its outputs. The compound node is labeled with the inputs of *op*.

```
UpdateFlowGraph(FG,op) {
  for each operation node op_i ∈ FG do
    if composable_horizontal(op,op_i,P)
      then { add_arrow(op,And_k);
             add_arrow(And_k,op_i);
             add_label_arrow(op,And_k,P);
             add_label_node(op,op.output);
             add_label_node(And_k,op.input);
             k = k + 1;    };
}
```

Fig. 6.7 Updating the Flow Graph

To illustrate the definition of a flow graph, we consider the example depicted in Figure 6.8. The example is related to the `get driving directions` sub-request (Figure 6.2). The operation `People Lookup` returns the *address* and *phone* number of a person (outputs), given her/his *name* and *state* of residence (inputs). The operation `Driving Directions Address` returns the *driving direction* (output) from a *source* to a *destination address* (outputs). Assume that `People Lookup` is horizontally composable with `Driving Directions Address`. Since `Driving Directions Address` requires two *address* parameters, it could be executed after executing `People Lookup` twice. The first execution of `People Lookup` returns the *source address* and the second execution gives the *destination address*.

The combination of `People Lookup` and `Driving Directions Address` as depicted in Figure 6.8 defines an "abstract operation" that returns the driving directions given the name and state of residence of two persons. The flow graph contains two operation nodes and one compound node. The arrow from `People Lookup` to And_1 contains the output parameter *address* twice. The compound node is labeled with the parameters *name*, *state*, *name*, and *state*. The operation node `Driving Directions Address` is labeled with the parameter *driving direction*.

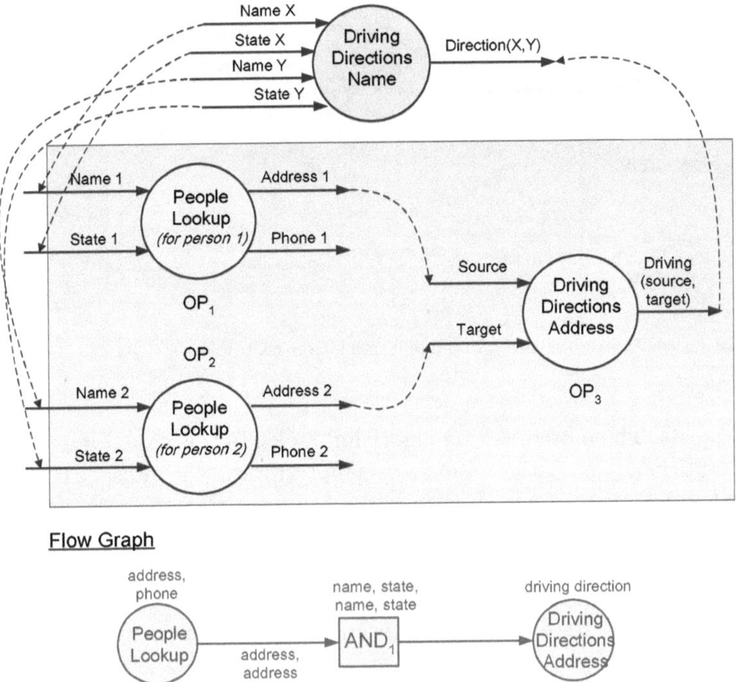

Fig. 6.8 Flow Graph for the Driving Directions Example

We depict in Figure 6.9 the flow graph of the language translation example. We assume that `English-French` is horizontally composable with `French-Chinese` and that `French-Chinese` is horizontally composable with `Chinese-Urdu`. The flow graph corresponding to these operations contains two compound nodes And_1 and And_2 and three operation nodes. And_1 and And_2 are labeled with the parameters *English word* and *French word* respectively. `English-French`, `French-Chinese`, and `Chinese-Urdu` are labeled with the parameters *French word*, *Chinese word*, and *Urdu word* rspectively. The combination of the three operations as depicted in Figure 6.9 defines three abstract operations. The first operation provides translation from English to Chinese, the second operation enables translation from English to Urdu, and the third operation allows translation from French to Urdu.

The flow graph is used to determine composition plans through 1:N vertical composition (Figure 6.10). Let *SR* be a composition sub-request. The issue is how to determine the operations to be outsourced from *SR*. We identify two cases based on the mode of *SR*. If *SR* is an *In/Out* sub-request, then the matchmaking algorithm looks for a compound node, say $And_{initial}$, so that *SR*'s input is composable with $And_{initial}$'s input message. It also looks for an operation node, say op_{final}, so that op_{final}'s output message is composable with *SR*'s output message. The second case of the algorithm concerns *Out/In*

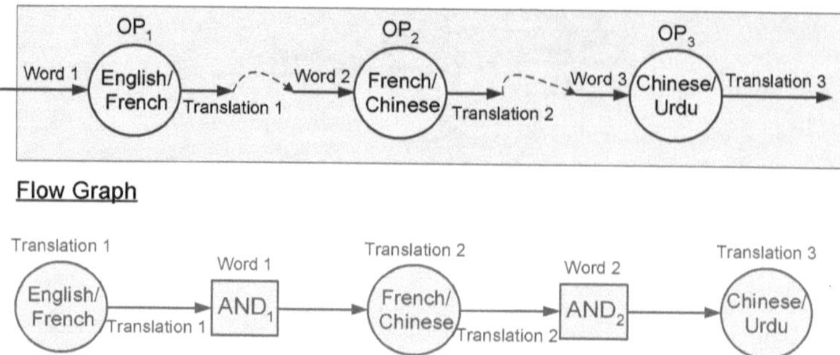

Fig. 6.9 Flow Graph for the Language Translation Example

sub-requests. The matchmaking algorithm looks, in this case, for a compound node, say $And_{initial}$, so that $And_{initial}$'s input message is message composable with *SR*'s output message. It also looks for an operation node, say op_{final}, so that op_{final}'s output message is message composable with *SR*'s input message. In both cases (*In/Out* and *Out/In* modes), $And_{initial}$'s predecessor is the initial operation of *SR*'s composition plan. Additionally, op_{final} is the final operation in that plan. To determine the intermediary operations, we calculate a *path* from $And_{initial}$ to op_{final} in the flow graph. We use the *breadth-first* search algorithm for this purpose [51].

```
Vert_Comp1:N(SR_p, Registry, Plans1:n, Profile, nb_plans) {
  while .true. do {
    if SR.mode = "In/Out"
        then { compound = search_compound_composable(FG,SR.input,found1);
               operation = search_operation_composable(FG,SR.output,found2); }
    if SR.mode = "Out/In"
        then { compound = search_compound_composable(FG,SR.output,found1);
               operation = search_operation_composable(FG,SR.input,found2); }
    if ¬found1 or ¬found2 then break;
    path = breadth_first_search(FG,compound,operation);
    Plans1:n = Plans1:n ∪ {path}
    nb_plans = nb_plans + 1
} }
```

Fig. 6.10 One-to-many Vertical Composition

To illustrate the 1:N composability algorithm, we consider the language translation example (Figure 6.9). Assume that *SR* (*In/Out* sub-request) aims at providing translation from English to Urdu. *SR*'s input and output are equal to the parameters *English word* and *Urdu word* respectively. *SR*'s input is message compatible with And_1's input and `Chinese-Urdu`'s output is message compatible with *SR*'s output. The algorithm then determines the path from And_1 to `Chinese-Urdu` using the *breadth-first* search algorithm. This gives the path $And_1 \rightarrow$ `French-Chinese` $\rightarrow And_2 \rightarrow$ `Chinese-Urdu`. By replacing And_1 by its predecessor and eliminating And_2, the composition plan generated for SR is `English-French` → `French-Chinese` → `Chinese-Urdu`.

6.3 Generating Composite Service Descriptions

At the end of the matchmaking phase, one or several composition plans are generated for each composition sub-request. The aim of the generation phase is to replace each sub-request by a composition plans. Composers first select a composition plan for each sub-requests. Based on the selected plans, we generate a composite service description. The generation process is conducted in three steps. We first replace each sub-request by the selected composition plan. We then insert the pre-operations and post-operations of each operation of the plan. We finally compute *Quality of Composition* (*QoC*) parameters to assess the quality of the generated plan. Composers have the possibility to select other plan if they do not like the quality of the generated composite service description.

6.3.1 Replacing Sub-requests by Composition Plans

Assume now that a composition plan is selected for each composable sub-request. Using those plans and the activity diagram (noted AD_s) specified by the composer, we generate an activity diagram (noted AD_g) for the composite service. Each sub-request SR is substituted by the operation in the corresponding plan. If the plan is obtained through 1:N composition, then the execution order of those operations in AD_g is similar to their execution order in the plan. Figure 6.11 illustrates the technique used for replacing a request in AD_s by its composition plan.

We sketch in Figure 6.12 the algorithm executed for replacing a subrequest SR by a plan P. Let SR_i and SR_j be a predecessor and succesor of SR in AD_s, respectively. We first create an activity A_i in AD_g for each operation op_i in P. For each arrow $op_i \rightarrow op_j$ in P, we then create a transition $A_i \rightarrow A_j$ in AD_g. The activity SR is then discarded. Finally, a transition is created from SR_i to the activity corresponding to the first operation in P. Likewise, a transition is created from the activity corresponding to the last operation in P to SR_j.

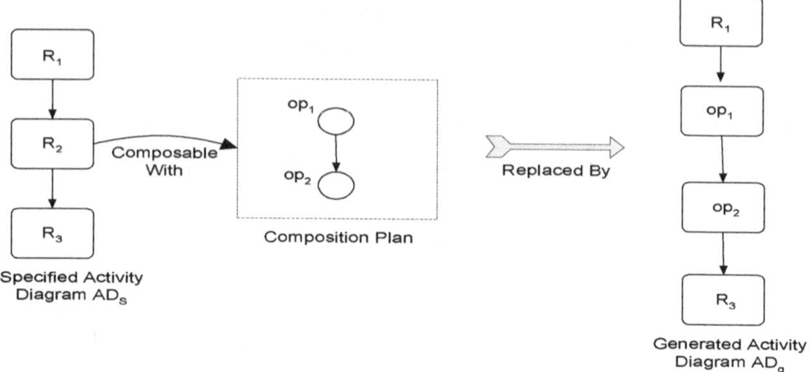

Fig. 6.11 Replacing a Sub-request by its Composition Plan

```
Replace(SR,Plan) {
    Let SR_i be a predecessor of SR in AD_s;
    Let SR_j be a succesor of SR in AD_s;
    Let op_1 be the first operation in Plan;
    Let op_n be the last operation in Plan;
    for each operation op_i ∈ Plan do
        create an activity A_i;
    for each op_i → op_j in Plan do
        create a transition A_i → A_j;
    create a transition SR_i → A_1;
    create a transition A_n → SR_j;
}
```

Fig. 6.12 Replacing a Sub-request by its Composition Plan

6.3.2 Inserting Pre and Post-Operations

Once, all sub-requests are replaced by their composition plans in the activity diagram, the final step of the generation phase is to include pre- and post-operations in AD_g. We determine the pre-operations and post-operations of every operation contained in AD_g. The idea is to "augment" each operation inserted in AD_g by its pre and post-operation relationships. We summarize in Figure 6.13, the algorithm used for that purpose.

Let op_i be an operation inserted in AD_g. The first step is to search for op_i in the OPD diagram. We use the well-known breadth-first algorithm for such task [51]. If op_i is found, we determine all operations that are related to op_i via pre and post operation relationships. For that purpose, we determine the set $\mathcal{P}$ of all OPD diagram's paths that contain op_i as a vertex. We use the Floyd-Warshall dynamic programming algorithm for computing these paths [51]. The OPD sub-diagram that contain all paths in $\mathcal{P}$ needs then to be inserted in AD_g. For that purpose, each arrow that exists in the sub-diagram is inserted into AD_g.

```
Insert(AD_g,OPD) {
    for each op_i ∈ AD_g do
      if found(op_i, OPD)
         then { sub-diagram = compute_paths(op_i, OPD);
                for each op_i ∈ sub-diagram
                  create an activity A_i;
                for each op_i → op_j ∈ sub-diagram
                  create a transition A_i → A_j in AD_g; }
}
```

Fig. 6.13 Inserting Pre and Post Operations

6.3.3 Quality of Composition

Once the activity diagram of a composite service is generated, the next step consists in checking its *quality*. We define a *Quality of Composition* (QoC) model for composite services. The model includes three parameters: *composition soundness*, *composition ranking*, and *composition completeness*.

Checking Composition Soundness – The first quality criterion we check is composition soundness (Chapter 4). A composition template *CT* is computed for the generated composite service. We use adjacency-matrix graph representation to model templates. Each composition template *CT* is represented by a $|OP(CT)| \times |P(CT)|$ matrix *T* where *OP(CT)* is the set of operations in the template. The entry T_{ij} corresponds to the operations op_i and op_j. It is equal to 1 *iff* there is an arrow from op_i to op_j. It is equal to 0 otherwise. Stored templates are represented in the same way as composition templates.

```
Sound(CT,Stored,result) {
    result = "not sound";
    for each ST ∈ Stored do {
       unification(CT,ST);
       R = matrix(CT) - matrix(ST);
       if R = 0 then result = "exactly sound";
       if R > 0 then result = "strongly sound";
       if R < 0 then result = "loosely sound";
       if result ≠ "not sound" then break;
} }
```

Fig. 6.14 Algorithm for Composition Soundness

We propose an algorithm for checking soundness based on comparing *CT* and *ST* matrices (Figure 6.14). The first step of the algorithm is the *unification* *CT* and *ST* vertices. This consists in adding to *CT* all vertices that belong to *ST-CT* and adding to *ST* all vertices that belong to *CT-ST*. In this way, both *CT* and *ST* will have the same set of vertices. The resulting templates are then represented by the matrices as explained previously. The next step consists in computing the classical substraction between matrices: R = matrix(CT) - matrix(ST). Four cases are then possible. If all elements in the matrix R are equal to 0, then CT and ST are similar. The composite service is hence exactly sound with respect to ST. If all elements in R are equal to 1/0, then ST is a subgraph of CT. The composite service is hence strongly sound with respect to ST. If all elements in R are equal to -1/0, then CT is a subgraph of ST. The composite service is hence loosely sound with respect to ST. If all elements in R are equal to -1, 1 or 0, then CT is not comparable with ST. CT should then be compared to another stored template (if any). If no stored template is left, then CT is not sound.

Composition Ranking – Assume that a composite service is sound with respect to stored template ST. We define a QoC parameter called *ranking* that gives an approximation of ST "importance". For each composite service, we determine its composition template CT. Assume that CT is *sound* with respect to a stored template ST_i. We define a function $\mathcal{R}$ ($\mathcal{R}$ stands for *reference*) so that $\mathcal{R}(\text{ST}_i)$ gives the number of times that composite services that are sound with respect to ST_i have been created. This assumes that a ranking coefficient is maintained for each stored template. The *ranking* of CT with respect to ST_i is the proportion of references to ST. If the composite service is not sound, then its ranking is equal to zero. We give below the formula used to compute the ranking of a sound composite service (s is the number of stored templates):

$$Ranking(CT, ST_i) = \frac{\mathcal{R}(ST_i)}{\sum_{k=1}^{s} \mathcal{R}(ST_k)}$$

Composition Completeness - This parameter, noted CC, is used to assess composite services that are not sound. It gives the proportion of composition sub-requests that are composable with participant service operations. CC allows the generation of composite service descriptions whose composition sub-requests are not "fully" composable with participant services. The value of CC is set by service composers in their profile and depends on their level of expertise. Indeed, if the value CC is relatively low (e.g., 25%), the algorithm might return composite services for which 75% of the composition sub-requests are not composable with participant service operations. In this case, composers may need to change their specification (e.g., data types) so that the desired sub-request can deal with participant services' features. The following formula defines the CC parameter for a composite service CS:

$$CC(CS) = \frac{\mid Composable(SubRequests) \mid}{\mid Sub - Requests \mid}$$

where *Composable*(SubRequests) is the set of sub-requests that are composable with participant services.

Chapter 7
Implementation and Performance

This chapter is devoted to the implementation and performance study of the proposed approach for composition. We provide an implementation in WebDG prototype. We use social and welfare services within the Family and Social Services Administration (FSSA). Then, we provide an extensive performance study of the proposed composition approach. For that purpose, we first define an analytical model for the proposed composition algorithms. We compare the performance of these algorithm using that model. The rest of this chapter is organized as follows. In Section 7.1, we describe the implementation of the composition approach in *WebDG* prototype. In Section 7.2, we present the performance study (analytical and experimental).

7.1 WebDG Prototype

WebDG is built with a *holistic* perception of e-government Web services. It aims at providing a Web service middleware that enables citizens and case officers to access government e-services via a rich, uniform, and flexible interface. The design and development of *WebDG* is directed by two key guidelines: the use of Web service standards (e.g., WSDL, SOAP, and UDDI) and extensibility (i.e., ability to add new functionalities).

7.1.1 WebDG Services

As a proof of concept, we implemented several FSSA applications in *WebDG*. These include *WIC*, *Medicaid*, and *TOP*. *WebDG* applications, developed in Java (JDK 1.3), access databases (Oracle 8.0.5) to retrieve/store government and citizens' information. *WIC* (Women, Infant, and Children) provides Federal grants to States for supplemental food, health care referrals,

B. Medjahed and A. Bouguettaya, *Service Composition for the Semantic Web*,
DOI 10.1007/978-1-4419-8465-4_7,

and nutrition education for low-income pregnant, breastfeeding, and non-breastfeeding postpartum women. It also provides nutritional assistance to infants and children who are found at nutritional risk. *Medicaid* is a jointly-funded (Federal and State) health insurance program for specific groups of low-income and needy people. It covers 36 million individuals including children, senior citizens, blind, and/or disabled, and people eligible for federally assisted payments. *TOP* (Teen Outreach Pregnancy) provides pregnant teens with childbirth and postpartum educational support, housing information, and adoption services.

To enable access to the aforementioned applications in *WebDG*, we "wrapped" them into Web services. We use state-of-the-art technologies for implementing *WebDG*. Table 7.1 gives a summary of these technologies. *WebDG* services are deployed using *Apache SOAP* (2.2). *Apache SOAP* provides not only server-side infrastructure for deploying and managing service, but also client-side API for invoking those services. Each service has a *deployment descriptor*. The descriptor includes the unique identifier of the Java class to be invoked, session scope of the class, and operations in the class available for the clients. Each service is deployed using the *service management client* by providing its descriptor and the URL of the *Apache SOAP servlet rpcrouter*.

Product	*Version*	*Role*
Oracle	8.0.5	WIC, Medicaid, and TOP databases. Used also as a template repository.
Java	JDK 1.3	WIC, Medicaid, and TOP "legacy" applications.
JDBC	2.0	Database connection.
Apache SOAP	2.2	SOAP server.
Systinet WASP UDDI	Standard 3.1	UDDI server.
J2EE Cloudscape	4.0	UDDI registry.
IBM WSTK	2.0	Convert applications into WSDL descriptions.
Tomcat	3.2.1	Web server and Java Servlet engine.

Table 7.1 Enabling Technologies

We use WSDL language to describe *WebDG* services. WSDL descriptions are extended with semantic features defined in the community ontology (e.g., purpose, business role). We use IBM Web Service Tool Kit (WSTK) to automatically generate WSDL files for Web services from Java class files. These WSDL files are accessible through tModels stored in the UDDI registry. We adopt *Systinet's WASP UDDI Standard 3.1* as a UDDI toolkit. *Cloudscape* (4.0) database is used as a UDDI registry. WASP UDDI provides client-side API (Application Programming Interface) for publishing and inquiring about Web services. Each Web service has one or more operations. For example,

WIC service has an operation `check_eligibility` which takes a citizen's eligibility information as input (e.g., salary, family size) and checks this information against categorical (e.g., pregnant women), financial (e.g., household income), and nutritional (e.g., children at risk) criteria. If the citizen's eligibility information satisfies all of the three criteria, the operation updates the eligibility status for this citizen to "eligible, wait for approval". Otherwise, the operation updates the status to "not eligible". In both cases, a message is returned to the customer.

7.1.2 Architecture

WebDG system is implemented across a network of *Solaris* workstations. We present the architecture of *WebDG* in Figure 7.1. The architecture is organized into four layers. The first layer contains a set of Oracle databases that store government and citizens' data. The second layer includes "proprietary" applications (e.g., WIC application) developed in Java. Each application access databases from the first layer. The third layer contains Web services. The Web service are either simple or composite. Simple Web services wrap proprietary applications defined in the lower layer. Composite services are automatically generated by the *WebDG manager*. The upper layer includes a *Graphical User Interface* (GUI) and *WebDG manager*. Citizens and case officers access *WebDG* via a GUI implemented using HTML/Servlet. Three types of requests are submitted through the GUI: discovery, invocation, and composition.

The *WebDG manager* is at the core of *WebDG* system. It is composed of several modules: *Request Handler*, *Matchmaker*, *Service Locator*, *One-to-One Composer*, *One-to-Many Composer*, *generator* and *QoC Manager*. The request handler is the router of the WebDG manager. The task it performs depends on the type of request it receives. If the request type is "discovery", it forwards it to the service locator which implements *UDDI Inquiry Client* using WASP UDDI API. If the request type is "invocation", the request handler invokes the corresponding operation through *SOAP Binding Stub* which is implemented using Apache SOAP API.

If the request type is "composition", the request handler forwards the composition specification (XML document) to the matchmaker. The matchmaker uses *JAXP* (*Java API for XML Processing*) to parse CSL specifications, check their correctness, and decompose them into sub-requests. For each sub-request, the matchmaker interacts with the service locator to get operations from the service registry. Then, it forwards these operations to the one-to-one composer which implements one-to-one algorithms for vertical composition. We currently consider the operation-centric algorithm.

At the end of its execution, the one-to-one composer returns a set of operations. Each operation could be used as a composition plan. If all operations

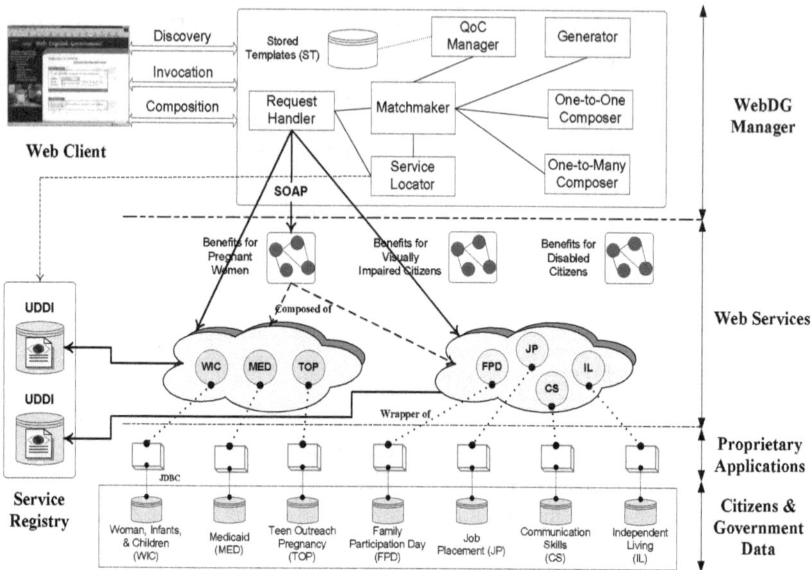

Fig. 7.1 WebDG Architecture

in the registry are checked and the maximum number of plans is not reached, the matchmaker invokes the one-to-many composer which implements the flow graph-based algorithm. At the end of its execution, the one-to-many composer returns a set of horizontally composed operations that could be used as composition plans. The matchmaker returns all generated plans to the user via the request handler. The user selects a composition plan for each sub-request and returns it to the matchmaker. The matchmaker sends the selected plans to the generator which augments them with pre and post-operations. The resulting composite service is forwarded to the QoC manager which checks QoC parameters. The composite service along with the values of its QoC parameters are finally returned to the user.

7.1.3 WebDG Scenario

We present a scenario that illustrates the main features of *WebDG*. We consider the case of a pregnant teen *Mary* visiting case officer *John* to collect social benefits to which she is entitled. *Mary* would like to apply for a government funded health insurance program. She also needs to consult a nutritionist to maintain an appropriate diet during her pregnancy. As *Mary* will not able to take care of the future newborn, she is interested in finding a foster family.

The fulfillment of the teen's needs requires accessing different services scattered in and outside the local agency. For that purpose, the case manager may either look for simple Web services that fit specific needs of the teen or specify all teen's needs through one single composite Web services. In the following, we describe the main steps for discovering and composing Web services using *WebDG*.

- **Step 1: Web Service Discovery** – To locate a specific Web service, *John* could provide either the service name, if known, or properties. This is achieved by selecting the "By Program Name" or "By Program Properties" nodes respectively (Figure 7.2). *WebDG* currently supports two properties: *Category* and *Agency*. Assume *John* is interested in a service that provides help in finding foster families. He would select the *adoption* and *pregnancy* categories and the *Division of Family and Children* agency. *WebDG* would return the `Teen Outreach Pregnancy` (`TOP`) service. `TOP` offers childbirth and postpartum educational support for pregnant teens.

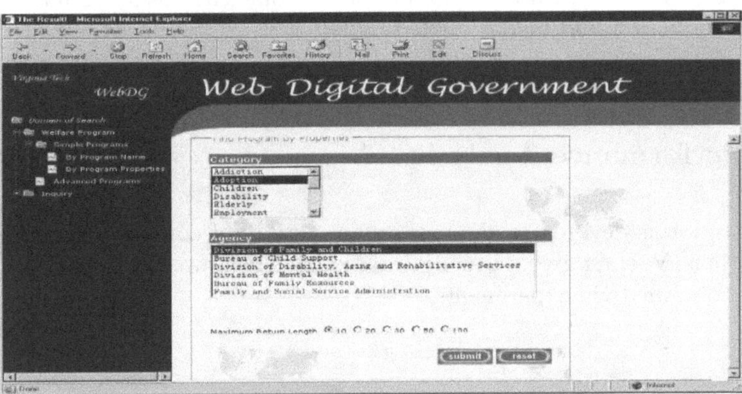

Fig. 7.2 Discovering E-Government Services

- **Step 3: Composing Web Services** – Assume now *John* wants to specify *Mary*'s needs through one single composite service called `Pregnancy Benefits` (`PB`). For that purpose, he selects the "Advanced Programs" node (Figure 7.3). Examples of `PB`'s operations include `Find Available Nutritionist`, `Find PCP Providers` (which looks for primary care providers), and `Find Pregnancy Mentors`. After checking composability rules, *WebDG* would return *composition plans* that conform to `BP` specification. Each plan has an ID (number). *John* would click on the plan's ID to display the list of outsourced services. In the scenario, `WIC`

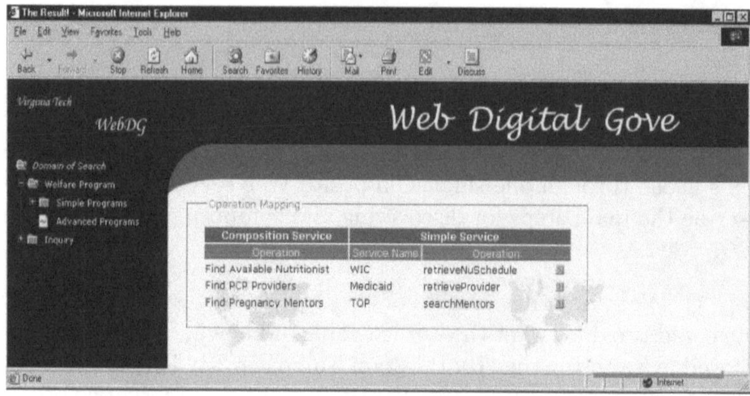

Fig. 7.3 Mappings of the Composite Service Operations

(a federally funded food program for `Women, Infants, and Children`), `Medicaid` (a healthcare program for low income citizens and families), and `TOP` services would be outsourced by `PB`.

7.2 Performance Analysis

This section is devoted to the performance study of composability checking algorithms. We first give the analytical model. Then, we give the performance results obtained via experiments.

7.2.1 Analytical Model

In this section, we present the analytical model for the operation-centric and community-based composability algorithms. We focus on computing the total time for checking composability of all target operations. This time will be the sum of the global time for checking static (T_{SS}) and dynamic (T_{DS}) semantic composability. Table 7.2 defines the parameters and symbols used in this section.

We compute the average execution time for each algorithm. Thus, T is equal to $(T_{min} + T_{max})/2$. To simplify the analysis, we assume that the times to retrieve a description from a service registry and parse that description are fixed values. In what follows, we focus on the time to check semantic composability. It is also reasonable to assume that time to check static semantic (at the operation granularity) composability for an operation is a constant. In contrast, message and business logic composability times depend on the number of message parameters and business logic rules, respectively. Thereby, U_t, O_t, t_{ST}, and t_{SS} are constants.

Variables	
N_{op}	Number of operations in the registry
N_T	Maximum number of target operations
N_C	Number of communities
n_{SO}	Number of source operations
P_M	Number of parameters per message
B_{op}	Number of business rules per operations
TC	Number of terms per condition
I_R	Number of inference rules
Performance measurement parameters and functions	
U_t	Time to obtain description from service registry
O_t	Time to parse a service description
T_{SS}^{min}	Minimum total static semantic composability time
T_{DS}^{min}	Minimum total dynamic semantic composability time
T_{SS}^{max}	Maximum total static semantic composability time
T_{DS}^{max}	Maximum total dynamic semantic composability time
t_{SS}	Time to check static semantic composability (operation granularity)

Table 7.2 Symbols and Parameters

Let us start by computing the minimum composability time T_{min} for the operation-centric algorithm. This time corresponds to the case where N_T iterations of the algorithm are executed. This means that we get a composability plan after each iteration. The total static semantic composability time T_{SS}^{min} is equal to $N_T \times (t_{SS} + T_{msg})$. Let us now compute the time T_{msg} for checking message composability. T_{msg} refers to the time of comparing a pair of message twice. At minimum, each parameter in a message would be compared to one parameter of the dual message. Hence, T_{msg} is equal to $2 \times P_M$ and T_{SS}^{min} is equal to $N_T \times (t_{SS} + 2 \times P_M)$. The last time to compute is T_{DS}^{min}. Since the algorithm performs vertical composability, dynamic semantic composability does not check plugin pre rule. Based on the definition of B-composability rules, there is a need to execute the theorem prover eight (8) times: two for exact post, two for plugin, and four for exact B-composability. At minimum, each business rule would be proved using the first inference rule. T_{DS}^{min} is then equal to $N_T \times (8 \times B_{op} \times TC)$. Based on the above analysis, we have:

$$T_{min} = N_T \times (U_t + O_t + t_{ST} + t_{SS} + 2 \times P_M + 8 \times B_{op} \times TC)$$

The maximum composability time T_{max} refers to the case where all operations in the registry are checked. This means that the number of iterations executed by the operation-centric algorithm is equal to N_{op}. Consequently, T_{SS}^{max} is equal to $N_{op} \times (t_{SS} + T_{msg})$. Let us now compute the formula for T_{msg}. The first parameter of each message should be compared to P_M parameters of the other message. The next parameter needs to be compared to P_M - 1 parameters, and so on. Hence, T_{msg} is equal to $2 \times (P_M + (P_M - 1) + ... + 1) = P_M \times (P_M + 1)$.

We need now to compute T_{DS}^{max}. As mentioned previously, we execute the theorem prover eight (8) times to check the different B-composability rules. We compare each rule in the sub-request with all rules of the current operations. The total of comparisons is then B_{op}^2. For each term, we need to go through all inference rules for a total of $TC \times I_R$. T_{DS}^{max} is then equal to $N_{op} \times (8 \times B_{op}^2 \times TC \times I_R)$. The maximum composability time is then given below:

$$T_{max} = N_{op} \times (U_t + O_t + t_{SS} + P_M \times (P_M + 1) + 8 \times B_{op}^2 \times TC \times I_R)$$

The previous formulas give composability times for one outsourcing request. In what follows, we specify the total execution time for the operation-centric algorithm when executed on n_{SO} source operations. In this case, we consider the times to access the registry and parse operation descriptions:

$$T = \frac{1}{2} \times N_{op} \times n_{SO} \times (U_t + O_t + t_{SS} + P_M \times (P_M + 1) + 8 \times B_{op}^2 \times TC \\ \times I_R) + \frac{1}{2} \times N_T \times n_{SO} \times (U_t + O_t + t_{SS} + 2 \times P_M + 8 \times B_{op} \times TC)$$

The minimum composition time T_{min} for the community-centric algorithm corresponds to the case where all outsourced operations are obtained during the first P_{max} iterations. It is thereby similar to that of the operation-centric algorithm:

$$T_{min} = P_{max} \times (U_t + O_t + t_{ST} + t_{SS} + 2 \times P_M + 9 \times B_{op} \times TC)$$

The maximum composition time T_{max} refers to the case where all operations are checked for composability. However, in contrast to the operation centric algorithm, only the operations within a specify community are checked. This means that the number of iterations executed by the algorithm equals N_{opc}. Let us now derive the relationship between N_{opc} and N_{op}. We assume that the operations within a registry are uniformly distributed across communities. Hence, $N_{opc} = \frac{N_{op}}{N_C}$. T_{max} can now be derived from the formula of the operation-centric algorithm by replacing N_{op} by $\frac{N_{op}}{N_C}$:

$$T_{max} = \frac{N_{op}}{N_C} \times (U_t + O_t + t_{ST} + t_{SS} + P_M \times (P_M + 1) \\ +9 \times B_{op}^2 \times TC \times I_R)$$

Finally, the composition times are as follows:

$$\begin{aligned} T_{SS} &= \frac{N_{op}}{2 \times N_C} \times C_{SR} \times (t_{SS} + P_M \times (P_M + 1)) + \frac{1}{2} \times P_{max} \times C_{SR} \\ &\quad \times (t_{SS} + 2 \times P_M) \\ T_{DS} &= \frac{9 \times N_{op}}{2 \times N_C} \times C_{SR} \times (B_{op}^2 \times TC \times I_R) + \frac{9}{2} \times P_{max} \times C_{SR} \times B_{op} \times TC \\ T &= \frac{N_{op}}{2 \times N_C} \times C_{SR} \times (U_t + O_t + t_{SS} + P_M \times (P_M + 1) + 9 \times B_{op}^2 \\ &\quad \times TC \times I_R) + \frac{1}{2} \times P_{max} \times C_{SR} \times (U_t + O_t + t_{SS} + 2 \times P_M \\ &\quad +9 \times B_{op} \times TC) \end{aligned}$$

7.2.2 Experiments

The aim of this section is threefold. First, we show the scalability of the proposed approach by computing the composability checking time for a large number of operations. We also compare the results of the analytical model with those obtained via experiments. Second, we assess the impact of the composability threshold τ on the number of composable operations. Third, we show the *efficacy* of the proposed approach, i.e., the usefulness of the composability algorithms to composers.

N_{op}	1000 - 30000	TC	10
$Tmax$	100	*Confidence level*	0.98
P_M	50 - 100	*Confidence accuracy*	0.02
B_{op}	10 - 20		

Table 7.3 Simulation settings

We built a simulation testbed to run the experiments. This has the advantage of allowing the generation of a large number of operations using various settings. The descriptions generated by the testbed are used to conduct the experimental study. We run our experiments on a *Sun Enterprise Ultra 10* server with a 440-MHz *UltraSPARC-IIi* processor, 1-GB of RAM, and under *Solaris* operating system. Table 7.3 shows the common settings for all simulation experiments. The *Confidence level* and *accuracy* are used to control the accuracy of the simulation results[1]. Users specify the values of confidence level and accuracy before starting simulation. The simulation is not complete until the expected confidence level and accuracy are achieved. Operation outsourcing requests are simulated through a random request generator. The generation of requests follows the exponential distribution. We generate 50 outsourcing requests generated (n_{SO} =50) during each simulation round.

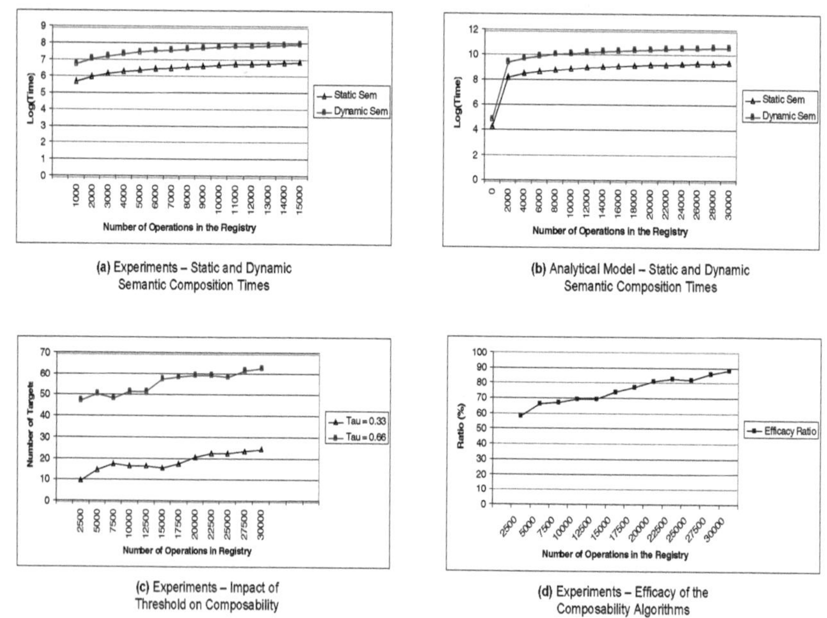

(a) Experiments – Static and Dynamic Semantic Composition Times

(b) Analytical Model – Static and Dynamic Semantic Composition Times

(c) Experiments – Impact of Threshold on Composability

(d) Experiments – Efficacy of the Composability Algorithms

Fig. 7.4 Performance of the Operation Centric Algorithm

[1] Given N sample results Y_1, Y_2, ..., Y_N, the *confidence accuracy* is defined as H/Y, where H is the *confidence interval half-width* and Y is the sample mean of the results ($Y = (Y_1 + Y_2 + ... + Y_N)/N$). The *confidence level* is the probability that the absolute value of the difference between the Y and μ (the true mean of the sample results) is equal to or less than $H = t_{\alpha/2;N-1} \times \sigma/\sqrt{N}$ where $\sigma^2 = \Sigma_i(Y_i - Y)^2/(N-1)$, and t is the standard t distribution.

In the first set of experiments, we evaluate the time for checking static and dynamic semantic composability (Figure 7.4.(a)). We vary the number of operations in the registry from 1000 to 15000 with an iteration range of 1000. To enable a better visualization of the figure, we represent T_{SS} and T_{DS} using logarithm function. Figure 7.4.(b) depicts the composition times obtained using the analytical model. Figure 7.4.(a) and 7.4.(b) show that most of the composability time is spent on checking dynamic composability. Indeed, static semantic composability compares simple ontological attributes (e.g., serviceability). However, B-composability compares each business logic rules of a source operation with each business logic rules of a target operation. Each pair of business logic rules involves the comparison of two pre-conditions and two post-conditions using the theorem prover (Figures 4.8).

In the second set of experiments, we assess the impact of τ on the number of target operations (Figure 7.4.(c)). We conducted experiments for $\tau = 33\%$ and $\tau = 66\%$. The results show that the number of generated targets is higher for $\tau = 33\%$. Indeed, in this case, target operations are generated if at least 33% of the composability rules are satisfied. However, for $\tau = 66\%$, target operations are generated if at least 66% of the composability rules are satisfied.

In the third set of experiments, we measure the *efficacy* of the proposed approach (Figure 7.4.(d)). Given a set $\mathcal{O}$ of outsourcing requests, we define the *efficacy ratio* by the expression $\frac{|\mathcal{T}|}{max\_target \times |\mathcal{O}|}$, where $\mathcal{T}$ is the set of targets returned by the composition engine for all outsourcing requests, *max_target* is the maximum number of generated targets (Figure 4.6), and $|\mathcal{O}| = n_{SO}$. This ratio gives the probability that the composition engine returns targets for a source operation. For each source operation, we consider a different value of the composability threshold τ (e.g., 0.33, 0.66). We set the variable *max_target* to 1. We also vary the number of operations available in the registry. Figure 7.4.(d) shows that the efficacy ratio varies from 58% to 88%. This means that the composition engine is able to find a composable operation for most of the outsourcing requests.

Figure 7.5 summarizes the experiments for the community-centric algorithm. Figure 7.5.a shows that the number of communities has an impact on the composition time. We consider two cases where the number of communities is 50 and 500. The figure states that the composition time for $N_C = 50$ is higher than then composition time for $N_C = 500$. The bigger is the number of communities, the smaller is the composition time. Indeed, the number of operations with which the algorithm checks composability is smaller in the case of $N_C = 50$. The main motivation behind designing different algorithms for composability was to decrease the composition time. Figure 7.5.b illustrates that the composition time for the operation-centric algorithm is bigger than the community-centric algorithm's time. Indeed, the first algorithm compares source operations with all operations in the registry. The second algorithm focuses on a subset of operations that belong to the same community. The results obtained through experiments are similar to the ones obtained via

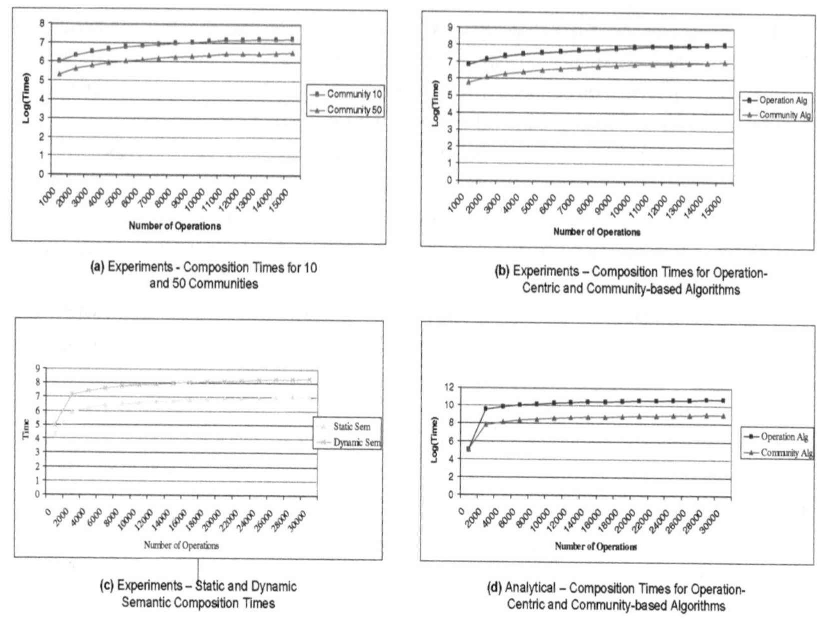

(a) Experiments - Composition Times for 10 and 50 Communities

(b) Experiments – Composition Times for Operation-Centric and Community-based Algorithms

(c) Experiments – Static and Dynamic Semantic Composition Times

(d) Analytical – Composition Times for Operation-Centric and Community-based Algorithms

Fig. 7.5 Performance of the Community-based Algorithm

the analytical model (Figure 7.5.d). We compare in Figure 7.5.c the times for static semantic and dynamic semantic composition. As for the operation-centric algorithm, the algorithm spends most of the time in checking dynamic semantic composability rules.

Chapter 8
Conclusion

In this chapter, we summarize the concepts and techniques described in this book. We also discuss future research directions for Web service composition.

8.1 Summary

Web service composition is emerging as *the* technology of choice for enabling inter-enterprise interactions on the Web [7, 140, 233]. However, current techniques for service composition are generally ad-hoc, time consuming, and error prone. In this book, we proposed an approach for the automatic composition of Web services. We summarize below the major contributions.

Ontology-based Organization and Description of Web Services [139, 142, 149, 17, 5] – Understanding the semantics of Web services is a key requirement for the automatic composition of those services. The first step in this book was thereby to define a framework for the semantic description of Web services. We proposed an *ontology-based framework for organizing Web services and describing their semantics.* Web Services are grouped into communities based on their domain of interest. Each community is an instance of an ontology, called community ontology. The community ontology includes a set of generic operations that can be used "as is" or customized by underlying services.

Multilevel Model for Web Service Composability [152, 143] – Assume now that the composition engine is able to "understand" the meaning and capabilities of each Web service. The issue then is to select "relevant" participants while making sure that those participants "can" actually interact with each other. For that purpose, we proposed a *composability model for semantic Web services.* The model is defined by a set of rules called composability rules. Each rule compares a specific feature of interacting

B. Medjahed and A. Bouguettaya, *Service Composition for the Semantic Web*,
DOI 10.1007/978-1-4419-8465-4_8, © Springer Science+Business Media, LLC 2011

Web services. It specifies the constraints and requirements for checking horizontal, vertical, and hybrid composability. We also introduced the notions of composability degree and τ-composability to cater for partial and total composability.

Context-Aware Matching of Semantic Web Services [138] – we proposed a novel matching framework for Web service composition. The framework combines the concepts of Web service, context, and ontology. We introduced an ontology-based categorization of contextual information in Web service environments. We defined a two-level mechanism for modeling Web service contexts. Finally, we presented a peer-to-peer architecture for matching context policies. The architecture relies on a context matching engine, context policy assistants, and context community services. Community services implement rule-based techniques for comparing context policies.

Supporting the Automatic Generation of Composite Services [148, 145, 234, 151] – Based on the proposed framework for semantic Web services and multilevel composability model, we designed a *technique for the automatic generation of composite services from high-level specifications of composition requests.* The proposed technique consists of three conceptually separate phases: specification, matchmaking, and generation. We defined a Quality of Composition (QoC) model to assess the quality of the generated composite service.

8.2 Directions for Future Research

We identify the following directions for future research: cloud services, service mashup, autonomic composition of Web services, dynamic composition of Web services, dependable service composition, and the support of mobile services.

Cloud Services – Cloud computing allows users to access applications running on large-scale remote computing environments. Cloud computing precursors include grid computing, which links disparate computers to form one large infrastructure; and utility computing, a metered service in which individuals work with programs kept on shared servers and, like a public utility, pay based on their usage level [119, 158, 93]. Major cloud-computing services include Amazon Web Services, Google Apps, and Force.com. Application developers face many challenges while creating new cloud services (e.g., when integrating end user services with billing and resource allocation services). Tools and techniques are needed to simplify the development, debugging, testing, change management, customization and integration of cloud services. Other research thrusts include complex event processing (e.g., Real-time data feeds such as location information for mobile devices) [70, 137, 111], cloud monitoring and management (e.g., failure prediction, performance and power management) [188], and security [20, 125].

Service Mashup – The Web 2.0 is commonly associated with applications that facilitate interactive information sharing and user-centered design and collaboration on the Web. One of the goals of Web 2.0 is to make it easy to create, use, describe, share, and reuse resources on the Web [126, 23, 26, 58]. Mashup is an application development approach that allows users to aggregate multiple services (e.g., Google Map and Amazon.com) to create a service that serves a new purpose. Unlike Web services composition where the focus is on the composition of business (process) services only, the mashup process goes further in that it allows more functionalities and can compose heterogeneous resources such as data services and User Interface (UI) services [126]. Service mashup currently receives a great deal of attention from academia and industry. Much of the current work involves tools and techniques that instrument the mashup process and subsequently visualize the results [112, 187]. Another issue is to define techniques for predicting or mining meaningful mashups.

Autonomic Composition of Web Services – The term "autonomic" was coined in the early-2000s by IBM's vision for self-managing complex and distributed computing environments [78]. The initiative identifies four fundamental "self" properties: self-healing, self-configuring, self-optimizing, and self-protecting [219]. One of the challenges is the autonomic composition of services, e.g., service composition that are self-configuring, self-optimizing, self-healing, and self-adapting. Self-configuring compositions are composite services that are capable of automatically discovering new participant services, selecting among available service providers, and choosing among different options available for contracts [177]. Self-optimizing compositions automatically select participants that would maximize Quality of Service (e.g., maximize benefits and reduce costs) [231, 234, 185, 232, 172]. Self-healing compositions automatically detect that some composition requirements (e.g., regulatory or business requirements) are no longer satisfied and react to requirement violations [83, 13]. Self-adapting compositions are able to function in spite of changes in behaviors of external services [91]; they reduce as much as possible the need of human intervention for adapting services to changes.

Dynamic Composition of Web Services – The number of services to be integrated may be large and continuously changing. Web service composition requires flexibility to dynamically adapt to changes that may occur in partners' applications [16, 192, 37]. Participants must be able to respond rapidly to changes where both operational (e.g., server load) and market (e.g., changes in regulations) environments are not easily predictable. Additionally, the competitive nature of the Web makes possible the availability of alternate services that provide "similar" functions. To stay competitive, businesses should team up with the "best" available services at any given time. They need to form *short term* relationships and then disband when it is no longer profitable to stay together. This form of partnership does not assume any *a priori* trading relationship. The support of dynamic composition will facilitate the establishment of *on demand* and *real-time* partnerships. Services will not statically be bound to each other. New partners with relevant features should be dynamically discovered and assembled. Currently, relationships among component services are mostly established at development time. While current service-oriented technologies provide capabilities for defining Web services, they clearly are not sufficient to facilitate the establishment of dynamic business relationships. More research effort is needed to enable the creation of dynamic relationships.

Dependable Composition of Web Services – Transaction support is required to provide reliable and dependable execution of composite services. Traditional transaction management techniques [68] are not appropriate in the context of composite services [86, 204, 11, 116]. The participants of a composite service may be heterogeneous and autonomous. They may not be transactional and if they are, their transactional features may not be compatible with each other. In addition, participant services may not be willing to comply with constraints such as resource locking, until the termination of the composite service execution. New transaction techniques are required in the context of Web services. For instance, it is important to extend the description of services by explicitly describing transactional semantics of Web service operations. An example is to specify that an operation can be aborted without effect from a requester's perspective. It is also imperative to extend service composition models to specify transactional semantics of an operation or a group of operations. An example is to specify how to handle the unavailability of a participant service. The effective handling of transactional aspects at the composite service level, should be facilitated by exploiting the transactional capabilities of participant services. A few industry standards such as *WS-Coordination* [105], *WS-Transaction* [106], and *Business Transaction Protocol (BTP)* [166] are already emerging for transaction support of composite services.

Support of Mobile Services – In this book, we focused on Web service composition in "wired" infrastructures with fixed or stationary users. An interesting research direction is to extend Web service composition to wireless environments [228, 229, 211]. Indeed, the past years have witnessed a boom in wireless technologies. Sophisticated wireless devices such as cellular phones and PDAs are now available at affordable prices. Emerging technologies including 3G and 4G (third and fourth generation) are developed to increase the bandwidth of wireless channels. However, most of the proposed Web service concepts cannot or may not be easily applicable to mobile services. This is due to the peculiarities of wireless environments including limited bandwidth, unbalanced client-server communication, limited power supply, and frequent unavailability of wireless networks. For example, using UDDI for discovering Web services requires multiple *costly* round-trips over wireless networks. Invoking Web services using SOAP/REST may increase mobile hosts' power consumption and waiting time. This calls for new techniques to adapt Web services to the wireless world.

References

1. M. S. Ackerman. Privacy in E-Commerce: Examining User Scenarios and Privacy Preferences. In *Proceedings of the ACM Conference on Electronic Commerce*, 1999.
2. N. Adam, O. Dogramaci, A. Gangopadhyay, and Y. Yesha. *Electronic Commerce: Technical, Business, and Legal Issues.* Prentice Hall (ISBN: 0139490825), August 1998.
3. N. R. Adam and Y. Yesha. Strategic Directions in Electronic Commerce and Digital Libraries: Towards a Digital Agora. *ACM Computing Surveys*, 28(4):818–835, December 1996.
4. R. Akkiraju, J. Farrell, J.Miller, M. Nagarajan, M. Schmidt, A. Sheth, and K. Verma. Web Service Semantics - WSDL-S. *A joint UGA-IBM Technical Note, version 1.0 (http://lsdis.cs.uga.edu/projects/meteor-s/wsdl-s)*, April 2005.
5. M. S. Akram, B. Medjahed, and A. Bouguettaya. Supporting Dynamic Changes in Web Service Environments. In *Proceedings of the International Conference on Service Oriented Computing*, pages 319–334, Trento, Italy, December 2003.
6. G. Alonso and F. Casati. Web Services and Service-Oriented Architectures. In *ICDE Conference*, page 1147, 2005.
7. G. Alonso, F. Casati, H. Kuno, and V. Machiraju. *Web Services: Concepts, Architecture, and Applications.* Springer Verlag (ISBN: 3540440089), June 2003.
8. Y. Atif. Building Trust in E-Commerce. *IEEE Internet Computing*, 6(1):18–24, February 2002.
9. ATIS. *Electronic Data Interchange Guideline Consistency Subcommittee (EGCS).* http://www.atis.org/atis/tcif.
10. F. Baader, D. Calvanese, D. L. McGuinness, D. Nardi, and P. F. Patel-Schneider, editors. *The Description Logic Handbook: Theory, Implementation, and Applications.* Cambridge University Press, 2003.
11. Y. Badr, D. Benslimane, Z. Maamar, and L. Liu. Guest Editorial: Special Section on Transactional Web Services. *IEEE T. Services Computing*, 3(1):30–31, 2010.
12. K. Baina, K. Benali, and C. Godart. A Process Service Model for Dynamic Enterprise Process Interconnection. In *Proceedings of the International Conference on Cooperative Information Systems*, pages 239–254, Trento, Italy, September 2001.
13. L. Baresi and S. Guinea. An Introduction to Self-Healing Web Services. In *International Conference on Engineering of Complex Computer Systems*, page 4, June 2005.
14. BEA. *WebLogic Integrator.* http://www.bea.com/products/weblogic/integrator.
15. BEA, IBM, and Microsoft. *Business Process Execution Language for Web Services (BPEL4WS).* http://xml.coverpages.org/bpel4ws.html.
16. B. Benatallah, M. Dumas, M. Sheng, and A. H. H. Ngu. Declarative Composition and Peer-to-Peer Provisioning of Dynamic Web Services. In *Proceddings of the IEEE*

B. Medjahed and A. Bouguettaya, *Service Composition for the Semantic Web*,
DOI 10.1007/978-1-4419-8465-4,

International Conference on Data Engineering, pages 297–308, San Jose, California, USA, February 2002.

17. B. Benatallah, B. Medjahed, A. Bouguettaya, A. Elmagarmid, and J. Beard. Composing and Maintaining Web-based Virtual Enterprises. In *Proceedings of the International Workshop on Technologies for E-Services*, pages 155–174, Cairo, Egypt, September 2000.
18. T. Berners-Lee. *Services and Semantics: Web Architecture.* http://www.w3.org/2001/04/30-tbl, April 2001.
19. T. Berners-Lee, J. Hendler, and O. Lassila. The Semantic Web. *Scientific American*, 284(5):34–43, May 2001.
20. E. Bertino, F. Paci, R. Ferrini, and N. Shang. Privacy-Preserving Digital Identity Management for Cloud Computing. *IEEE Data Eng. Bull.*, 32(1):21–27, 2009.
21. R. Bhatti, E. Bertino, and A. Ghafoor. A Trust-Based Context-Aware Access Control Model for Web-Services. *Distributed and Parallel Databases*, 18(1):83–105, July 2005.
22. M. Bichler, A. Segev, and J. L. Zhao. Component-based E-Commerce: Assessment of Current Practices and Future Directions. *ACM SIGMOD Record*, 27(4):7–14, December 1998.
23. M. B. Blake. Knowledge Discovery in Services. *IEEE Internet Computing*, 13(2):88–91, 2009.
24. A. Bouguettaya, B. Benatallah, and A. K. Elmagarmid. *Interconnecting Heterogeneous Information Systems.* Kluwer Academic Publishers (ISBN 0792382161), July 1998.
25. A. Bouguettaya, A. Elmagarmid, B. Medjahed, and M. Ouzzani. Ontology-Based Support for Digital Government. In *Proceedings of the International Conference on Very Large Databases*, pages 633–636, Roma, Italy, September 2001.
26. A. Bouguettaya, S. Nepal, W. Sherchan, X. Zhou, J. Wu, S. Chen, D. Liu, L. Li, H. Wang, and X. Liu. End-to-End Service Support for Mashups. *IEEE T. Services Computing*, 3(3):250–263, 2010.
27. A. Bouguettaya, M. Ouzzani, B. Medjahed, and J. Cameron. Managing Government Databases. *IEEE Computer*, 34(2):56–64, February 2001.
28. P. Brezillon. Context-Based Modeling of Operators' Practices by Contextual Graphs. In *Human Centered Processes: 14th Mini Euro Conference*, 2003.
29. M. Brodie. The B2B E-commerce Revolution: Convergence, Chaos, and Holistic Computing. In *Information System Engineering: State of the Art and Research Themes. S. Brinkkemper, E. Lindencrona, and Solvberg (editors)*, London, England, June 2000.
30. M. H. Burstein, C. Bussler, M. Zaremba, T. W. Finin, M. N. Huhns, M. Paolucci, A. P. Sheth, and S. K. Williams. A Semantic Web Services Architecture. *IEEE Internet Computing*, 9(5), 2005.
31. C. Bussler. B2B Protocol Standards and their Role in Semantic B2B Integration Engines. *IEEE Data Engineering Bulletin*, 24(1):3–11, March 2001.
32. C. Bussler. *B2B Integration.* Springer Verlag (ISBN: 3540434879), May 2003.
33. C. Canal, L. Fuentes, E. Pimentel, J. M. Troya, and A. Vallecillo. Adding Roles to CORBA Objects. *IEEE Transactions on Software Engineering*, 29(3):242–260, March 2003.
34. F. Casati, U. Dayal, and M.-C. Shan. E-Business Applications for Supply Chain Automation: Challenges and Solutions. In *Proceddings of the IEEE International Conference on Data Engineering*, pages 71–78, Heidelberg, Germany, April 2001.
35. F. Casati, D. Georgakopoulos, and M.-C. Shan, editors. *Proceedings of the International Workshop on Technologies for E-Services*, Roma, Italy, September 2001.
36. F. Casati, S. Ilnicki, L. Jin, V. Krishnamoorthy, and M.-C. Shan. Adaptive and Dynamic Service Composition in eFlow. In *Proceedings of the International Conference on Advanced Information Systems Engineering*, pages 13–31, Stockholm, Sweden, June 2000.

37. F. Casati, S. Ilnicki, L.-J. Jin, V. Krishnamoorthy, and M.-C. Shan. eFlow: a Platform for Developing and Managing Composite e-Services. Technical Report HPL-2000-36, HP Laboratoris, Palo Alto, California, USA, 2000.
38. F. Casati, M. Sayal, and M.-C. Shan. Developing E-Services for Composing E-Services. In *Proceedings of the International Conference on Advanced Information Systems Engineering*, pages 171–186, Interlaken, Switzerland, June 2001.
39. F. Casati and M.-C. Shan. Dynamic and Adaptive Composition of E-services. *Information Systems*, 26(3):143–163, 2001.
40. F. Casati and M.-C. Shan. Models and Languages for Describing and Discovering E-Services (Tutorial). In *Proceedings of the International ACM SIGMOD Conference on Management of Data*, Santa Barbara, California, USA, May 2001.
41. D. Chakraborty, F. Perich, S. Avancha, and A. Joshi. DReggie: A Smart Service Discovery Technique for E-Commerce Applications. In *Workshop at the 20th Symposium on Reliable Distributed Systems*, October 2001.
42. D. Chakraborty, F. Perich, A. Joshi, T. Finin, and Y. Yesha. A Reactive Service Composition Architecture for Pervasive Computing Environments. In *7th Personal Wireless Communications Conference*, pages 53–62, October 2002.
43. H. Chesbrough and J. Spohrer. A Research Manisfesto for Services Science. *Communications of the ACM*, 49(7):43–47, July 2006.
44. S. A. Chun, V. Atluri, and N. R. Adam. Using Semantics for Policy-Based Web Service Composition. *Distributed and Parallel Databases*, 18(1):37–64, 2005.
45. E. Cobb. The Evolution of Distributed Component Architectures. In *Proceedings of the International Conference on Cooperative Information Systems*, pages 7–21, Trento, Italy, September 2001.
46. C. Collet, T. Coupaye, and T. Svensen. NAOS: Efficient and Modular Reactive Capabilities in an Object-Oriented Database System. In *Proceedings of the International Conference on Very Large Databases*, pages 132–143, Santiago, Chile, September 1994.
47. CommerceNet. *eCO.* http://eco.commerce.net.
48. RosettaNet Consortium. *RosettaNet.* http://www.rosettanet.org.
49. X12 Consortium. *EDI (Electronic Data Interchange) ANSI X12.* http://www.x12.org.
50. XML/EDI Consortium. *XML/EDI.* http://www.xmledi-group.org.
51. T. H. Cormen, C. E. Leiserson, R. L. Rivest, and C. Stein. *Introduction to Algorithms.* MIT Press (ISBN: 0262032937), September 2001.
52. F. Curbera, M. Duftler, R. Khalaf, and W. Nagy. Unraveling the Web Services Web. *IEEE Internet Computing*, 6(2):86–93, March 2002.
53. F. Curbera, R. Khalaf, N. Mukhi, S. Tai, and S. Weerawarana. The Next Step in Web Services. *Commun. ACM*, 46(10):29–34, 2003.
54. cXML Consortium. *cXML.* http://www.cxml.org.
55. K. Czajkowski, D. F. Ferguson, I. Foster, J. Frey, S. Graham, I. Sedukhin, D. Snelling, S. Tuecke, and W. Vambenepe. The WS-Resource Framework. *http://www.globus.org/wsrf/specs/ws-wsrf.pdf*, May 2004.
56. DAML. DAML-S (and OWL-S) 0.9 Draft Release. *http://www.daml.org/services/daml-s/0.9/*, 2004.
57. U. Dayal, M. Hsu, and R. Ladin. Business Process Coordination: State of the Art, Trends, and Open Issues. In *Proceedings of the International Conference on Very Large Databases*, pages 3–13, Roma, Italy, September 2001.
58. P. de Vrieze, L. Xu, A. Bouguettaya, J. Yang, and J. Chen. Process-Oriented Enterprise Mashups. In *GPC Workshops*, pages 64–71, 2009.
59. A. K. Dey. Providing Architectural Support for Building Context-Aware Applications. *Ph.D. Dissertation, Georgia Tech*, December 2000.
60. Y. Ding, D. Fensel, and and B. Omelayenko M. Klein. The Semantic Web: Yet Another Hip? *Data and Knowledge Engineering*, 41(3):205–227, May 2002.

61. A. Doan. Learning to Map between Structured Representations of Data. *Ph.D. Dissertation, University of Washington*, 2002.
62. A. Dogac. A Survey of the Current State-of-the-Art in Electronic Commerce and Research Issues in Enabling Technologies. In *Proceddings of the Euro-Med Net Conference, Electronic Commerce Track*, pages 50–53, Nicosia, Cyprus, March 1998.
63. A. Dogac, editor. *Special Issue on Electronic Commerce, ACM SIGMOD Record*, 27(4), December 1998.
64. A. Dogac, editor. *Special Issue on Electronic Commerce, Distributed and Parallel Databases, an International Journal*, 7(2), April 1999.
65. A. Dogac and I. Cingil. A Survey and Comparison of Business-to-Business E-Commerce Frameworks. *ACM SIGecom Exchanges*, 2(2):16–27, June 2001.
66. Drala. *Drala Event Broker.* http://www.dralasoft.com.
67. S. Dustdar and W. Schreiner. A Survey on Web Services Composition. *IJWGS*, 1(1):1–30, 2005.
68. A. K. Elmagarmid, editor. *Database Transaction Models for Advanced Applications.* Morgan Kaufmann (ISBN:1558602143), December 1992.
69. H. Elmeleegy, M. Ouzzani, and A. K. Elmagarmid. Usage-Based Schema Matching. In *ICDE*, pages 20–29, 2008.
70. P. Th. Eugster, P. Felber, R. Guerraoui, and A.-M. Kermarrec. The Many Faces of Publish/Subscribe. *ACM Comput. Surv.*, 35(2), 2003.
71. D. Fensel. *Ontologies: A Silver Bullet for Knowledge Management and Electronic Commerce.* Springer Verlag (ISBN: 3540003029), September 2003.
72. D. Fensel and C. Bussler. The Web Service Modeling Framework WSMF. 2002.
73. R. T. Fielding and R. N. Taylor. Principled Design of the Modern Web Architecture. *ACM Trans. Internet Techn.*, 2(2):115–150, 2002.
74. D. Florescu, A. Grunhagen, and D. Kossmann. XL: An XML Programming Language for Web Service Specification and Composition. In *Proceedings of the International World Wide Web Conference*, pages 65–76, Honolulu, Hawaii, USA, May 2002.
75. D. Florescu, A. Grunhagen, D. Kossmann, and S. Rost. XL: Platform for Web Services. In *roceedings of the International ACM SIGMOD Conference on Management of Data*, page 625, Madison, Wisconsin, USA, May 2002.
76. I. Foster and C. Kesselman. *The Grid: Blueprint for a New Computing Infrastructure, 2nd Edition.* Morgan Kaufmann (ISBN: 1-55860-933-4), November 2004.
77. E. Gamma, R. Helm, R. Johnson, and J. Vlissides. *Design Patterns: Elements of Reusable Object-Oriented Software* . Addison-Wesley (ISBN: 0201633612), January 1995.
78. A. G. Ganek and T. A. Corbi. The Dawning of the Autonomic Computing Era. *IBM Systems Journal*, 42(1):5–18, 2003.
79. D. Garlan, R. Allen, and J. Ockerbloom. Architectural Mismatch: Why Reuse Is So Hard. *IEEE Software*, 12(6):17–26, November 1995.
80. D. Geer. Taking steps to secure web services. *IEEE Computer*, 36(10):14–16, 2003.
81. D. Georgakopoulos, editor. *Information Technology for Virtual Enterprises*, Proceedings of the International Workshop on Research Issues on Data Engineering, Sidney, Australia, March 1999.
82. D. Georgakopoulos, H. Schuster, A. Cichocki, and D. Baker. Managing Process and Service Fusion in Virtual Enterprises. *Information Systems*, 24(6):429–456, September 1999.
83. D. Ghosh, R. Sharman, H. R. Rao, and S. Upadhyaya. Self-Healing Systems - Survey and Synthesis. *Decision Support systems*, 42:2164–2185, 2007.
84. A. Gomez-Perez and O. Corcho. Ontology Languages for the Semantic Web. *IEEE Intelligent Systems*, 17(1):54–60, January 2002.
85. A. J. Gonzales and R Ahlers. Context-Based Representation of Intelligent Behavior in Training Simulations. *International Transactions of the Society for Computer Simulation*, pages 153–166, 1999.

86. P. Greenfield, A. Fekete, J. Jang, D. Kuo, and S. Nepal. Isolation Support for Service-based Applications: A Position Paper. In *Third Biennial Conference on Innovative Data Systems Research (CIDR)*, pages 314–323, 2007.
87. Object Management Group. *Unified Modeling Language Specification (Version 1.3)*. http://www.omg.org/technology/documents/formal/uml.htm, 1999.
88. WSMO Working Group. Web Service Modeling Language (WSML). *http://www.wsmo.org/wsml*, 2004.
89. WSMO Working Group. Web Service Modeling Ontology (WSMO). *http://www.wsmo.org/*, 2004.
90. X. Gu, K. Nahrstedt, W. Yuan, D. Wichadakul, and D. Xu. An XML-based Quality of Service Enabling Language for the Web. *J. Vis. Lang. Comput.*, 13(1):61–95, 2002.
91. R. Hamadi, B. Benatallah, and B. Medjahed. Self-adapting Recovery Nets for Policy-driven Exception Handling in Business Processes. *Distributed and Parallel Databases*, 23(1):1–44, 2008.
92. J. M. Hancock and M. J. Zvelebil. *Dictionary of Bioinformatics and Computational Biology*. Wiley-Liss (ISBN: 0471436224), August 2004.
93. B. Hayes. Cloud computing. *Commun. ACM*, 51(7):9–11, 2008.
94. T. Heinis, C. Pautasso, O. Deak, and G. Alonso. Publishing Persistent Grid Computations as WS Resources. In *e-Science*, pages 328–335, 2005.
95. J. V. D. Heuvel, J. Yang, and M. P. Papazoglou. Service Representation, Discovery and Composition for E-marketplaces. In *Proceedings of the International Conference on Cooperative Information Systems*, pages 270–284, Trento, Italy, September 2001.
96. J. Hopkins. Component Primer. *Communications of the ACM*, 43(10), October 2000.
97. I. Horrocks. DAML+OIL: a Description Logic for the Semantic Web. *IEEE Data Engineering Bulletin*, 25(1):4–9, March 2002.
98. I. Horrocks. OWL: A Description Logic Based Ontology Language. In *International Conference on Logic Programming*, pages 1–4, 2005.
99. I. Horrocks and P. F. Patel-Schneider. The Generation of DAML+OIL. In *Description Logics*, 2001.
100. HP. *NetAction*. http://www.hp.com.
101. M. N. Huhns. Agents Web Services. *IEEE Internet Computing*, 6(4):93–95, July 2002.
102. M. N. Huhns and M. P. Singh. Service-Oriented Computing: Key Concepts and Principles. *IEEE Internet Computing*, 9(1):75–81, 2005.
103. R. Hull, M. Benedict, V. Christophides, and J. Su. E-services: A Look Behind the Curtain. In *PODS Conference*, pages 1–14, California, USA, June 2003.
104. IBM. *WebSphere*. http://www.ibm.com.
105. IBM. *WS-Coordination*. http://www-106.ibm.com/developerworks/.
106. IBM. *WS-Transaction*. http://www-106.ibm.com/developerworks/.
107. IBM, BEA Systems, Microsoft, SAP AG, Sonic Software, and VeriSign. WS-Policy Specification. *http://www.ibm.com/developerworks/library/specification/ws-polfram*, March 2006.
108. IBM, BEA Systems, Microsoft, SAP AG, Sonic Software, and VeriSign. WS-PolicyAttachment Specification. *http://www.ibm.com/developerworks/library/specification/ws-polatt*, March 2006.
109. IETF. *EDIINT*. http://www.ietf.org.
110. IETF. *The Internet Engineering Task Force*. http://www.ietf.org.
111. K. R. Jayaram and P. Th. Eugster. Scalable Efficient Composite Event Detection. In *COORDINATION*, pages 168–182, 2010.
112. A. Jhingran. Enterprise Information Mashups: Integrating Information, Simply. In *VLDB*, pages 3–4, 2006.
113. L. Kagal, M. Paolucci, N. Srinivasan, G. Denker, T. W. Finin, and K. P. Sycara. Authorization and Privacy for Semantic Web Services. *IEEE Intelligent Systems*, 19(4):50–56, 2004.

114. R. Kalakota and A. B. Whinston. *Frontiers of Electronic Commerce*. Addison Wesley (ISBN: 0201845202), February 2000.
115. G. M. Kuper and J. Simeon. Subsumption for XML Types. In *ICDT Conference*, pages 331–345, London, UK, January 2001.
116. N. Ben Lakhal, T. Kobayashi, and H. Yokota. FENECIA: Failure Endurable Nested-Transaction Based Execution of Composite Web Services with Incorporated State Analysis. *VLDB J.*, 18(1):1–56, 2009.
117. G. Larsen. Component-based Enterprise Frameworks. *Communications of the ACM*, 43(10):24–26, October 2000.
118. A. Lazcano, H. Schuldt, G. Alonso, and H. J. Schek. WISE: Process based E-Commerce. *IEEE Data Engineering Bulletin*, 24(1):46–51, March 2001.
119. N. Leavitt. Is Cloud Computing Really Ready for Prime Time? *IEEE Computer*, 42(1):15–20, 2009.
120. C. Lee and S. Helal. Context Attributes: An Approach to Enable Context- awareness for Service Discovery. In *2003 Symposium on Applications and the Internet (SAINT'03)*, 2003.
121. S. M. Lewandowski. Frameworks for Component-based client/server Computing. *ACM Computing Survey*, 30(1):3–27, March 1998.
122. F. Leymann. The (Service) Bus: Services Penetrate Everyday Life. In *Third International Conference on Service-Oriented Computing (ICSOC)*, pages 12–20, December 2005.
123. F. Leymann, D. Roller, and M.-T. Schmidt. Web Services and Business Process Management. *IBM Systems Journal*, 41(2):198–211, 2002.
124. L. Li and I. Horrocks. A Software Framework for Matchmaking Based on Semantic Web Technology. In *WWW 2003 Conf.*, pages 331–339, May 2003.
125. D. Lin and A. C. Squicciarini. Data Protection Models for Service Provisioning in the Cloud. In *SACMAT*, pages 183–192, 2010.
126. G. Di Lorenzo, H. Hacid, H.-Y. Paik, and B. Benatallah. Data Integration in Mashups. *SIGMOD Record*, 38(1):59–66, 2009.
127. H. Ludwig and Y. Hoffner. Contract-based Cross-Organisational Workflows - The CrossFlow Project. In *Proceedings of the International Joint Conference on Work Activities Coordination and Collaboration*, pages 1–6, San Francisco, California, USA, February 1999.
128. Z. Maamar, D Benslimane, and N. C. Narendra. What Can Context do for Web Services. *Communications of the ACM*, to appear in 2006.
129. Z. Maamar, S. K. Mostefaoui, and H. Yahyaoui. Toward an Agent-Based and Context-Oriented Approach for Web Services Composition. *IEEE Transactions on Knowledge and Data Engineering (TKDE)*, 17(5):686–697, 2005.
130. Z. Maamar, S. Kouadri Mostefaoui, and Q. H. Mahmoud. On Personalizing Web Services Using Context. *International Journal of E-Business Research*, 1(3), 2005.
131. Z. Maamar, G. Kouadri Mostfaoui, D. Benslimane, S. Sattanathan, and C. Ghedira. Developing Interoperable Business Processes Using Web Services and Policies. In *2nd International Conference on Interoperability for Enterprise Software and Applications*, 2006.
132. Z. Malik and A. Bouguettaya. RATEWeb: Reputation Assessment for Trust Establishment among Web services. *VLDB J.*, 18(4):885–911, 2009.
133. D. V. McDermott. Estimating-Regression Planning for Interactions with Web Services. In *International Conference on Artificial Intelligence Planning Systems*, pages 204–211, Toulouse, France, April 2002.
134. S. A. McIlraith, T. C. Son, and H. Zeng. Semantic Web Services. *IEEE Intelligent Systems*, 16(2):46–53, March 2001.
135. M. Mecella, B. Pernici, and P. Craca. Compatibility of e -Services in a Cooperative Multi-platform Environment. In *Proceedings of the International Workshop on Technologies for E-Services*, pages 44–57, Roma, Italy, September 2001.

136. B. Medjahed. Semantic Web Enabled Composition of Web Services. *Ph.D. Dissertation, Virginia Tech*, May 2004.
137. B. Medjahed. Dissemination Protocols for Event-Based Service-Oriented Architectures. *IEEE T. Services Computing*, 1(3):155–168, 2008.
138. B. Medjahed and Y. Atif. Context-Based Matching for Web Service Composition. *Distributed And Parallel Databases, an International Journal*, 21(1):5–37, February 2005.
139. B. Medjahed, B. Benatallah, A. Bouguettaya, and A. Elmagarmid. WebBIS: A Framework for Agile Integration of Web Services. *International Journal of Cooperative Information Systems*, 13(2), June 2004.
140. B. Medjahed, B. Benatallah, A. Bouguettaya, A. Ngu, and A. Elmagarmid. Business-to-Business Interactions: Issues and Enabling Technologies. *The VLDB Journal*, 12(1):59–85, May 2003.
141. B. Medjahed, B. Benatallah, A. Bouguettaya, A. H. H. Ngu, and A. K. Elmagarmid. Business-to-Business Interactions: Issues and Enabling Technologies. *The VLDB Journal*, 12(1):59–85, May 2003.
142. B. Medjahed and A. Bouguettaya. A Dynamic Foundational Architecture for Semantic Web Services. *Distributed And Parallel Databases, an International Journal*, 17(2):179–206, March 2005.
143. B. Medjahed and A. Bouguettaya. A Multilevel Composability Model for Semantic Web Services. *IEEE Transactions on Knowledge and Data Engineering*, 17(7):954–968, July 2005.
144. B. Medjahed and A. Bouguettaya. A Multilevel Composability Model for Semantic Web Services. *IEEE Transactions on Knowledge and Data Engineering (TKDE)*, 17(7):954–968, July 2005.
145. B. Medjahed and A. Bouguettaya. Customized Delivery of E-Government Service. *IEEE Intelligent Systems*, 20(6):77–84, December 2005.
146. B. Medjahed and A. Bouguettaya. Customized Delivery of E-Government Web Services. *IEEE Intelligent Systems*, 20(6):77–84, December 2005.
147. B. Medjahed, A. Bouguettaya, and B. Benatallah. Introduction to Special Issue on Semantic Web Services. *ACM Trans. Internet Techn.*, 8(1), 2007.
148. B. Medjahed, A. Bouguettaya, and A. Elmagarmid. Composing Web Services on the Semantic Web. *The VLDB Journal*, 12(4):333–351, November 2003.
149. B. Medjahed, A. Bouguettaya, and M. Ouzzani. Semantic Web Enabled E-Government Services. In *Proceedings of the NSF Conference for Digital Government Research*, pages 250–253, Boston, Massachussets, USA, May 2003.
150. B. Medjahed, S. Hadi, and W. I. Grosky. A Service-Oriented Framework for Controlling Invasive Species in Agriculture. *IJMSO*, 4(1/2):34–41, 2009.
151. B. Medjahed, M. Ouzzani, and A. Bouguettaya. Using Web Services in E-Government Applications. In *Proceedings of the NSF Conference for Digital Government Research*, pages 371–376, Los Angeles, California, USA, May 2002.
152. B. Medjahed, A. Rezgui, A. Bouguettaya, and M. Ouzzani. Infrastructure for E-Government Web Services. *IEEE Internet Computing*, 7(1):58–65, January 2003.
153. B. Meyer. On To Components. *IEEE Computer*, 32(1):139–140, January 1999.
154. Microsoft. *Distributed Component Object Model (DCOM)*. http://www.microsoft.com.
155. Microsoft. *.NET*. http://www.microsoft.com/net/.
156. Sun Microsystems. *Java RMI (Remote Method Invocation)*. http://java.sun.com/products/jdk/rmi.
157. Sun Microsystems. *Sun ONE*. http://www.sun.com.
158. P. Mika and G. Tummarello. Web Semantics in the Clouds. *IEEE Intelligent Systems*, 23(5):82–87, 2008.
159. G. Kouadri Mostefaoui. Towards a Conceptual and Software Framework for Integrating Context-Based Security in Pervasive Environments. *Ph.D. Dissertation, University of Fribourg*, October 2004.

160. P. Muth, D. Wodtke, J. Weissenfels, A. K. Dittrich, and G. Weikum. From Centralized Workflow Specification to Distributed Workflow Execution. *Journal of Intelligent Information Systems*, 10(2):159–184, March 1998.
161. S. Narayanan and S. A. McIlraith. Simulation Verification and Automated Composition of Web Services. In *WWW 2002 Conf.*, pages 77–88, 2002.
162. NASA. *Scientific and Engineering Workstation Procurement (SEWP).* http://www.sewp.nasa.gov.
163. United Nations. *United Nations Directories for Electronic Data Interchange for Administration, Commerce and Transport (UN/EDIFACT).* http://www.unece.org/trade/untdid/welcome.htm.
164. Netscape. *Secure Socket Layer (SSL) 3.0 Specification.* http://wp.netscape.com/eng/ssl3/.
165. H. S. Nwana and D. T. Ndumu. An Introduction to Agent Technology. *Lecture Notes in Artificial Intelligence, Number 1198, Springer Verlag*, 1997.
166. OASIS. *Business Transaction Protocol.* http://www.oasis-open.org/cover.
167. OASIS and United Nations. *ebXML.* http://www.ebxml.org.
168. OBI. *OpenBuy.* http://www.openbuy.org.
169. Oracle. *Integration Server Starter Pack.* http://otn.oracle.com/software.
170. R. Orfali and D. Harkey. *Client/Server Programming With Java and CORBA.* Wiley Computer Publishing (ISBN: 047124578X), March 1998.
171. M. Ouzzani, B. Benatallah, and A. Bouguettaya. Ontological Approach for Information Discovery in Internet Databases. *Distributed and Parallel Databases, an International Journal*, 8(3):367–392, July 2000.
172. M. Ouzzani and A. Bouguettaya. Efficient Access to Web Services. *IEEE Internet Computing*, 8(2):34–44, 2004.
173. M. Ouzzani and A. Bouguettaya. Query Processing and Optimization on the Web. *Distributed and Parallel Databases, an International Journal*, 15(3):187–218, May 2004.
174. M. Ouzzani, B. Medjahed, and A. Bouguettaya. Optimized Querying of E-Government Services. In *Proceedings of the NSF Conference for Digital Government Research*, pages 363–366, Boston, Massachussets, USA, May 2003.
175. A. Paepcke, C. K. Chang, H. Garcia-Molina, and T. Winograd. Interoperability for Digital Libraries Worldwide. *Communications of the ACM*, 41(4):33–43, April 1998.
176. M. Paolucci, T. Kawamura, T. R. Payne, and K. Sycara. Semantic Matching of Web Services Capabilities. In *First International Semantic Web Conference*, pages 333 – 347, 2002.
177. M. P. Papazoglou, P. Traverso, S. Dustdar, and F. Leymann. Service-Oriented Computing: a Research Roadmap. *Int. J. Cooperative Inf. Syst.*, 17(2):223–255, 2008.
178. J. Pascoe. The Stick-e Note Architecture: Extending the Interface beyond the User. In *Intelligent User Interfaces*, pages 261–264, 1997.
179. T.R. Payne, M. Paolucci, , and K. Sycara. Advertising and Matching DAML-S Service Descriptions (position paper). In *Int'l Semantic Web Working Symp.*, pages 76–78, 2001.
180. C. Petrie and C. Bussler. Service Agents and Virtual Enterprises: A Survey. *IEEE Internet Computing*, 7(4):68–78, July 2003.
181. S. Ran. A Model for Web Services Discovery with QoS. *SIGecom Exchanges*, 4(1):1–10, March 2003.
182. A. Rezgui, A. Bouguettaya, and M. Y. Eltoweissy. Privacy on the Web: Facts, Challenges, and Solutions. *IEEE Security&Privacy*, 1(6):40–49, 2003.
183. A. Rezgui, M. Ouzzani, A. Bouguettaya, and B. Medjahed. Preserving Privacy in Web Services. In *Proceedings of the International ACM Workshop on Web Information and Data Management*, pages 56–62, Virginia, USA, November 2002.
184. E. Roman, S. W. Ambler, and T. Jewell. *Mastering Enterprise JavaBeans.* Wiley Computer Publishing (ISBN: 0471417114), December 2001.

185. F. Rosenberg, M. B. Müller, P. Leitner, A. Michlmayr, A. Bouguettaya, and S. Dustdar. Metaheuristic Optimization of Large-Scale QoS-aware Service Compositions. In *IEEE SCC*, pages 97–104, 2010.
186. S. Russell and P. Norvig. *Artificial Intelligence: A Modern Approach.* Prentice Hall (ISBN: 0137903952), December 2002.
187. M. Sabbouh, J. Higginson, S. Semy, and D. Gagne. Web Mashup Scripting Language. In *WWW*, pages 1305–1306, 2007.
188. F. Salfner, M. Lenk, and M. Malek. A Survey of Online Failure Prediction Methods. *ACM Computing Surveys*, 42(3):1–42, 3 2010.
189. C. Schuler, H. Schuldt, G. Alonso, and H.-J. Schek. Workflows over Workflows: Practical Experiences with the Integration of SAP R/3 Business Workflows in WISE. In *Proceedings of the Informatik'99 Workshop "Enterprise-wide and Cross-enterprise Workflow Management: Concepts, Systems, Applications"*, pages 65–72, Paderborn, Germany, October 1999.
190. H. Schuster, D. Baker, A. Cichocki, D. Georgakopoulos, and M. Rusinkiewicz. The Collaboration Management Infrastructure. In *Proceddings of the IEEE International Conference on Data Engineering*, pages 485–487, San Jose, California, USA, March 2000.
191. H. Schuster, D. Georgakopoulos, A. Cichocki, and D. Baker. Modeling and Composing Service-Based and Reference Process-Based Multi-enterprise Processes. In *Proceedings of the International Conference on Advanced Information Systems Engineering*, pages 247–263, Stockholm, Sweden, June 2000.
192. M. Shen, B. Benatallah, M. Dumas, and E. O.-Y. Mak. SELF-SERV: A Platform for Rapid Composition of Web Services in a Peer-to-Peer Environment. In *Proceedings of the International Conference on Very Large Databases*, pages 1051–1054, Hong Kong, China, August 2002.
193. A. P. Sheth and J. A. Larson. Federated Database Systems for Managing Distributed, Heterogeneous, and Autonomous Databases. *ACM Computing Surveys*, 22(3):183–236, September 1990.
194. S. S. Y. Shim, V. S. Pendyala, M. Sundaram, and J. Z. Gao. Business-to-Business E-Commerce Frameworks. *IEEE Computer*, 33(10):40–47, October 2000.
195. M. P. Singh. Physics of Service Composition. *IEEE Internet Computing*, 5(3):6, May 2001.
196. M. P. Singh and M. N. Huhns. *Service-Oriented Computing : Semantics, Processes, Agents.* John Wiley and Sons (ISBN: 0470091487), January 2005.
197. E. Sirin, B. Parsia, and J. A. Hendler. Filtering and Selecting Semantic Web Services with Interactive Composition Techniques. *IEEE Intelligent Systems*, 19(4):42–49, 2004.
198. B. Spitznagel and Garlan D. A Compositional Formalization of Connector Wrappers. In *Proceedings of the International Conference on Software Engineering*, pages 374–384, Portland, Oregon, USA, May 2003.
199. J. Spohrer and D. Riecken. Services Science (Guest Editors Introduction). *Communications of the ACM*, 49(7):31–34, July 2006.
200. N. Sriharee, T. Senivongse, K. Verma, and A. P. Sheth. On using WS-Policy, Ontology, and Rule Reasoning to Discover Web Services. In *INTELLCOMM 2004*, pages 246–255, 2004.
201. U. Srivastava, J. Widom, K. Munagala, and R. Motwani. Query Optimization over Web Services. In *VLDB Conference*, 2006.
202. K. Sycara, M. Klush, , and S. Widoff. Dynamic Service Matchmaking among Agents in Open Information Environments. *ACM SIGMOD Record*, 28(1):47–53, 1999.
203. C. Szyperski. *Component Software - Beyond Object-Oriented Programming.* Addison-Wesley (ISBN: 0201745720), November 2002.
204. S. Tai, T. A. Mikalsen, E. Wohlstadter, Nirmit Desai, and I. Rouvellou. Transaction Policies for Service-Oriented Computing. *Data Knowl. Eng.*, 51(1):59–79, 2004.

205. The Stencil Group. *How Web Services Will Beat the "New New Thing" Rap.* http://www.stencilgroup.com/ideas_scope_200106newnew.html.
206. TIBCO. *ActiveEnterprise.* http://www.tibco.com.
207. A. Tsalgatidou and T. Pilioura. An Overview of Standards and Related Technology in Web Services. *Distributed and Parallel Databases*, 12(3):135–162, November 2002.
208. S. Tsur, S. Abiteboul, R. Agrawal, U. Dayal, J. Klein, and G. Weikum. Are Web Services the Next Revolution in e-Commerce? (Panel). In *Proceedings of the International Conference on Very Large Databases*, pages 614–617, Roma, Italy, September 2001.
209. R. M. Turner. Context-Mediated Behavior for Intelligent Agents. *Int. J. Hum.-Comput. Stud.*, 48(3):307–330, 1998.
210. S. D. Urban, S. W. Dietrich, A. Saxena, and A. Sundermier. Interconnection of Distributed Components: An Overview of Current Middleware Solutions. *Journal of Computer and Information Sciences and Engineering*, 1(1):23–31, March 2001.
211. U. Varshney and R. J. Vetter, editors. *Special Issue on Mobile Commerce*, MONET 7(3), June 2002.
212. K. Verma, R. Akkiraju, and R. Goodwin. Semantic Matching of Web Service Policies. In *Second International Workshop on Semantic and Dynamic Web Processes*, pages 79–90, 2005.
213. S. Vinoski. Web Services Interaction Models, Part 1: Current Practice. *IEEE Internet Computing*, 6(3):89–91, May 2002.
214. Vitria. *BusinessWare.* http://www.vitria.com.
215. W3C. *Simple Object Access Protocol (SOAP).* http://www.w3.org/TR/soap.
216. W3C. *Universal Description, Discovery, and Integration (UDDI).* http://www.uddi.org.
217. W3C. *Web Services Description Language (WSDL).* http://www.w3.org/TR/wsdl.
218. W3C. Web Services Architecture. *http://www.w3.org/TR/ws-arch/*, 2003.
219. R. Want, T. Pering, and D. L. Tennenhouse. Comparing Autonomic and Proactive Computing. *IBM Systems Journal*, 42(1):129–135, 2003.
220. WebMethods. *WebMethods.* http://www.webmethods.com.
221. G. Weikum, editor. *Special Issue on Organizing and Discovering the Semantic Web*, IEEE Data Engineering Bulletin, 25(1), March 2002.
222. J. Weissenfels, M. Gillmann, O. Roth, G. Shegalov, and W. Wonner. The Mentor-Lite Prototype: A Light-Weight Workflow Management System. In *Proceddings of the IEEE International Conference on Data Engineering*, pages 685–686, San Diego, California, USA, February 2000.
223. M. Wooldridge and N. R. Jennings. Intelligent Agents: Theory and Practice. *Knowledge Engineering Review*, 10(2):115–152, 1995.
224. M. Wooldrige and N. R. Jennings. Intelligent Agents: Theory and Practice. *Knowledge Engineering Review*, 10(2):115–152, 1995.
225. C. Wroe, R. Stevens, C. A. Goble, A. Roberts, and R. M. Greenwood. A Suite of Daml+Oil Ontologies to Describe Bioinformatics Web Services and Data. *International Journal on Cooperative Information Systems*, 12(2):197–224, 2003.
226. D. Wu, B. Parsia, J. Hendler, and D. Nau. Automating DAML-S Web Services Composition using SHOP2. In *International Semantic Web Conference*, pages 195–210, Florida, USA, October 2003.
227. J. Yang and M. P. Papazoglou. Interoperation Support for Electronic Business. *Communications of the ACM*, 43(6):39–47, June 2000.
228. X. Yang and A. Bouguettaya. Semantic Access to Multichannel M-Services. *IEEE Trans. Knowl. Data Eng.*, 21(2):259–272, 2009.
229. X. Yang, A. Bouguettaya, B. Medjahed, W. He, and H. Long. Organizing and Accessing Web Services on Air. *IEEE Transactions on Systems, Man, and Cybernetics - Part A: Systems and Humans*, 33(6):742–757, November 2003.

230. D. M. Yellin and R. E. Strom. Protocol Specifications and Component Adaptors. *ACM Transaction on Programming Languages and Systems*, 19(2):292–233, March 1997.
231. Q. Yu and A. Bouguettaya. Framework for Web Service Query Algebra and Optimization. *TWEB*, 2(1), 2008.
232. Q. Yu and A. Bouguettaya. Computing Service Skyline from Uncertain QoWS. *IEEE T. Services Computing*, 3(1):16–29, 2010.
233. Q. Yu, X. Liu, A. Bouguettaya, and B. Medjahed. Deploying and Managing Web Services: Issues, Solutions, and Directions. *The VLDB Journal*, 17(3):537–572, May 2008.
234. Q. Yu, M. Rege, A. Bouguettaya, B. Medjahed, and M. Ouzzani. A Two-phase Framework for Quality-aware Web service Selection. *Service Oriented Computing and Applications*, 4(2):63–79, June 2010.
235. A. M. Zaremski and J. M. Wing. Specification Matching of Software Components. *ACM Transactions on Software Engineering and Methodology*, 6(4):333–369, October 1997.
236. L. Zeng, B. Benatallah, M. Dumas, J. Kalagnanam, and Q. Z.Sheng. Quality Driven Web Services Composition. In *Proceedings of the International World Wide Web Conference*, pages 411–421, Budapest, Hungary, May 2003.

Zeitfracht Medien GmbH
Ferdinand-Jühlke-Straße 7
99095 Erfurt, Deutschland
produktsicherheit@kolibri360.de